Self-Examination and the Old Testament

Self-Examination and the Old Testament

MARC COGEN

RESOURCE *Publications* • Eugene, Oregon

SELF-EXAMINATION AND THE OLD TESTAMENT

Copyright © 2024 Marc Cogen. All rights reserved. Except for brief quotations in critical publications or reviews, no part of this book may be reproduced in any manner without prior written permission from the publisher. Write: Permissions, Wipf and Stock Publishers, 199 W. 8th Ave., Suite 3, Eugene, OR 97401.

Resource Publications
An Imprint of Wipf and Stock Publishers
199 W. 8th Ave., Suite 3
Eugene, OR 97401

www.wipfandstock.com

PAPERBACK ISBN: 979-8-3852-0730-5
HARDCOVER ISBN: 979-8-3852-0731-2
EBOOK ISBN: 979-8-3852-0732-9

VERSION NUMBER 01/08/24

Contents

Preface | xi

Introduction | 1

PART I: THE FIVE BOOKS OF MOSES OR PENTATEUCH

Genesis

Reading 1	The Evil of Man	25
Reading 2	The brothers of Joseph ask for forgiveness.	31

Exodus

Reading 3	Pharaoh's insincere regret	36
Reading 4	Tablets of the Covenant and God's compassion	40

Leviticus

Reading 5	Individual confession	46
Reading 6	Atonement for the community	48
Reading 7	Sending away the transgressions	50
Reading 8	Day of Atonement: Yom Kippur	54
Reading 9	Upholding the Covenant and restoring the relationship with God	57

Numbers

Reading 10	Individual confession and forgiveness	61
Reading 11	Moses prays to spare God's unfaithful people	63
Reading 12	Idolatry and a return to God	67
Reading 13	Balaam keeps up appearances, but his true character is revealed.	69

Deuteronomy

Reading 14   God shall be among His exiled people who return to Him. | 74

PART II: THE PROPHETS

Joshua

Reading 15   Achan transgresses and confesses but is executed under emergency powers. | 79

Judges

Reading 16   The Israelites are rebuked by an angel and weep. | 83

1 Samuel

Reading 17   Samuel calls for a return to God—Israel confesses its idolatry and returns to God. | 87

Reading 18   Saul disobeys God and loses his kingship. | 92

Reading 19   Saul asks David for forgiveness. | 98

Reading 20   Abigail begs David for mercy for her foolish husband Nabal. | 101

2 Samuel

Reading 21   David transgresses, seeks God's forgiveness and is forgiven but there is divine justice. | 104

1 Kings

Reading 22   Solomon, when he Dedicated the Temple, prayed for forgiveness for the mistakes of future generations. | 106

Reading 23   After being rebuked by Elijah, king Ahab rends his clothes and puts sackcloth on his body. | 111

2 Kings

Reading 24   Josiah rends his clothes when he hears that the scroll of the teaching has been discovered in the Temple by the high priest Hilkiah. | 116

Isaiah

Reading 25   Angels prepare Isaiah for his prophetic mission and the Lord promises forgiveness. | 120

Jeremiah

Reading 26   God does not look in anger for He is compassionate. | 126

Ezekiel
Reading 27   Individual responsibility and salvation | 132

Hosea
Reading 28   Return, O Israel, to the Lord, your God! | 138

Joel
Reading 29   The Lord is gracious and compassionate, slow to anger, abounding in kindness. | 143

Amos
Reading 30   Seek the Lord and you will live. | 146

Obadiah
Reading 31   Humanitarian action prevents transgressions. | 150

Jonah
Reading 32   Nineveh is saved by regret. | 153

Micah
Reading 33   God forgives the remnant of His people. | 156

Nahum
Reading 34   God is slow to anger but does not remit all punishment. | 159

Habakkuk
Reading 35   Though angry, may You remember compassion. | 161

Zephaniah
Reading 36   Seek the Lord before the day of the Lord's anger. | 164

Haggai
Reading 37   The returned exiles repent and rebuild the House of the Lord. | 166

Zechariah
Reading 38   Humanity is not inherently evil and can cleanse itself from its mistakes. | 168

Malachi
Reading 39   All the nations shall account you happy because you returned to Me. | 171

PART III: THE WRITINGS

Psalms

Reading 40	A plea for forgiveness and protection from enemies	177
Reading 41	The decision to acknowledge transgression.	181
Reading 42	But I wait for You, O Lord.	184
Reading 43	Teach me wisdom about secret things so that I do not stumble.	187
Reading 44	Out of the depths	192

Proverbs

Reading 45	Rely on the wisdom of the Lord.	194

Job

Reading 46	The self-righteous Job examines himself.	197

The Song of Songs

Reading 47	Dark but comely	200

Ruth

Reading 48	A change of heart	204

Lamentations

Reading 49	Take us back, O Lord!	207

Ecclesiastes

Reading 50	God will call everyone to account.	211

Esther

Reading 51	We should not hide who we are.	214

Daniel

Reading 52	Daniel's prayer on behalf of the people, confessing transgressions and seeking forgiveness.	217

Ezra

Reading 53	Ezra's prayer to send away idolatry.	221

Nehemiah

Reading 54	Nehemiah's prayer for success.	224

1 Chronicles

| Reading 55 | Satan induces David to transgress, and David repents. | 227 |

2 Chronicles

| Reading 56 | God promises that His forgiveness shall heal the Land. | 231 |

Appendix: Structure and Indicative Timeline of the Old Testament | 235

Preface

EXAMINING ONESELF IS ONE of the most important exercises to maintain the quality of life and perhaps human life itself, yet it is at the same time one of the most difficult to do. It is like looking in the mirror to see your own mind and feelings, to contemplate with care and find out if repair is needed. Often people find it painful because they are afraid to discover or be confronted with flawed elements, black places that they do not understand, and memories about damage done to themselves or to others. It is easy to comprehend that abstaining from self-examination is a comfortable yet a false way out of problems, a denial of facts and an excuse for not doing what we ought to do. The book is the result of many exercises of self-examination, sometimes difficult times of life when sound judgment and good choices were vital. Schooling in self-examination can save us from dark thoughts and feelings that paralyze, pave the ground for depression and anxieties, and may open an abyss of despair. How can we free ourselves if we are stuck in this kind of transition?

Self-examination with the help of the Bible is the chosen way of the book for getting to grips with diverse troubling issues. Moreover, reading the Bible is anchored in Western civilization and history for whom the Bible is the book of books, divinely inspired, to guide humans through all kinds of challenging circumstances. Of course, the existence of God is accepted, and it is a belief that needs no scientific proof. As a matter of fact, no proof of God's existence can be offered by science. In the Bible, God is seen as the father of mankind who cares for his children. He is the Creator of the universe and everything and He created man to be free so that he or she can make choices, either good or bad ones. Humans were not created as perfect but can err, are able to examine themselves, change and choose for a righteous way of living. If humans were perfect, no freedom would be possible, they would be like robots. However, considering the worldview of the Bible, it stands out that human life is blessed and the earth full of promises. Genesis is the first book of the Bible, and it speaks about every majestic life that God created while Psalm 118 praises the earth as marvelous in our sight. When examining oneself this picture of beauty and joy should always be kept in mind because it is our best gift.

In the very long history of Christianity, the Old Testament has always been regarded as a strong appeal to spirituality and a way to find God. Especially the early Church was immersed in the Old Testament with the books of Isaiah and the Psalms as favorites. For example, Jerome (Hieronymus) wrote in his Commentary on Isaiah "… permit me to explain Isaiah, showing that he was not only a prophet, but an evangelist and an apostle as well. For he says about himself and the other evangelists: How beautiful are the feet of those who preach good news, of those who announce peace. And God speaks to him as if he were an apostle: *Whom shall I send, who will go to my people?* And he answers: *Here I am; send me.*" Jerome lived for about 40 years among the Jews in their homeland; he called them 'the Hebrews', living among them and learning from them, although some criticized him because of it. He is known for his radical return to the 'hebraica veritas', the 'Hebrew truth', or Hebrew scholarship. His understanding of the Hebrews is still relevant as explained by Michael Graves, Jerome's Hebrew Philology, Leiden, Brill, 2007. As a matter of fact, Jerome had in mind the words of Jesus Christ when He said, "Do not think that I have come to abolish the Law or the Prophets. I have not come to abolish them but to fulfill them." (Matthew 5:17). The fulfillment is understood as the complete revelation of God's will, God communicating with humanity for which He constantly cares, also for future generations. Moreover, the teachers in the Temple were astonished of the twelve years old Jesus' understanding and answers about the Old Testament (Luke 2:42, 46-47).

Many of the beautiful Gregorian chants refer to verses of the Old Testament expressing the hope that God would establish His justice on earth. Gregorian chant also contains prayers to be spared from affliction and rejection, finally trusting that He will save us, there is no reason for fear or sadness. It is God, our heavenly Father, who cares for us. This message of hope and trust in divine help arranges very well in the exercise of self-examination, the way of improving ourselves and finding peace of mind. Faith in the divinely inspired words of the Bible also helps to heal and bind together society. The early Church took over the older words for gathering of the believers or assembly, the Hebrew word 'qahal', which was translated in the Septuagint as 'Ἐκκλησία' (ekklēsia) while the word 'συναγωγή' (synagogue) was used for assembly in the Gospel of John 9:22, the Book of Revelation 2:9, and the epistle of James 2:2. Finally, the Greek word 'καθολικός' (catholic) means universal and refers to the openness of the church and the gathering of believers to everyone who accepts the Bible as the basis of his or her faith, regardless of social class, ethnicity, or wealth. Even slaves were welcome based on equality, a revolutionary step in that time. The Bible shows God as our Heavenly Father who cares about humanity. This view is a radical break with the pagan worldview of antiquity which regards humans as mere play-toys for entertainment of the gods, a cynical and sometimes cruel entertainment. Or as Mary Lefkowitz put it rather mildly in the New York Times (2003), "Zeus did not create humankind, and he is not primarily concerned with their welfare."

Because the Old Testament is a constant reminder of the Jewish setting and legacy, several references are made to well-known historical Jewish commentaries, especially the Talmud, Rashi, and Maimonides. By doing so, the uninterrupted line of biblical thought and teachings is better preserved. Concern to maintain the uninterrupted line was also in the mind of the Church Fathers. They had acquainted themselves with the religious documents of Judaism and had nurtured personal relations with Jews. The Talmud of Jerusalem and the oldest Midrashic documents, which became the bedrock of Jewish doctrine, served as learning material for the transmission of theological viewpoints to the early Church. They were a theological bridge between Judaism and Christianity notwithstanding some polemical arguments in the teachings of the Church Fathers towards the 'old belief' of Judaism.

The book does not read like a novel but should be used from time to time or in a moment of doubt about oneself. It is divided in 56 readings which are stand-alone readings and do not require much time although they challenge the reader to reflect and possibly act. The book is written for the general reader who is interested in the Bible, spirituality, and the inner self. It invites any reader to reflect on what is important in life. Schools and teachers may find the book useful for some readings in Religion Courses, Social Studies Courses, Ethics Courses, and Introductory Courses of Psychology. Educational purposes were very much in the mind when writing the book because learning how to make an honest and balanced self-examination has always been part of a well-rounded young adulthood. If the book can contribute to this end, it was worthwhile to write it.

MARC COGEN

Introduction

WHY UNDERTAKE SELF-EXAMINATION IF we are constantly examined and judged by others? Why reading the Old Testament in connection with self-examination? Many other questions reverberate from the previous ones to say the least. The answer of this book is to explore self-examination through the eyes of the Old Testament, a collection of writings that are divinely inspired according to the opinion of the believer or a collection of ancient wisdom and a great source of human experiences for non-believers. By reading the Old Testament and spending some time to reflect about yourself you allow a deeper understanding and gain an ability of problem solving, whether you acted appropriately, righteously, and honestly. If we are putting enough time and effort in this kind of action, we will discover and learn how to improve and correct ourselves instead of a teacher doing it for us, or worse, a judge or an angry harmed person. Considering that nobody is perfect, self-examination and healing is a necessary lifelong challenge as well as the best-known approach to prevent the same errors in the future and the mental pain that comes with it. Self-correction as an outcome, if necessary, makes us more powerful because we avoid a repetition of errors that weaken us, condemn us to go through the same errors again with the same disappointing results. Equally so, an absence of self-examination and needed self-correction sets into motion a negative dynamic that frustrates us, squeezes out the joy of life and may stir up bitter feelings of failure. A refusal to take responsibility for our own life is often a gliding path to self-perceived victimhood, a great temptation that tends to glorify victimhood and ultimately ourselves. What is more, the best way not to become a victim is to stop thinking about yourself as a victim. We cannot change the world, but we have the power to change ourselves.

The 56 'readings' in the book go through all 'books' of the Old Testament and offer at least one quotation from each book dealing with self-examination, healing as well as personal and sometimes communal change. Together, the quotations come close to a complete overview of the Old

Testament teachings on self-examination and healing.[1] Each quotation is placed in its proper historical context and ends with a final thought about the essence of the quotation. Hopefully, the readings will encourage the reader to start reading the Old Testament itself because much more is to be discovered that opens a path to spirituality and personal wisdom. In a widely secularized Western society, reading the Old Testament has become rather an exception, hence the appeal to read the Old Testament itself because it is as meaningful today as it was for the numerous generations before us. Moreover, reading the Old Testament is a spiritual activity that is embedded in a long tradition. Each of the 56 readings can be read as a stand-alone for a quick reflection and inspiration. Numerous references are made to other verses and parts of the Old Testament that relate to the quoted verses.

The selected readings remain as close as possible to the words and mindset of some of the most remarkable personalities in the Old Testament. Engaging with the text of the quotations requires an involvement in interpreting and applying the biblical quotations in daily life as well questions about society, a task and challenge of any time. It is commonly accepted that reading the Bible cannot remain a passive act but insistently demands a personal effort or at least an attempt to bring into practice the messages contained in it. Obviously, a clear-cut answer to specific questions is not always possible although a proper understanding of the Bible verses is always a good and reliable guide for help. Today, even more than in the past, every person is required to make deliberate choices in life instead of being dictated by an authority. Emphasis on personal effort and free choice opens a window of opportunities for introspection that can answer our needs when the time is right. Not surprisingly, centuries-old rules and interpretations, including those written in the Old Testament, are put into question. How relevant are they today?

Seeking spirituality can begin with an enquiry of the Bible as a leading book with two fundamental principles in mind. First, the 'unity principle' of

---

1. The three-parts order of the Old Testament is maintained. The tripartite canon was for the first time mentioned by the Jewish writer Ben Sira (around 180 BC) and his grandson. Later it was used in the writings of Philo of Alexandria (around 30 CE), a Hellenistic Jewish philosopher, and Josephus, a Hellenistic Jewish historian of the first century CE. The Bible is written in Biblical Hebrew with some of the later works, such as Daniel and Ezra, in Biblical Aramaic. The Bible itself does not mention 'Hebrew' but refers to Canaanite (Isaiah 19:18) or Judahite (2 Kings 18:26), the Semitic language spoken by the Israelites. The Hebrew Bible is in various writing systems, namely the Phoenician script, the later developed Paleo-Hebrew script which was replaced by the Aramaic script. The Bible translations are not copied from an existing edition. It should be reminded that many Bible translations exist and many of the words used in them are the same or similar.

the material world and the universe itself can be understood as an emanation of the existence of one God who transcends the material world and the universe. God connects everything with everything else and is the only reality that remains in eternity. Humans are aware that they are dependent on this kind of unity but cannot know all that exist. A second fundamental principle is the 'principle of uncertainty' that applies to both the material and spiritual worlds and implies that not only humans can change but that God may also change His plans with humanity and each of us.

Acceptance of the existence of one God, and one God only, is the basic tenet of Judaism and Christianity. It requires faith, a spiritual step that cannot be defined. We cannot underline enough the fundamental difference between faith and science although science is all too often presented and even abused by a strictly secular public as evidence that God does not exist. Such misconception is called Scientism which is a mischievous attempt to explain the world and the universe while denying other ways of awareness of the universe, humanity, and their creation. The Old Testament itself contains self-revelations of God as well as His directives regarding righteous behavior. In the biblical narrative God is not only the Creator of the universe and the sole source of everything that exists but He also interacts constantly with humanity for which He deeply cares. When and how God interacts with our life is God's decision alone, although we may be confident that He will answer our prayers in His ways.

The Old Testament contains some prayers and desperate cries to God, doubting whether He is listening. Although we may expect God's answer as we imagine it, God chooses His own way and timing to answer our prayers. For example, the book of the prophet Habakkuk starts with the complaint 'How long, O LORD, shall I cry out and You do not listen …' (Habakkuk 1:2—Reading 35). King David, although steadily aware of God's presence in his life, lamented one day 'My God, I cry by day—but You answer not; by night, and I have no respite.' (Psalm 22:3). And in the Book of Job, Job not only complains that God has treated him cruelly but also that He is not answering his prayers 'I cry to You, but You do not answer me; I wait, but You do not think about me. You have turned to be cruel to me; with Your powerful hand You persecute me.' (Job 30: 20-21). Waiting for God's answer is accepting with humility that God cannot be subject to our desires or needs how justified they may be, even when we are on the verge of collapse. Waiting for God is the true believer's upright spirit, as King David said, 'But I wait for You, O LORD; You will answer, O LORD, my God.' (Psalm 38:16) and 'I look to the LORD; I look to Him; I await His word. I am more eager for the LORD than watchmen for the dawn, watchmen for the dawn.' (Psalm 130:5-6—see Reading 44). Confidence in God's chosen moment of reply and action is also in the words of the prophet Isaiah when he declares 'Truly, the LORD is waiting to show you His love, truly, He will arise to forgive you. For the LORD is a God of justice; happy are those who wait for His help.' (Isaiah 30:18).

Taking on a distressful event or a difficult time in life is always a big challenge. Therefore, it is generally recognized that a person's greatness is not measured because of success, wealth, intelligence, or talents but on how he or she deals with the challenges in life. We may say that the biblical meaning of personal greatness is different from the historian's interpretation that is usually focused on important historical personalities who influenced and even determined the outcome of events. According to the Old Testament, every person can become a great person in the eyes of God.

To address God is part of life of the believer for whom the ultimate purpose of life is to maintain or restore a close relationship with God. We can rely on other humans, as we do so often and even by necessity, but in the end one can only truly reckon on God. A prayer is an address to God. It is not ritual, but a truthful and loving dialogue with our Father. How we should address God is a question that was answered in different ways throughout the Old Testament and numerous examples show how to do it.

The great Israelite leaders and the prophets have usually addressed God starting with an expression of regret for mistakes and a plea for forgiveness, either for their own mistake or on behalf of the Israelites. So why is a request for forgiveness often the beginning of a prayer in the Old Testament? Why asking for forgiveness is the first to do in a prayer? According to the ancient biblical view it is an expression of a profound awareness of the evil part of human nature while we address God who is perfectly good and without flaws. From the beginning of the prayer, it creates the right perspective on the true relationship between man and God. An early example of a biblical prayer starting with acknowledgment of transgression is Moses' prayer on behalf of the Israelite people at Mount Sinai 'If it is true that I have gained Your favor, O LORD then walk with us O LORD, even though this is a stubborn and rebellious people. Forgive our iniquity and our sins and take us as Your own people!' (Exodus 34:9—Reading 4). In 1 Samuel 7:5-6 the people started to fast for one day and admitted their transgressions before Samuel acted as their chieftain (Reading 17). When King Solomon dedicated the Temple, his prayer even addressed future transgressions of the Israelites and contained a plea for forgiveness if the people repented 'If Your people be defeated by an enemy because they have transgressed against You, and if they turn back to You and acknowledge Your name and pray to You here in Your House, oh, hear in heaven and forgive the transgressions of Your people Israel and return them to this land You gave to their forefathers.'

(1 Kings 8:33-34—Reading 22). Daniel's prayer on behalf of the people is another example of a prayer starting with acknowledgment of evildoing and transgression: 'I prayed to the LORD my God and confessed thus: "O LORD, great and awesome God! You stay always faithful to Your covenant with those who love You and keep Your commands! We have transgressed; we have done wrong; we have acted wickedly;' (Daniel 9:4-5—see Reading 52).[2]

According to the best observations, human nature has two inclinations, the good one ('yetzer hatov') and the evil one ('yetzer hara'). The inherent capacity of the two gives man a free choice how to behave, what kind of choices to make, although it also bestows on him personal responsibility for his actions, emotions, or thoughts.[3] If man is only able to make the good choices, he would not be truly free. Control over our evil inclination makes us human. Moreover, since the evil desire is an inherent part of humanity, a daily possibility of making the wrong choices and mistakes is always near. The evil inclination of man is mentioned in Genesis 6:5 'The LORD noticed how immense was man's wickedness on earth, and how everything they thought and planned was nothing but evil all the time.' (Reading 1). And in Genesis 8:21 the LORD said to Himself 'Never again will I destroy the earth because of man, since the thoughts of man are evil from his youth.' The Book of Habakkuk opens with a cry of despair when the prophet sees that violence is everywhere and there is no justice 'Raiding and violence are before me, enmity continues and contention goes on. The law has become perverted and the courts are corrupted.' (Habakkuk 1:3-4—Reading 35). Awareness of our inclination to transgress can only mean that we should behave with humility and care when considering our actions and opinions. It is the prerequisite of what is called wisdom in the sense of a good and unbiased judgment. Part of this quality is the recognition of our limitations and eventual shortcomings.

No man or woman is without blame or fault, regardless of the efforts made, which is proof how forceful the evil inclination is. Thus, even the

---

2. The Hebrew word for sin or transgression is 'chet' (אְטָח) which means 'missing the mark'. The Old Testament makes use of around 20 different words which denote 'sin' or transgression. The three most used words are 'chet', 'pesha' and 'avon'.

3. Children are in full development and do have neither the full power to supress the evil inclination nor the mental ability to distinguish clearly between good and evil. In the catholic church, a child at age 13 takes part in the solemn communion, marking his/her awakening of conscience. According to rabbinical tradition, a child develops the 'yetzer hatov' from the age of thirteen and gains control over his/her actions. The transition in a child's life is marked by the Bar Mitzvah ritual in Judaism when the child becomes a 'bar mitzvah'. Christianity uses the ritual of 'solemn communion' at the age of twelve for the same reason.

most righteous man or woman will make mistakes during life. Clearly, the gravity of the many kinds of transgressions can differ widely and have very different effects. Yet, one should be aware that no one is blameless. Recognition of this reality is the great lesson of the Book of Job (Reading 46). Job was a righteous man who thought that he was blameless. Finally, after many calamities, he acknowledged before God his self-righteousness which is a transgression. An example of an intense awareness of man's evil inclination is the grandiose opening of the Book of Isaiah. After beholding the LORD seated on a high and lofty throne, Isaiah cried 'Woe is me! I am doomed! For I am a man of unclean lips and I live among a people of unclean lips.' (Isaiah 6:5—see Reading 25). God knows that His creation, mankind, is prone to transgression but He does not destroy mankind for its evil inclination. Regret, a change of heart and a return to God are enough to be purified and restored in good faith. When the Accuser (usually translated as Satan) accused the high priest of being dressed in filthy clothes, symbolizing not only his transgressions but also all transgressions of mankind, he sought the condemnation of mankind. However, the angel of the LORD came to the defense of mankind and rebuked the Accuser (Zechariah 3 in Reading 38). There is no need to draft a catalogue of transgressions like we do in a penal code; instead, we refer to basic characteristics of transgressive behavior which are laid out in the Bible and are always related to human freedom and responsibility for the consequences of choices we made. For this reason, transgression is part of humanity only and the Old Testament does not recognize evil as an independent force opposing God or humanity.

Our views on what constitutes transgression are open to interpretation but, fortunately, the Old Testament provides divine guidance. At Mount Sinai the Ten Sayings (traditionally called the Ten Commandments) were given by God and are ever since the backbone of the moral code. They are mentioned in Exodus 20:1-17 and Deuteronomy 5:4-21. Etched in stone, the Ten Sayings are ten categories—see comments in Reading 4. Other parts of the Bible and Jewish-Christian history have worked out the ten categories into many more transgressions, an ongoing work that is punctuated from time to time by an attempt of codification. According to traditional Judaism, the most authoritative codification was made by Moshe Maimonides in his 'Sefer Hamitzvot' (Book of Commandments), written between 1170 and 1180 AD. In it he argued that the Written Law and the Oral Law together contained 613 commandments or 'mitzvah', consisting of 248 positive commandments—an allusion to the number of limbs in the human body—and 365 negative commandments or prohibitions—an allusion to the number of days in a solar year. He then identified and qualified these commandments as the basis of transgressions. The number of 613 commandments dates from the third century sermon of Rabbi Simlai as mentioned in the Talmud, Makkot 23b. Traditional Judaism still accepts Maimonides' codification of the 613 commandments and requires any observant orthodox Jew to behave accordingly. Christian history also witnessed attempts to codify instructions and transgressions, like the famous 'Summa Theologica' of Thomas Aquinas in the 13th century. It is divided in 614 questions. However, interpreting and re-interpreting the Bible is an effort of any generation so that the sacred book remains a living book for the present and future generations.

Clearly, a person's behavior is not only based on his/her consciousness and the rules of a religious or non-religious belief but are also influenced by the enforcement of the laws of the country. It is enough to bring in mind the penal code which lists the criminal offences that are punishable by the administration of justice. In some cases, it can lead to an inner conflict if the laws of the country contradict religious laws and the personal conscience. However, it is good to remind that divine justice cannot be compared with the administration of justice by man. As we witnessed in the 20th century, laws and the administration of justice can become perverted and corrupted too and be used as an instrument of oppression or, even worse, the extreme denial of human dignity by allowing or justifying genocide—see the Nuremberg laws enacted in September 1935 by the Reichstag, a pseudo-parliament, in Nazi Germany.

When reflecting on transgression, a good starting point is the notion of corruption which is dishonest or fraudulent practice that makes someone morally damaged or depraved. Usually, corruption involves the abuse of power or position to acquire a personal benefit. Personal integrity, which is based on being oneself without feigning, is lost and impaired by corruption. Sometimes protection of our integrity can require us to resist social pressure to make a better impression for personal advancement to which you are not entitled if you were true, whole, or innocent. An integer person remains 'complete', unimpaired and enjoys a simplicity of life. Jeremiah 44:7 warns us that we harm ourselves when we transgress 'Why are you doing such great harm to yourselves ...' A second manifestation of corruption is the process by which a word or expression is changed from its original meaning to one regarded as erroneous or debased or even the opposite which is a perversion. Corruption of words is often used to conceal the truth or to manipulate a situation to one's advantage. An authentic life is noticed, certainly by God. In 1 Samuel 16:7 the LORD said to Samuel when he was ordered to anoint the boy David as the future king '... Don't judge him by his appearance or his height, for I have rejected him' (Saul). According to 1 Samuel 9:2 Saul was a handsome and tall man '... an excellent young man; no one among the Israelites was handsomer than he; he was a head taller than any of the people.' The LORD doesn't see things a man sees. People judge by outward appearances but 'the LORD sees into the heart.' (1 Samuel 16:7) A third criterion of transgression is lack of respect towards others which may lead to denigrate or ridicule the other or to intentionally damage his or her reputation. This kind of transgression is aggressive behavior which can escalate into violence and assault. In an open and free society, we need to distinguish between freedom of expression and transgressive verbal behavior even if the borderline can be a precarious one. However, there are ways of expressing a judgment or opinion, stating your point, in a more neutral way without the intent of hurting another person. This attitude is the right choice for any righteous person to avoid harmful behavior and show respect towards others, even enemies. Hurtful or hateful speech is repeatedly regarded as a serious flaw by Isaiah—see Reading 25. Finally, when we doubt about what transgression is, we can always pray to the LORD with confidence: 'let me know Your paths, O LORD, teach me Your ways' so that I do not stumble (Psalm 25:4).[4]

It happens that others warn for our own mistakes, perhaps by reproaching us openly. Any justified admonition can help to regain a proper awareness of our deeds and allow us to correct harmful behavior. As a matter of fact, it is a very common way. We constantly and most often unconsciously assess the behavior of people around us and call on them to stop unwanted or harmful speech and actions, if any. By doing so we help each other to walk upright. The Talmud (Sotah 22a) teaches that one lapse, if repeated, becomes permissible to the transgressor. Moreover, small missteps can easily become a slippery slope of ever more serious transgressions. Regarding private or public reproach, there is a difference between shaming and guilt. Some societies believe in shaming which implies our moral conduct depends on conformity to commonly held standards, rules, and expectations. In these societies people are required to do what others expect you to do. Examples are 'political correctness' arguments and woke culture which intend to limit and guide our thoughts and expressions of opinion. In an environment driven by shaming, the judgment of others can easily become the basis for our own opinion and social interaction. A person who is accused of transgressing political correctness and woke behavior can be subjected to a wide variety of social sanctions such as shame, ridicule, disapproval, and even exclusion. In a shaming culture, emphasis is put on how you appear in the eyes of others. On the other hand, Judaism and Christianity teach the

---

4. The same hope of being taught by the LORD is expressed in Micah 4:2 'And the many nations shall go and shall say: "Come ... That He may instruct us in His ways, and that we may walk in His paths." For instruction shall come forth from Zion, the word of the LORD from Jerusalem.'

importance of personal conscience about what is right and wrong grounded on internalized values. As rabbi Jonathan Sacks wrote, 'The emergence of a guilt culture in Judaism flowed from its understanding of the relationship between God and humankind. From a Jewish perspective, we are not actors on a stage with society as the audience and a judge. We can fool society, but we cannot fool God. All pretense and pride, every mask and persona, the cosmetic cultivation of public image are irrelevant.' Sacks warns us about the dangers of the use of mainstream media and social media as tools of public shaming, illustrating both the power and the danger of a culture of shame.[5]

Harmful behavior can have communal consequences. By its nature it is contagious and, if not stopped, can become accepted in everyday life. Uncorrected mistakes and lack of attention by others can give the wrong signal that such conduct may go unsanctioned which undermines our sense of justice and righteousness and becomes socially destructive. Transgression produces negative dynamic effects which are well described in the Book of Leviticus—see Leviticus in Reading 6. Sin is regarded as an impurity which can provoke a societal breakdown and even defile the divinely created order. Nowhere else in the Old Testament is the contagious nature of sin so vividly presented as in Leviticus dealing with leprosy.[6] Fearing the spread of the infection, the leper is ritually removed from society and must live outside the Israelite camp until his health is fully restored.[7] His healing is extensively examined by a prescribed priestly ritual in Leviticus 14. 'Outside the camp' stands for death, disease, expulsion, and brokenness. The use of running water in the re-entry ritual of the healed leper symbolizes the removal of sin or transgression. In Leviticus again, sending away the goat to Azazel confirms the contagious nature of transgression—see Reading 7.

The most damaging form of socially destructive behavior is uncorrected transgression by those in power who can harm many persons under their control. In the Book of Micah, the prophet rebuked the political and

---

5. Rabbi Jonathan Sacks, "The Power of Shame," 14 April 2016—http://blogs.timesofisrael.com/the-power-of-shame-metsorah-covenant-conversation-5776-on-spirituality/

6. The physical effects of leprosy are shortly mentioned in Aaron's and Moses' prayer for the healing of their sister Myriam in Numbers 12:10-13: 'As the cloud withdrew from the Tent, there was Myriam stricken with snow-white scales! When Aaron turned toward Myriam, he saw that she was stricken with scales. And Aaron said to Moses, "O my lord, account not to us the sin which we committed in our folly. Let her not be as one dead, who emerges from his mother's womb with half his flesh eaten away." So Moses cried out to the LORD, saying, "O God, pray heal her!"'

7. The unclean state of the leper falls in the same category as someone who encountered a corpse. Hence, a purification is necessary. Although leprosy is a disease, not a sin, Leviticus portrays leprosy as the contagious nature of sin like an infectious disease.

religious leaders for being immoral, oppressing the people and being corrupt. The prophet Amos also condemned the corrupted leadership which was only preoccupied with their own rights and privileges and oppressed the poor and needy despite their root ritual performances in the Temple (Reading 30). However, blaming the leadership alone is not always precise as the people should have revolted against unjust leaders and, by failing to do so, became complicit in the transgressions and crimes of the leaders (Micah in Reading 33). In our time, an example of the people's complicity is the lack of resistance by the German people to the crimes of their national-socialist government in the fateful 1930s and during the Second World War.

Our own conscience entails the willingness to take responsibility for own mistakes while excluding responsibility for mistakes of others. In the later books of the Old Testament the principle of individual responsibility was raised, especially after the destruction of Jerusalem which was seen as a divine punishment for the mistakes of the forefathers. Already during the Babylonian captivity, the exiled Israelites complained about their punishment for the mistakes of the forefathers.[8] Ezekiel answered that individual regret, change and acceptance of responsibility are the cornerstone of personal salvation. Moreover, blaming the forefathers is an easy excuse for failing to act. In his view self-examination is the starting point for individual improvement (Reading 27). However, the Old Testament makes it also clear that mistakes of the forefathers can serve as a warning not to act in the same way. It is the message in Zechariah 1:4 'Do not act like your fathers!' (Reading 38) and in Psalm 78:8 '. . . and not be like your forefathers, a stubborn and rebellious generation, a generation whose heart was devoted to God, whose spirit was not faithful to God.' A good knowledge and understanding of history may help to prevent that the same mistakes are made again and again. The Old Testament itself is the first great history book containing useful lessons regarding past mistakes, even in a distant past—see the timetable of the Old Testament in Annex.

Individual responsibility is confirmed in Habakkuk 2:4 '. . . the righteous man is rewarded with life for his faithfulness.' Referring to Sheol, the abode of the dead, the book continues by teaching us that a wicked man does not really live, he is already dead although he is not aware of this reality. Yet, a widespread pattern of misbehaviour can lead to national disaster and have even negative effects on later generations. Many contemporary academic studies demonstrate the intergenerational consequences of policies and attitudes in almost any domain of life. Mistakes of today can lead

---

8. This was a widely held belief and repeated in Lamentations 5:7 'Our fathers sinned and are no more; and we must bear their guilt.'

to harmful effects beyond the present generation which is a major argument for stopping environmental degradation as an example. Having this in mind, it is said in Exodus 34:7 'But He does not excuse the guilty. He visits the wickedness of parents upon children and grandchildren, into the third and fourth generation.' (Reading 4). Aware of the grave intergenerational effects of wicked behaviour, King Solomon, when he dedicated the Temple, prayed for forgiveness for the mistakes of future generations (Reading 22).

'Teshuvah', from the Hebrew verb הבושת, means turn or return and, in this context, it means a (re)turn to God. The word is usually translated as 'repentance' although this is not an accurate translation since the Hebrew verb contains two connected elements at the same time: regret for mistakes and a return to God because of a change of heart and mind. English and some other languages do not have a word that combines the two elements. It proves how the Hebrew language is deeply influenced by the ancient belief that every emotion or thought is known by God. 'Teshuvah' is so central in the Old Testament or Hebrew Bible that Maimonides wrote 'All the prophets preach teshuvah.'[9] We will now look at the several elements in the process of teshuva, namely regret, a change of heart and mind with a return to God, and forgiveness.

REGRET AND CONFESSION

Regret deals with remorse for the mistake we made because we have accepted responsibility for wrongdoing. It can provoke many emotions and always involves sorrow or disappointment and distress. However, a warning is needed regarding "regret" because of sorrow for the negative consequences of transgression. It happens that people regret the consequences of their action without having regret over the decision itself to make the mistake. For example, a thief can regret that he was caught by the police, without having regretted that he stole something. Or we regret that we have not taken the right turn on our way home so that we had to make a long detour. Confession has a different meaning and implies that we regret our behaviour because we acted morally wrong, and we look back with a sense of loss. As a matter of fact, any morally wrong behaviour degrades to some extent our personal integrity. The distress can affect our wellbeing to such extent that we are not only vexed by our transgressions, but we physically suffer from it. In Psalm 32 David felt very ill when thinking about his transgression, his vigour waned, and it felt as if his limbs wasted away (Readings 40 and 41).

---

9. Moshe Maimonides, Mishneh Torah, Sefer Madda, Hilchot Teshuva, Chapter Seven, Halacha 5.

Hosea was the first prophet to announce publicly the paramount importance of 'teshuvah' and he was the most articulate and persuasive on this (Reading 28). Throughout history, both rabbinical thought and secularist views agree that sincere self-examination and introspection are essential for improving life and restoring personal integrity.

The prophets called on the people to regret, to confess and to return to God. When they made their denunciations and frightful maledictions, they had only one purpose in mind which is to wake up the people from their lethargic state. Their warning was a call to be honest and accept responsibility for own mistakes. Only by doing so can punishment and disaster be averted. The prophets always hoped that their warning would be heeded so that their calling would become self-defeating. Notwithstanding the many prophetic calls, the Old Testament contains numerous examples of a denial of guilt with punishing consequences. The story about King Saul illustrates that an unrepentful transgressor or insincere repentant is doomed to repeat his mistakes which may lead to his downfall (Reading 19). Insincere regret is the same as no regret although with a veneer of hypocrisy. The Old Testament includes several cases of insincere regret that were uncovered and finally sanctioned (Readings 3 and 13).

Self-examination as a way of self-improvement was an essential element in the works of the Greek philosopher Socrates (470-399 BC). Max Maxwell writes about it as follows: 'Socrates lived most of his life constantly examining his own ideas and character. He saw such self-examination, whether conducted by himself or in companionship with conversation partners, to be the greatest good of a life worth living. His constant habit of examining himself and others was not an obsession with idle philosophy games. Socrates' focus was to determine how to become a better human. In this Socratic perspective, the quality and persistence of the attention we pay to living an examined life is at the heart of living well.'[10]

Regret is not complete without accepting responsibility for transgressions and confessing them. Confession of transgression before God ('viduy' or וִדּוּי in Hebrew) is an act of honesty which demands that we have no excuses or false justifications for a morally wrongful act (Reading 15). Confession of transgression is not only required on Yom Kippur but is also necessary at the end of life. As the moments of dying bring the conclusion of the soul's dwelling on earth, it also heralds the beginning of the soul's passage to eternal life in Heaven, the dwelling place of God. The catholic church regards confession as the intention of returning to God like the prodigal son

---

10. quoted from The Fundamentals of Education—www.socraticmethod.net/how_to_use_the_socratic_method/page3.html

(Luke 15:11-32) and to acknowledge our transgressions with true sorrow before a priest. After confession the repentant should thank God for His forgiveness.[11]

Confession or acceptance of responsibility can be a very hard step to make because it's an admission of failure and error (Psalm 32 in Reading 41). According to Daniel Kahneman, the Israeli Nobel laureate and father of behavioural economics, regret and acceptance of responsibility are rare. People find a way to explain what happened and blame somebody, the general pattern when things go wrong, and people are afraid.[12] From early childhood humans seem to have developed clever mechanisms to avoid confronting own mistakes. One such mechanism is denial of evident facts or observed consequences that distorts our view on reality. Isaiah 6:9 gives a suitable description of denial 'Listen indeed, but do not understand. See, indeed, but do not comprehend.' (Reading 25). If denial no longer works, people may start to rationalize their transgressive conduct by logically sounding arguments, a second defense line. An early critique of this kind of reasoning is Plato's dialogue called "Sophist" ('Σοφιστής') written in 360 BC which described sophists, a kind of orators in his time, as paid hunters for the young and wealthy, as merchants of knowledge who do not offer true knowledge but only an opinion, an insincere kind of conceited mimicry. In the Book of Jeremiah, the wicked people rationalized their immoral conduct by accusing Jeremiah of treason (Reading 26). In 1 Chronicles 21:1 rationalization is personified by Satan inducing King David to count the number of Israelites notwithstanding God's prohibition and support for Satan's message by his commander Joab who argued that the Israelites were all subjects of King David (Reading 55). David accepted this logical but false argument for which he would be punished. A third defense line is the bad habit that hardens us to perceive the transgression we commit. Moreover, a repeated transgression creates an appearance of righteousness or entitlement to act wickedly. A fourth defense is to blame others so that our transgression remains in the shadows or even appears justified. Non-reciprocity in confession and acceptance of responsibility is an important principle since a transgression by another does not justify us to make the same mistake. A fifth defense line is trivializing our transgressions as minor occurrences that do not really matter although it puts us on a slippery slope to more and more harmful deeds. God knows that confession may require a long time and He gives enough time to confess although a persistent denial

---

11. www.catholic.org/prayers/confession.php

12. The Telegraph, June 5, 2016—www.telegraph.co.uk/business/2016/06/05/british-voters-succumbing-to-impulse-irritation-and-anger---and/

of transgression will be punished. God waited before He destroyed the generation of the Flood (Genesis 6-9), the people of Sodom (Genesis 19), and the unremorseful Pharaoh (Exodus in Reading 3).

To whom should we confess? We should confess our transgressions to God and, if we harmed a person, also to that person. King David gave the example of a contrite heart by regretting sincerely, confessing directly to God and God forgave him (Readings 21 and 43). Regret without confession locks us into the past and causes us to live with a bad conscience. It may be difficult or embarrassing to confess directly to the person we harmed but it is a matter of fairness and honesty to do so. In traditional Judaism, confession of transgressions is done by a terminally ill person, although he should first endeavor to ask forgiveness from those whom he may have caused pain or hardship.

Confession can also be done by a community. During Yom Kippur services, the 'Text of Al Chet' or 'confession of sins' is said ten times and includes the plea 'For all these, God of pardon, pardon us, forgive us, atone us.' The Old Testament mentions numerous events when the Israelite community confessed its transgressions. For example, the Book of Leviticus contains important elements of communal confession of guilt and a plea to be forgiven. It is part of the priestly ritual whereby the priest makes expiation for the people and the people shall be forgiven (Reading 6). The second example is 1 Samuel 7 which mentions that the Israelites removed the idolatrous images and confessed that they had transgressed before the LORD (Reading 17). The third example is Nehemiah 9 which contains the communal confession by the people who were fasting in sackcloth and with earth upon them (Reading 54). Confession of error and sin can be necessary for political leaders on behalf of a failing government. The Catholic Church reinstated communal confession by Vatican II which emphasized the social as well as the personal consequences of sin. Communal confession is now part of the 'Ordo Paenitentiae' of 1974 although a private confession is still needed for grave sins. The bishops predicted that the communal setting would become the ordinary one for penance.[13]

A CHANGE OF HEART AND MIND

Genesis 1:26 tells us that man was created in the image and likeness of God, one of the most important statements of the Old Testament. It implies that we have a spark of the divine in our self and that we have the

---

13. Edward B. Fiske, "Vatican Revises Sacrament of Penance," The New York Times, February 7, 1974.

capacity to be in a close personal relationship with God. By growing into adulthood from the age of 13 and during our adult life we become defiled by errors and mistakes since we are prone to the evil inclination. However, even when we go astray, we keep the capacity to access the divine spark in ourselves, to return to this dimension deep inside ourselves. Yet, the more we transgress, the more the divine spark is buried and the harder it is to reconnect with it. The consequences are far-reaching because by burying our divine spark we also estrange from God, our Creator and source of life. For every person maintaining a close relationship with God is the greatest joy in life which becomes more difficult or can even be lost by our transgressions. Thus, a return after self-examination means a return to our inner self and a return to God at the same time. According to the Old Testament and Jewish-Christian teachings, any transgression damages the relationship with God.

A change of heart and mind is the transformation that is taking place in anyone involved in returning after self-examination. Instead of hardening our heart, we open our heart and mind to make a necessary change possible and regain personal integrity. It also implies that we assert never to make the same mistake again. Trust in our capacity to change ourselves and our actions liberates us from the negative forces of the past and offers a new beginning. When we really change our heart and mind, we should not dwell on the transgressions of the past. A repeat of this view is part of the beautiful Gregorian chant 'Rorate Caeli desuper' that is sung in the advent in all abbeys. Its verses are framed on Isaiah 45:8 in the Vulgate translation.

> 'quare maerore consumeris,
> quia innovavit te dolor?
> Salvabo te, noli timere,
> ego enim sum Dominus Deus tuus,
> Sanctus Israel, Redemptor tuus.'
>
> Why would you fade away in sadness?
> Why has sadness stayed with you?
> I will save you, fear not,
> for I am the Lord your God,
> the Holy One of Israel, your Redeemer.

Trust in our capacity to change renews personal strength while a spirit of defeat is a sign on the wall that we are disconnecting from God (Reading 37). In the story of Ahab, God changed His mind because of the change of heart and mind of the wicked Ahab although it is much harder for him to continue following the right path for the rest of his life (Reading 23).

A return to God as a change of heart and mind is the eternal call of the prophets. According to the Bible, God and man act together in a process of restoring their relationship. While God reaches out to mankind, He cannot be sure that man will reach out to Him. Certainly, a man reaching out to God can be sure of God's positive response (Lamentations in Reading 49). In Malachi 3:7 God declares 'Return to Me, and I will return to you.' (Reading 39). And in Amos 5:4 the LORD said, 'Seek Me and you will live!' (Reading 30). A return to God is the overriding concern in Jeremiah's prophecy even if it means that the law must be broken (Reading 26). In numerous instances a return to God resulted in a divine turning in the sense that God changed His plan with humanity. Instead of punishing humanity, God showed mercy and compassion. One example is the repentant city of Nineveh in the Book of Jonah (Reading 32). Another example is Hosea 11:8-9 'I have had a change of heart and My compassion overflows. I will not unleash My fierce anger, I will not turn to destroy Israel. For I am God, not man, the Hole One living among you. I will not come to destroy you.' (Reading 28).

Sometimes a dramatic event was needed to make the people aware of their transgressions so that they could prepare themselves for a return to God. This is the message of the Book of Lamentations with the assurance that God shows an abundant kindness once we are cleansed and reunited with Him in heart and mind (Reading 49). The Book of Lamentations is a call not to despair or become embittered in times of distress and catastrophe but seize the moment to change for the better. As the first, Moses revealed that God shall always be with His people if they search for the LORD and seek Him with all their heart and soul (Deuteronomy 4 in Reading 14).

FORGIVENESS

Forgiveness is central in the Old Testament as expressed in Numbers 14:20 'And the LORD said, "I will forgive you, as you have asked."' Exodus 34:6-7 shows God reaching out for human pleas for forgiveness. He sets the example, even giving us words to use in our prayers for forgiveness. The same verses reveal God's nature as compassionate and gracious, abounding in kindness and faithfulness, forgiving iniquity and transgressions. They are known in Judaism as 'God's 13 Attributes of Mercy'. (Reading 4). In summary, the Bible tells us that God is inclined to forgive, and this divine attribute embraces the world because God has told that He is the Father of all people. He shows compassion and forgiveness to anybody who is truly responsive and open-minded to His call. This lesson was taught to Jonah who could not believe that God's forgiveness would be granted to Nineveh, a truly wicked although regretful city (Reading 32). When asking God's forgiveness, a truly contrite heart seeks forgiveness based on God's abundant mercy and loving-kindness, not one's own righteousness, as we can read in Psalm 51 (Reading 43) and in the Book of Job (Reading 46).

The liberating effect of God's forgiveness is expressed in verse 1 of Psalm 32 'How happy is he whose transgression is forgiven!' (Reading 41). It is echoed in the Song of Songs '... do not stare at me because I am swarthy...' (Reading 47) which is an allegorical expression of an awareness of past mistakes but with the comforting belief that these mistakes are overcome and forgiven. Thus, when we are truly regretful and ask God's forgiveness, we will be granted it. The promise of restoration and forgiveness is most often repeated in the Book of Jeremiah (Reading 26). However, part of regret and a plea for forgiveness is the acceptance of God's justice: He afflicts us, forgives us, and then rebuilds us (Lamentations in Reading 49).

Repentance atones only for mistakes between man and God while a wrongdoer should ask the wronged person to forgive him (Leviticus in Reading 8). In case we have wronged another, we should address the wronged and ask forgiveness, if necessary, several times. In daily life, many people are too embarrassed or ashamed or too proud to ask forgiveness to the person they wronged. The Old Testament teaches us to overcome this mental obstacle and expressly ask for forgiveness while Maimonides confirmed this moral and religious duty (Leviticus in Reading 8). As a matter of fact, asking for forgiveness is at the same time telling the truth.

Can a person ask forgiveness for the transgression of another person? This question is addressed in Abigail's request to David to forgive her deceitful and ruthless husband Nabal. David showed mercy for Nabal although this could not save his life for Nabal died soon afterwards (Reading 20). It signifies that only the transgressor can ask for forgiveness. Religious and secular views converge on the idea that the process of asking for forgiveness and granting it is necessary for both a reconciliation between persons and peace in society. Clinical practitioners argue that '... forgiveness is a decision to let go resentment and thoughts of revenge. The act that hurt or offended might always be part of your life, but forgiveness can lessen its grip on you and help you focus on other, more positive parts of your life. Forgiveness can even lead to feelings of understanding, empathy, and compassion for the one who hurt you. Forgiveness doesn't mean that you deny the other person's responsibility for hurting you, and it doesn't minimize or justify the wrong. You can forgive the person without excusing the act. Forgiveness brings a kind of peace that helps you go on with life.'[14]

One of the greatest biblical examples of forgiveness is the story of Joseph who forgave his brothers for their betrayal and selling him into slavery (Reading 2). Nevertheless, by reason of the seriousness of their crime, it was a painful process for Joseph, and it took a long time for him to recover. It can also be seen as the ultimate example of brotherly love. The wronged person, if asked for forgiveness, should grant it. If not, he himself commits a transgression. And a person who forgives, but holds a grudge, is also a transgressor because his forgiveness was not sincere (Readings 2 and 10). For the same reason a person who forgave may not seek revenge. Once the transgressor regrets his mistakes and asks for forgiveness to the wronged person, it should be given. Hatred and revenge or prohibited after regret and a plea for being forgiven, as stated in Leviticus 19:17-18 'Do not hate your relatives in your heart. Confront your relatives with their transgressions so that you will not be held responsible for their transgressions. Do not seek vengeance or bear a grudge against your fellows. Love your fellows as yourself. I am the LORD.'

Finally, in the view of the Old Testament a person is not forgiven if he does not ask for forgiveness to the wronged other. Sometimes forgiveness is given without remorse or an apology by the wrongdoer. In this case, the word 'forgiveness' is used in a non-Biblical sense and should be avoided. It is better to say that we let go the past without seeking revenge, although this is not an act of forgiveness but rather a healing step for the victim and even society in some cases.

HEALING

Healing is the most important positive outcome of regret, change and forgiveness. According to the Bible healing refers to either the restoration of the body to health and soundness, relief from emotional distress or the restoration of a good relationship with God.

In Exodus 15:26 God declared 'I will not inflict upon you any of the diseases that I brought upon the Egyptians, for I am the LORD who heals you.' According to this verse God punished the Egyptians by means of successive diseases whereas the healing of the Israelites was their national and spiritual liberation, from a subdued mind to a free spirit (Reading 3). The prophets Isaiah and Jeremiah used the word 'healing' quite often.

---

14. Source: Mayo Clinic—www.mayoclinic.org/healthy-lifestyle/adult-health/in-depth/forgiveness/art-20047692

Isaiah 38 starts with King Hezekiah who fell dangerously ill. When the prophet Isaiah informed him to prepare for his death, the king prayed and asked God for a longer life, referring to his sincere and wholehearted devotion to God. God then commanded Isaiah to tell the king that fifteen years were added to his life. The book continues with the poem by King Hezekiah when he recovered from the illness, thanking God for his compassion 'I walk humbly all my years because of this anguish of my mind. My LORD, despite all this suffering my life was restored in good health; You have restored my health and let me live.' (Isaiah 38:15-16). God changed His mind by the prayer of the loyal king. It illustrates that the future is contingent on the human response to the prophetic word and that God can change His plans.

In Jeremiah 33 God announces the healing of the nation of the Israelites after the cleansing of their transgressions and His forgiveness: 'The time has come that I will heal them and reveal to them abundance of true favor. And I will restore the fortunes of Jerusalem and Israel, and I will rebuild their towns. And I will cleanse them of all the sins against Me, and I will forgive all the sins which they committed against Me, by which they rebelled against Me.' (Jeremiah 33:6-8). God's promise was made at a time when the people of Judah refused to consider the possibility of the destruction of Jerusalem and the subsequent Babylonian captivity (Reading 26). Jeremiah 33 shows God's desire to intervene and save humanity, not to destroy it.

The prophet Hosea uses the parent-child metaphor when the prophet describes God's feelings towards the Israelites in Hosea 11:3 'I have fondled Ephraim, embraced them; but they didn't see My healing care.' The Israelites turned away from their caring Father, not appreciating what He did for them. They rebelled and got into serious problems with the ascending power of the Assyrians who brought the downfall of the Northern Kingdom (Reading 28). Yet, in Hosea 11:8 God asks, 'How can I give you up, O Israel?' A father does not give up his rebellious son but has the patience to welcome the lost son back in the family. Hosea 11:8-9 speaks about the change of heart of God, forgiving the mistakes of the lost son 'I have had a change of heart and my compassion overflows. I will not unleash my fierce anger, I will not turn to destroy Israel. For I am God, not man, the Hole One living among you. I will not come to destroy you.' The healing compassion of God serves as an example for us.

The Psalms contain several verses appealing for the healing power of God. In Psalm 6:3 David cries 'How long O LORD will You wait until You heal me? Have mercy on me, O LORD, for I am sick.' As so often in his life, David was pursued and terrorized by his enemies who wanted him dead. It caused such emotional distress that his bones were shaken with terror, and his eyes were wasted by vexation. God's healing power is embedded in his belief that his life will be saved by God, restoring his mental health and stability, while his enemies will be frustrated and stricken with terror. The same idea is expressed in Psalm 30:3.

The Book of Job is about the testing of Job's faith in God notwithstanding the debilitating diseases that were inflicted on him by the Accuser with God's permission (Reading 46). Seriously ill by diseases, Job's first reaction was to curse the day that he was born (Job 3:1). Yet, Job 5:17-18 tells us that he understands God's power to test his sincerity of faith and the power of healing if he stood firm. 'See how happy the man is who is corrected by God's word; do not reject the healing power of the Almighty. He punishes, but He also heals; He wounds, but His hands heal.' The Book of Job ends with his full recovery and restoration to health, and he lived up to 140 years. He died old and peacefully.

In the closing book of the Old Testament, 2 Chronicles 7:13-14 God told the Israelites that He had punished them with calamities, such as sending the pestilence, although His only purpose was to make possible a change of heart and spirit. If the people return to the LORD, He will forgive their transgressions and heal the land '. . . when My people, who bear My name, will humble themselves, pray, and seek My face and turn from their evil doings, I will hear from heaven and forgive their sins and heal their land.' (2 Chronicles 7:14).

SELF-EXAMINATION AND SELF-DEFENSE

Sometimes we are entangled in a vicious circle of own mistakes and at the same time being the victim of mistakes or attacks by others. A psychological chaos caused by intermingled mistakes can provide an opportunity to use it as an excuse for not regretting own mistakes. Otherwise, it is possible that a person, paralyzed by his mistakes, can delve too deeply in his own mistakes while not reacting adequately to defend himself while under attack. It can become even more extreme when someone unscrupulously exploits the mistake of another to conceal his own and more vicious mistakes.

When King David found himself in this bewildering situation, he sought God's refuge against his enemies, and he started questioning whether he had done wrong things to deserve their hate and anger (Psalm 46 in Reading 40). After weighing in the many confounding events, he concluded he was righteous and blameless, he had even rescued his foe, King Saul, who was now his pursuer. In later life King David encountered life-threatening conspiracies such as the one devised by his son Absalom. Not surprisingly, many Davidic psalms express a plea for God's protection from enemies who have no reason to be hostile. However, David confessed his grave transgression—the provoked killing of one of his soldiers, Uriah—directly to God and was forgiven (Readings 21 and 43). One of the reasons for David's greatness was his ability to distinguish between his own transgressions, which he sincerely regretted, and those of his enemies who repeatedly slandered him without remorse. There is no moral equivalence between David's mistakes and the unrelenting hate campaign of his enemies. At least David returned to God which cannot be said about his pursuers and slanderers who continued to conspire against him without justification except their hunger for power. It teaches us that misrepresentations and false accusations against a person are a character assassination and therefore acts of evil (Zechariah in Reading 38). Scapegoating and character assassination are often the preferred weapons of a group against a person whom the group wants to expel or destroy, like an unpopular colleague in the workspace.[15] It is a heinous crime, and in many cases not even sanctioned because the targeted person will most likely be falsely accused or misrepresented by that social group which holds power. Victims of such social attacks may find comfort in David's plea to God in of Psalm 35:4 'Let those who seek my life be shamed and frustrated; humiliate those who plan to harm me.'

We may conclude that self-examination helps us greatly to distinguish between our mistakes and responsibility and the mistakes of others. This in turn strengthens our personal self-defense against false accusations and slander. To some extent the same is true regarding countries and governments which might be caught in the same kind of political entanglements with a mixture of true and false accusations, either domestically or by foreign governments. If the political system works well and is transparent and honest, governments will be able to have a clearer view and make the right decisions.

---

15. The expression 'scapegoat' means the one that is made to bear the blame of others. It refers to the goat sent to Azazel in the Book of Leviticus (Reading 7).

Part I

THE FIVE BOOKS OF MOSES OR PENTATEUCH

Genesis

Reading 1   The Evil of Man

Genesis 6:5-8

5. And the LORD saw that the evil of man was great in the earth, and every imagination of his heart was only evil all the time.

6. And the LORD regretted that He had made man on the earth, and He became grieved in His heart

7. And the LORD said, "I will blot out man, whom I created, from upon the face of the earth, from man to cattle to creeping thing, to the fowl of the heavens, for I regret that I made them."

8. But Noah found favor in the eyes of the LORD.

GENESIS 6:5-8 IS A strong introductory statement about man's evil, the expression of God's regret and His desire to punish humanity by destroying it, although God ultimately saves humanity because of His mercy and the righteous man Noah. The circumstances leading to God's regret are the creation of Adam ('ish' or 'man') and Eve ('isha' or 'woman') in the Garden of Eden. After the creation of the universe, with all living creatures, God decided to create man '. . . in Our image, after Our likeness...' (Genesis 1:26). The creation of man in God's image and likeness is fundamental to understand the existence and nature of mankind and the many implications following from it. Foremost is man's ability or gift to be in personal relationship with God and to communicate with God at any time. Creation in the image and likeness of God also implied a guaranteed eternal life of the soul of man, an eternal existence in God's presence. Tragically, this condition was lost by man's disobedience in the Garden of Eden, and can only be won again, individually, by leading a God-loving and righteous life. The creation of man in God's image and likeness necessarily implies the obligation that man should respect other men, including his enemies, since they too are created in God's image and likeness.

The nature of mankind is further explained in Genesis 2:7 where it is written that '. . . the Lord GOD formed man from the dust of the ground, and He breathed into his nostrils the soul of life, and man became a living soul.' The formation of man from dust relates to the body or physical form of man, and the inevitability that the body will return to dust or atoms and their subatomic particles. We know that man's body was mortal since his creation because God feared that man, after a transgression of his prohibition not to eat from the Tree of Knowledge of good and evil, could '. . . reach out and take from the Tree of Life and eat and live forever.' (Genesis 3:22). The kind of eternal existence of man in the Garden of Eden remains unexplained and unanswered.

But the body, as much as it is important, does not relate to the image and likeness of God since all living creatures have bodies. Only man was made in the image and likeness of God by breathing into man's nostrils the soul of life. This marks the spiritual dimension of man, transcending earthly or other cosmological categories, which is necessary to remain in God's presence in eternity. For that reason, it is said that man is made from earthly matter (dust) and heavenly matter (soul). The latter refers to the condition that man is made in the image and likeness of God. It sets humanity apart from all other living creatures which do not have a soul. And from this viewpoint God decided that man should '. . . rule over the fish in the sea and over the birds in the skies and over the animals over all the earth and over all the small animals that creep upon the earth.' (Genesis 1:26). God's decision gives mankind the ability and entitlement to rule and to explore the universe since no other living being has been given a soul.

God commanded man by saying 'Of every tree of the garden you may freely eat. But of the Tree of Knowledge of good and evil you shall not eat of it, for on the day that you eat from that tree, you shall surely die.' (Genesis 2:16-17). The creation of the Tree of Knowledge of good and evil also means that God created good and evil, symbolized by a forbidden tree and its fruit. There is only one reason for God's creation of evil: everything, material or immaterial in the universe and beyond, is the creation of God. Nothing can exist outside God's will and power. This can never be fully understood but at least we can be aware of God creating and holding everything together or destroying what has been created. And the prophet Isaiah said: 'I am the LORD, and there is no other God. I will make you more powerful although you have not known Me. In order that they know from the east to the west that there is no other God; I am the LORD and there is no other. I create light and darkness, I make peace and bring bad times; I am the LORD, who makes all these.' (Isaiah 45: 5-7). The fact that man can neither fully understand nor enquire God was made clear to Moses when he asked to see God. The LORD answered: ". . . you may not see My face, for man may not see Me and live." And the LORD continued, "See, there is a place near Me on the rock; as My Presence passes by, I will put you in a crevice of the rock and shield you with My hand until I have passed by. Then I will take My hand away and you will see My back; but My face will not be seen." (Exodus 33:20-23). God's words go to the heart of the religious consciousness and experience.

Humans have the capacity to be aware of God's existence but cannot gain knowledge about God except by the self-revelations of God as recorded in the Bible. Science and knowledge are the domain of humans, but science or human reasoning alone cannot add anything about God. Today we live in an age of technological revolution and rapid scientific advances, there is always the temptation to explain away God by means of science. The religious person is intensely aware about God's existence but does not strife to know God as we know subjects by scientific efforts. Here is a potential pitfall of any scientific education, namely the belief that one day in a distant future science will be able to explain everything that exists. Without a spiritual or religious point of view, any scientific temptation can easily lead to a denial of God's existence. Unfortunately, universities and schools, as the centers of knowledge and science, are becoming a cultural environment that is prone to reject what cannot be understood by science, including faith. God's only prohibition was not to eat from the Tree of Knowledge of good and evil although Adam and Eve were granted the freedom to obey or disobey God. Man, from his creation, was given a freedom of choice regarding the only prohibition in the Garden of Eden. Freedom of choice will remain a privilege and a daily responsibility of man in all times. 'Man is the last in creation and the first in responsibility.' (Vayikra Rabbah 14).

Finally, Genesis 4:7 calls for continuous self-examination so that we not trespass: 'If you do not improve, however, at the entrance, sin is lying, and to you is its longing, but you can rule over it.' The expression 'At the entrance sin is lying' means that at the entrance of your grave, your transgression is preserved. The expression 'but you can rule over it' means that if you wish, you will overpower your evil inclination which constantly longs and lusts to cause you stumble—see Rashi comment on 4:7

The fateful event that resulted in sin is man's decision to disobey the only prohibition by eating from the Tree of Knowledge of good and evil (see Genesis 3:6). Immediately before this act, as if in an uncontrolled state of mind, the tree was very desirable because it made one wise, in the sense that wisdom is gained by knowing the difference between good and evil. But wisdom and knowledge come with pain and anxiety, with regret and sorrow, like it is said in Ecclesiastes 1:18: 'For in much wisdom is much sorrow, and he who acquires knowledge increases pain.'[1] Knowledge and awareness of having done evil causes pain and anxiety, not only temporarily, but also at an existential level, since the personal bond with God is harmed or can even be lost forever. From the moment that Adam and Eve disobeyed God, transgression and 'teshuvah' or repentance became two separate although related acts. It starts with transgression or disobedience of God's commandments and instructions and is as such a factual element, namely a deed, a thought, an emotion, or an omission.

In the beginning, transgression or disobedience of God's commandment was only possible regarding one prohibition. After the eating from the forbidden tree and the subsequent expulsion from the Garden of Eden, the possibilities of wrongful conduct dramatically expanded because Adam and Eve were expelled from the Garden of Eden or paradise. The dramatic increase in possible transgressions is not explained by Genesis but can be deduced from the event that Cain killed his brother Abel and was punished by God. Cain became a wanderer and an exile in the land (Genesis 4:8-16). From this event we also learn that wrongful conduct, by unlawfully harming another human, is at the same time a transgression against God. The acquired post-Adam and Eve knowledge of good and evil remains connected to free choice after transgressive conduct, namely the freedom to atone or not. A transgressor can deny or disregard his wrongdoing, as all too often happens, but he has the freedom to regret, to acknowledge responsibility and to return to God with sincerity of heart and mind. Regret and the humble question for forgiveness is not only a matter between men, but also between man and God which we discover in many stories of the Bible.

God's regret in Genesis 6:6 is sometimes called 'the repentance of God' although this expression is misguided because God is without fault or moral imperfection and God's decisions cannot be subject to human doubt or judgment. God's regret is a change in God's plan or intention, sometimes because of man's return to God according to later books of the Old

---

1. The early secularist movement developed a similar thought, for example Jean-Jacques Rousseau (1712–78). See Craig Calhoun et al. (eds), Classical Sociological Theory, Oxford, Wiley-Blackwell, 2020, p. 26: "Rousseau was passionate about the exercise of individual reason ... Shockingly, he argued that progress in science actually brought humanity unhappiness by separating people from nature." However, Rousseau misses the point that unhappiness results from lack of a moral code as the Old Testament teaches us. In the 20th century Nazi Germany was a highly developed country and at the forefront of science and technology but abandoned the biblical moral code.

Testament.[2] In Genesis 6:5, God wanted to destroy humanity because '... how great was man's wickedness on earth, and how every plan they devised by his mind was nothing but evil all the time.' Nevertheless, God rejected His thought because of the righteous man Noah and God's inclination to mercy and compassion whenever there is a good reason. God's change of mind is not always the result of regret or human pleading because God also shows His will to intervene and save humanity at critical moments, even by changing His original plan.[3]

We learn from God's change of mind that one righteous man, Noah, can save humanity. Such is the power of one individual leading a righteous life, even considering that no man can live a perfect life.[4] Judah HaNasi, also called Rabbeinu HaKadosh, emphasized the potential power of one righteous individual to save the world: 'And whoever saves a single life, the Old Testament considers it as if he saved an entire world'. Moreover, according to the Talmud (Yoma 86b), God forgives the misdeeds of a whole community on account of the true repentance of only one man. It is explained by the goodness of God as God's main attribute (Talmud Yer. Hag. 77c). God is the Supreme Judge and Father, tempering justice with mercy and compassion.

Finally, God's change of mind may involve His intention to punish. God said to Noah: 'The end of all flesh has come before Me, for the earth has become full of robbery because of them, and behold I am destroying them from the earth.' (Genesis 6:13). He commanded Noah to build an ark of gopher wood to save Noah and his family from the global flood which devastated all living creatures on the earth. Noah, his wife and children, and all living animals—two of each (male and female) were brought into the ark—and spared during the catastrophic flood. The ark came to rest in the seventh month of the flood, on the mountains of Ararat. After this destruction, the LORD said to Himself 'Never again will I doom the earth because of man, since the devisings of man's mind are evil from his youth.' (Genesis 8:21).

---

2. See Exodus 32:14; Deuteronomy 32:36; Judges 2:18; 1 Samuel 15:10-11.

3. In particular, the Book of Jeremiah contains the articulation of hope by God's intention. One remarkable revelation of God's intention of giving hope happened while Jeremiah was in the prison compound: 'This said the LORD who is planning it, the LORD who is shaping it to bring it about, whose name is LORD; call to Me, and I will answer you, and I will tell you wondrous things, secrets you have not known.' (Jeremiah 33:2-3)

4. That no man can live a perfect life will be dealt with in the considerations about the Book of Job (Reading 46).

For the first time the Bible mentions a covenant between God and mankind in the person of Noah (Genesis 6:18). The Noahite covenant is God's promise to righteous men, while the ark became the symbol of God's presence among His people. At that moment the idea of the Ark of the Covenant was born, and it will reach its climax when Moses has his meetings with God at Mount Sinai (Exodus 19:3). However, the covenant between God and men is conditional on a righteous life and recognition of God as the Creator of the universe. If people forsake the LORD, they will suffer because they broke the covenant. Divine punishment is a recurring theme throughout the Old Testament if the covenant with God is violated.

Reading 2   *The brothers of Joseph ask for forgiveness.*

Genesis 42:21

21. They said to one another, "Alas, we are being punished for what we did to our brother, because we merely looked on at his anguish when he begged us, and we did not listen. That is why this calamity has come upon us."

...

Genesis 50:16-21

16. So they sent these words to Joseph, "Before he died your father left this instruction:

17. So shall you say to Joseph, "Please, forgive now your brothers' transgression and their sin, for they did evil to you. Now please forgive the transgression of the servants of the God of your father." Joseph wept when they spoke to him.

18. His brothers went to him, fell before him, and said, "We are prepared to be treated as your slaves."

19. But Joseph promptly said to them, "Do not fear! Am I a replacement for God?

20. Besides, although you intended to harm me, God intended it for good, He wanted to bring about the present outcome—the survival of many people.

21. Fear not. I will sustain you and your children." Thus he comforted them, speaking kindly to them!

A GREAT FAMILY CRIME and drama is at the root of this brotherly expression of regret and a plea for forgiveness. Jacob, also called 'Israel,'[1] who was the

---

1. Jacob's second name was 'Israel' since the day that he met an angel with whom

grandson of Abraham, dwelt with his family in the land of Canaan. Genesis 37:3-4 mentions that Israel, who had twelve sons, loved Joseph more than all his sons, because he was a son of his old age.[2] His brothers saw that their father loved Joseph more than all his brothers, so they hated him, and they could not speak with him in a friendly manner. As the oldest son of his favored wife Rachel, Jacob loved Joseph dearly and gave him preferential treatment, causing Joseph's brothers to envy him and, finally, sell him into slavery. Maimonides criticizes Jacob because he should not have differentiated between his children: 'Our Sages commanded that a person should not differentiate between his children in his lifetime, even regarding a small matter, lest this spawn competition and envy as happened with Joseph and his brothers.'[3]

Joseph was known for his dream interpretations about which he spoke frequently and openly. One day Joseph told his brothers that he had dreamed they were binding sheaves in the middle of a field and his sheaf rose and stood upright while his brothers' sheaves encircled it and prostrated themselves to Joseph's sheaf. His brothers became even more angry. This time even his father Jacob rebuked Joseph for some of his dreams, although Jacob did not consider the dreams without meaning and waited to look forward in expectation of what would come—see Rashi comment on Verse 37:11.

It happened that Joseph was on his way to meet his brothers in a field, when they planned to kill him. But his brother Reuben saved him by proposing the alternative of throwing him in a pit. The brothers acted accordingly. When a caravan was coming from Gilead and heading to Egypt, his brother Judah proposed to sell Joseph as a slave to the caravan leaders. The brothers of Joseph pulled him out of the pit and sold him as a slave to the

---

he wrestled until the break of dawn. When the angel said, 'Let me go, for dawn is breaking', Jacob said 'I will not let you go before you have blessed me.' Then the angel asked, 'What is your name?' and he said 'Jacob'. And the angel said, 'Your name shall be called no more Jacob, but Israel, for you have striven with God and humans, and have prevailed.' (Genesis 32: 25-29). God confirmed the new name of Jacob on Jacob's arrival from Paddan-aram in a place called Bethel. God said to him 'Your name is Jacob, you shall not be called anymore Jacob, but Israel shall be your name.' (Genesis 35:10).

2. Jacob had twelve sons who established the twelve tribes of Israel. 'The sons of Leah: Reuben (Jacob's first-born), Simeon, Levi, Judah, Issachar, and Zebulun. The sons of Rachel: Joseph and Benjamin. The sons of Bilhah, Rachel's maid: Dan and Naphtali. And the sons of Zilpah, Leah's maid: Gad and Asher. These are the sons of Jacob who were born to him in Paddan-aram.' (Genesis 35:22-26).

3. Moshe Maimonides, Mishneh Torah, Sefer Mishpatim, Hilchot Nehalot, Chapter Six, Halacha 13.

caravan people for twenty silver pieces. Jacob is deceived when his sons tell him that a wild beast had killed Joseph.[4]

While Jacob was mourning, Joseph was bought by Potiphar, the Pharaoh's chamberlain, and served the household of the Pharaoh. After explaining the Pharaoh's dream about seven years of abundance and seven years of drought in Egypt, the Pharaoh appointed Joseph over the entire land of Egypt. During a period of extreme drought and famine, Jacob sent his sons to Egypt to buy grain, except the youngest son Benjamin who stayed at home. When the brothers met Joseph, he recognized them, but he made himself not known to them. Joseph accused his brothers of spying and put them in jail for three days. Then Joseph sent his brothers home to bring with them Benjamin. At this point, although they did not know that the Pharaoh's Vizier was Joseph, the brothers expressed first-time regret because they had sold one of them and said that they had come in trouble because of their crime (Genesis 42:21). But Joseph's mercy was stirred towards his brothers, and he wanted to weep, so he went into another room and wept there. After some time, Joseph made himself known to his brothers, and he kissed all his brothers and wept over them, and afterwards his brothers spoke with him. When the brothers went back home again Jacob decided that the whole family would go to Egypt to meet Joseph. Then God appeared to Jacob in a nightly vision, and He said: 'Do not be afraid to go down to Egypt, for there I will make you into a great nation. I will go down with you to Egypt, and I will also bring you back again' (Genesis 46:3-4).[5]

Joseph settled his father Jacob and his brothers and gave them property in Egypt, in the fertile Land of Goshen, as Pharaoh had mandated. After Jacob's death, the brothers started to fear that Joseph would hate them and return to them all the evil that they had done to him. Because of their fear, they asked Joseph forgiveness for their grave transgressions. Joseph forgave his brothers and comforted them, saying that God had designed it for good. God's purpose was to save many lives in Egypt, the lives of the Joseph's

---

4. In the Old Testament, 'evil beasts' is an expression of God's punishment, along with the sword, famine, and pestilence. See Ezekiel 5:17, 14:15 and 33:27; Jeremiah 15:3 and Leviticus 26:22. It is likely that the brothers suggested that Joseph had sinned because of his dreams, and therefore was punished by God.

5. Here Gods reveals the place where the descendants of Jacob will become a great nation, namely in Egypt. Before, at Bethel, God had promised Jacob to become the forefather of a great nation and to acquire the land that God had promised to Abraham and Isaac, namely the land of Canaan. God said at Bethel: 'I am El Shaddai (meaning 'God pays attention'). Be fertile and increase; a nation, an assembly of nations, shall descend from you. Kings shall issue from your loins. The land that I gave to Abraham and Isaac I give to you; and to your descendants will I give the land.' (Genesis 35:11).

family and to prepare the Israelite tribe for becoming a great nation in Egypt and their later liberation and exodus to Canaan.

The religious idea underlying the narrative is that 'Yahweh was with Joseph', recalling Yahweh's promise to the patriarchs Abraham, Isaac, and Jacob that He would always be with them and their descendants. In the many life-threatening situations, Yahweh protected and favored Joseph. One is mentioned by Genesis 39:2-3 'The LORD was with Joseph, and he became a successful man while he stayed in the house of his Egyptian master. Potiphar noticed that the LORD was with Joseph and that the LORD lent him success to everything he undertook; he began to like Joseph.'

Regarding regret and forgiveness, several lessons can be learned from the interactions between Joseph and his brothers. One is that we should not hold grudges but forgive those who have injured us and have asked for forgiveness.[6] Ultimately, a grudge turns against him who holds a grudge; it will make a man bitter. Another lesson is the state of mind of the transgressor. Joseph's brothers could never forget their criminal act, even when it was done in a concealed way, and this created fear, anxiety, and doubtfulness in their mind. They felt the need to recognize their transgression or criminal act before Joseph and God—they called themselves 'the servants of the God of your father'—and to accept whatever may come, even slavery. The brothers were ultimately saved by Joseph. Forgiveness was their reward and anger replaced by brotherly love.

Joseph's words of forgiveness are among the finest in the Bible: 'Now do not be afraid for I will sustain you and your children. And he reassured them and spoke with kindness.' (Genesis 50:21). However, Joseph had been the victim of a serious crime committed by his brothers and it took a long time to heal from it as Joseph wept on several occasions when seeing back his brothers. Indeed, Joseph's forgiveness was a long and painful process because of the seriousness of the crime. A consequence of forgiveness is that the wronged person (in this case Joseph) does not seek revenge but draws a dividing line between the past and the future. It means that one should not bring the wrongdoing up again.

A final lesson is given in the very beginning. If we witness the distress of a man's soul who begs for our compassion and support, we have the obligation to listen and to help as much as we can. If not, remorse will haunt us; our mind will be troubled because we could have saved somebody from anguish and pain. A final lesson reveals God's plan. What Joseph's brothers meant for evil, God meant for good. Their wrongdoing was overshadowed by God's will to save. Joseph's brothers and Joseph himself were instruments

---

6. Not to bear a grudge is a commandment according to Leviticus 19:18

in God's plan for the salvation of the Israelites because God secretly blessed and preserved Jacob's family. At a fundamental level, it implies that humans can never read or predict the mind of God, no matter how great the suffering can be or how righteously we live. Joseph became gradually aware of this truth as the story unfolded. Even in great injustices, God creates a future for those and their descendants who show a steadfast belief in God's goodness, protection, and loving kindness for His people. Experiencing injustices and enduring hard times are a test of life, character, and faith.

Exodus

Reading 3 Pharaoh's insincere regret

Exodus 9:27-35

27. So Pharaoh sent messengers and summoned Moses and Aaron and said to them, "I am guilty this time. The LORD is the righteous One, and I and my people are the guilty ones.

28. Entreat the LORD, and let it be enough of God's thunder and hail, and I will let you go, and you will be free to leave.

29. And Moses said to him, "When I leave the city, I will spread my hands to the LORD. The thunder will cease, and there will be no more hail, in order that you know that the land is the LORD's.

30. But I know that you and your servants still do not fear the LORD God,

31. though the flax and the barley have been broken, for the barley is in the ear, and the flax is in the stalk.

32. The wheat and the spelt, however, have not been broken because they ripen late."

33. Moses went away from Pharaoh, out of the city, and he spread out his hands to the LORD, and the thunder and the hail ceased, and rain did not come down to earth.

34. And Pharaoh saw that the rain, the hail, and the thunder had ceased; he continued to sin, and he hardened his heart, and his servants acted accordingly.

35. And Pharaoh's heart became rock-hard, and he did not let the children of the Israelites go out, as the LORD had spoken through Moses.

…

Exodus 10:16-20

16. Pharaoh hastened to summon Moses and Aaron, and he said, "I have sinned against the LORD your God and against you.

17. But now, forgive my transgression only this time and entreat the LORD your God, and let him remove from me just this death."

18. So Moses left Pharaoh and pleaded with the LORD,

19. and the LORD reversed a very strong west wind, and it picked up the locusts and blew them into the Sea of Reeds; not one locust remained in the land of Egypt.

20. But the LORD hardened Pharaoh's heart, and he did not let the children of the Israelites leave the country.

The Book of Exodus begins with the death of Joseph and his brothers as well as the succession of the deceased Pharaoh. The new Pharaoh, whose name is not mentioned, started to oppress the Israelites because they became too numerous in his eyes, and he feared that they might one day rule over Egypt. Step by step the Pharaoh made the Israelites slaves and their life very hard. When the Israelites cried for help, God rose and remembered His covenant with Abraham, Isaac, and Jacob. 'God looked upon the Israelites, and God took notice of them' (Exodus 2:25).[1] The greatest prophet, teacher and political leader in the Torah, Moses, now enters the stage as the liberator of the Israelites.[2] He was raised at the court by one of the daughters of the Pharaoh who had found him as a baby boy in a basket on the Nile while she was bathing. Although she assumed that it was an Israelite baby, she took pity and cared for his education and upraising. 'She named him Moses, explaining, "I drew him out of the water."' (Exodus 2:10). Moses had an official position in the court but was aware of his Israelite origins. One day he had to flee for his life after having killed an Egyptian who had beaten a Hebrew, one of his kinsmen. When Moses was at mount Horeb, the mountain of God in the wilderness, an angel appeared to him at a burning bush that was not consumed by the fire. God called Moses out of the bush and appointed him as the liberator of the Israelites with these words: 'Hear! The cry of the Israelites has reached Me; and I have seen how the Egyptians oppress them. Come now, I will send you to Pharaoh, and you shall free My people Israel from Egypt.' (Exodus 3:

---

1. 'God took notice of them' refers to Genesis 35:11 where God said at Bethel: 'I am El Shaddai' meaning 'God pays attention'.

2. God considered Moses as His most trusted prophet by saying '. . . if there be among you, I the LORD make Myself known to him in a vision, I speak with him in a dream. Not so with My servant Moses, he is trusted in all My house. With him I speak mouth to mouth, in plain language and not with evasive words, and he beholds the likeness of the LORD.' (Numbers 12:6-8).

9). But God knew that the Pharaoh would not let go the Israelites voluntarily and said: 'Yet I know that the king of Egypt will not let you go unless he is forced to do so by a greater might. So I will raise My hand and afflict Egypt with various miracles with which I will strike upon them; after that he shall let you go.' (Exodus 3: 19-20). Ultimately, Yahweh inflicted upon Egypt ten plagues.[3] Only after the tenth plague—the death of every first born, both men and animals—did the Pharaoh let the Israelites go.

Before Moses went to the Pharaoh, Yahweh said to Moses 'But I will stiffen Pharaoh's heart, and I will multiply My signs and My wonders in the land of Egypt' (Exodus 7:3). It should not be understood that Yahweh excluded the free choice of the Pharaoh to repent sincerely. Yahweh knew that the Pharaoh was wicked and had defied Him; that the Pharaoh had no delight to make a wholehearted attempt to repent. By hardening Pharaoh's heart, Yahweh made public to the whole world that the Pharaoh was insincere in his expression of regret. However, God waits for every transgressor to repent; He gives time and an opportunity for change. God had waited before He destroyed the generation of the Flood,[4] the people of Sodom,[5] and the Egyptians.

God knows what is in the heart of a person, whether he or she is sincere or not. The LORD said to the prophet Samuel: 'Pay no attention to his appearance or his stature, for I have rejected him. The LORD knows things a man does not see. People often judge by outward appearances, but the LORD sees into the heart.' (1 Samuel 16:7). Because of his insincerity, the Pharaoh repeated his mistakes and even lost his judgmental abilities. The borderline between good and bad behavior became erased and made the Pharaoh's mind blind. Someone who does neither examine himself nor regret but repeats his transgression becomes like a blind man, ultimately falling into a pit. The severity of repetitive transgression by lack of timely regret and change was underlined by Yonah Ben Avraham of Gerona who died in 1263 AD in Toledo: '. . . if one repeats his sin, his repentance is difficult, for the sin becomes permissible to him and, consequently, extremely severe … Our Sages of blessed memory have said, "When a man has committed a

---

3. The ten plagues were inflicted in this order: (1) water which turned into blood and killed all fish and other aquatic life; (2) frogs; (3) lice; (4) swarms of insects; (5) disease on livestock (horses, asses, camels, cattle, and the sheep); (6) unhealable boils on man and beasts; (7) very heavy hail and thunder; (8) locusts; (9) darkness; and (10) death of the first born of all Egyptian humans and animals. During the tenth plague, the Israelites had to bring blood of a lamb on their door to be spared.

4. Genesis 7:1-10; the period was seven days.

5. Genesis 18:26-33. The period of waiting is not mentioned.

transgression and repeated it, it has become permissible to him" (Kiddushin 40a)'[6]

The way of God rests on divine justice that demands a free and sincere will of the transgressor to regret and change. He saves only those who are willing to repent with a sincere heart. Insincerity has its consequences too. Yahweh made use of the insincere Pharaoh and his administration to favor the Israelites. God's decision to punish not only the Pharaoh but also all Egyptians is explained by Maimonides[7] that '... a country whose sins are great will immediately be obliterated as implied by Genesis 18:20: The outcry of Sodom and Amorah is great ... Regarding the entire world as well, were its inhabitants' sins to be greater than their merits, they would immediately be destroyed as Genesis 6:5 relates: God saw that the evil of man was great ... and God said: 'I will destroy man'. Maimonides explains the ten plagues as the collective punishment inflicted by God on the Egyptians and their leaders because every Egyptian had the free choice how to behave towards the Israelites: '... in regard to the Egyptians, each and every one of the Egyptians who caused hardship and difficulty for Israel had the choice to refrain from harming them, if he so desired, for there was no decree on a particular person.'[8] Punishment of a society was already questioned by Abraham with regard to the people of Sodom: 'Abraham stepped forward and said, 'Will You sweep away the innocent along with the wicked?'' (Genesis 18:23). The kind and life-saving treatment of Moses by Pharaoh's daughter is an exception and a testimony to the free choice granted to all persons, even in Pharaonic Egypt.

---

6. Yonah Ben Avraham of Gerona, Shaarei Teshuvah (The Gates of Repentance), first published in Fano, 1505, translated reprint in Jerusalem, Feldheim Publishers, 1967, pp. 7-8 (First Gate concerning the Principles of Repentance, V)

7. Moshe Maimonides, Mishneh Torah, Sefer Madda, Hilchot Teshuva, Chapter Three, Halacha 2.

8. Moshe Maimonides, Mishneh Torah, Sefer Madda, Hilchot Teshuva, Chapter Six, Halacha 5.

Reading 4 *Tablets of the Covenant and God's compassion*

Exodus 34:4-10

4. So Moses carved two tablets of stone, like the first, and early in the morning he went up on Mount Sinai, as the LORD had commanded him, taking the two stone tablets with him.

5. The LORD came down in a cloud; He stood with him there and proclaimed the name of the LORD.

6. The LORD passed before him and the LORD proclaimed: "The LORD! The LORD! A God compassionate and gracious, slow to anger, abounding in kindness and faithfulness,

7. extending kindness to the thousandth generation, forgiving iniquity, transgression, and sin; yet He does not remit all punishment, but visits the iniquity of parents upon children and children's children, upon the third and fourth generations.

8. Moses hastened to bow low to the ground in homage,

9. and said, "If I have gained Your favor, O LORD, pray, let the LORD go in our midst, even though this is a stiff-necked people. Pardon our iniquity and our sin and take us for Your own!"

10. He said: "I hereby make a covenant. Before all people I will work such wonders as have not been wrought on all the earth or in any nation; and all the people who are with you shall see how awesome are the LORD's deeds which I will perform for you."

THE QUOTATION RECORDS A pivotal event in the Old Testament when the LORD came down on the top of Mount Sinai and called Moses. There God inscribed the 'Ten Sayings' in the tablets: 'The tablets were God's work, and the words written on them were God's words' (Exodus 32:16). The 'Tablets of the Covenant' ('Luchot HaBrit'), also called the 'Tablets of Stone' or the 'Tablets of Testimony', were two pieces of a precious stone inscribed with the 'Ten Sayings'. Moses remained on the top of Mount Sinai, inside the cloud, for 40 days and 40 nights. As soon as Moses went down with the tablets and came near the Israelite camp, he saw that the Israelites were worshipping a golden calf with the help of Aaron, his older brother, and a prophet. Moses became enraged, hurled the tablets from his hands and shattered them at the foot of the mountain. He took the golden calf and burned it; then he grounded it to powder and strewed it on the water and so made the Israelites drink it. Thereafter, the LORD sent a plague upon the Israelites for what they did with the golden calf that Aaron made. Without hesitation, Moses soon addressed the LORD asking to lead the Israelite people forward and to consider that this nation was His nation (Exodus 33:12-13). At the top of Mount Sinai again, also called Mount Horeb,[1] God called Moses who stayed there for 40 days and 40 nights, and the LORD inscribed the 'Ten Sayings' again in two tablets of precious stone. When Moses came down from the mountain, bearing the two tablets of the covenant, he was not aware that the skin of his face was radiant since he had spoken with the LORD. Both the first shattered tablets and the second tablets were stored in the 'Ark of the Covenant'.[2]

Verses 6 and 7 are known as 'God's Thirteen Attributes of Mercy'. They are the heart of the prayers for 'regret, sorrow, and forgiveness—see also Reading 8—and are among the oldest texts in the liturgical calendar. Remarkably, verses 6 and 7 portray God reaching out for human pleas for forgiveness. God sets the example, even giving us the words to use in our prayers for forgiveness. Verses 6 and 7 record God's self-revelation with the 13 attributes of mercy:

1. The LORD!: God is merciful before a person transgresses because God is aware that future transgressions will be done—see 1 Kings in Reading 22.

---

1. The name Horeb is mentioned for the first time in the story of Moses and the 'Burning Bush' (Exodus 3:1): 'Moses was keeping the flocks of Jethro, his father-in-law, the priest of Midian, and he led the flocks to the farthest end of the wilderness, and came to the mountain of God, unto Horeb.' Here it is called the mountain of God in view of the events of the future. See Rashi comment on Exodus 3:1: "to the farthest end of wilderness" means to distance himself from the possibility of theft so that the flocks would not pasture in others' fields (from Exodus Rabbah 2:3).

2. According to Exodus 40:20-21, Moses took the Covenant and placed it in the Ark, and he fixed the poles to the Ark Then he placed the cover on top of the Ark and brought the Ark inside the Tabernacle. Next, he put up the curtain for screening off the Ark. The same lay-out was used for the building of the Temple of Jerusalem.

2. The LORD!: God is merciful after the sinner has transgressed and repented.

3. God: God is the ruler over nature and humans and God is mighty in compassion to meet the needs of humans.

4. Compassionate: God is filled with loving kindness for mankind and eases the suffering and the punishments.

5. Gracious: God shows mercy even to those who have transgressed and do not deserve it. God consoles the afflicted and raises up the oppressed.

6. Slow to anger: God gives the transgressor time and opportunity to regret.

7. Abundant in kindness: God provides support and blessing, considering the imperfect nature of humans.

8. Truth: God will always reward those who recognize and follow Him.

9. Preserver of kindness for thousands of generations: God always remembers the good deeds of the righteous people and their deeds are beneficial to all later generations. God's inter-generational kindness saves humanity in the darkest of times.

10. Forgiver of iniquity: God will always grant forgiveness, even for the greatest crimes, if one regrets.

11. Forgiver of willful sin: God will forgive rebellious behavior against God if one regrets.

12. Forgiver of error: God forgives transgressions committed out of carelessness, thoughtlessness, or apathy.

13. Who cleanses: God forgives and pardons, wiping out sins of those who repent. He renews life.

The Old Testament often repeats that God is compassionate,[3] gracious,[4] kind[5] and inclined to forgive.[6] Jewish liturgy revolves around the thirteen attributes of mercy on fasts, during the month Elul and on Yom Kippur. Elul is the sixth month of the Jewish calendar (late summer/early fall) which is set apart for repentance in preparation for the Jewish New Year (Rosh Hashanah) and, ten days later, the Day of Atonement (Yom Kippur). The ten days between the Jewish New Year and the Day of Atonement are called the 'Days of Awe' because it is a period for introspection and considering the transgressions of the previous year. Every year the period of 'teshuvah' runs 40 days from the first day of the month Elul to Yom Kippur and is called 'Days of Favor'. It is not only intended to wake up from a state of mental unconsciousness induced by transgression, but it is also a call to be reborn by returning to God, or 'teshuvah'. The 40 days refer to the 40 days and nights when Moses stayed at the top of Mount Sinai before he received the 'Ten Sayings' from God. The 40 days were needed to let the Israelites repent for their idolatrous sins. God knows that a change of heart and mind requires time. The ritual blowing of the 'shofar', or ram's horn, in

---

3. Genesis 43:14; Exodus 33:19; Deuteronomy 13:18; Isaiah 54:8,10; Isaiah 55:7; Jeremiah 31:19; Ezekiel 39:25; Hosea 2:25; Micah 7:19; Malachi 3:17; Psalm 86:15; Psalm 145:8; Lamentations 3:32.

4. Exodus 22:26; 2 Kings 12:23; Isaiah 30:18; Isaiah 60:10; Joel 2:13; Amos 5:15; Jonah 4:2; Zechariah 12:10; Psalm 67:2; Psalm 84:12; Psalm 86:15; Psalm 103:8; Psalm 111:4; Psalm 112:4; Psalm 116:5; Psalm 145:8; Job 33:24; Nehemiah 9:17,31; 2 Chronicles 30:9.

5. Genesis 19:19; Genesis 32:11; Exodus 15:13; Numbers 14:19; Deuteronomy 5:10; Deuteronomy 7:9,12; 2 Samuel 22:51; Isaiah 54:8,10; Jeremiah 9:23; Jeremiah 16:5; Jeremiah 31:2; Jeremiah 32:18; Jeremiah 33:11; Hosea 2:21; Joel 2:13; Jonah 4:2; Micah 7:18; Psalm 5:8; Psalm 6:5; Psalm 13:6; Psalm 18:51; Psalm 21:8; Psalm 25:6,7,10; Psalm 26:3; Psalm 31:8,17; Psalm 33:5,18,22; Psalm 36:6,8,11; Psalm 40:11,12; Psalm 42:9; Psalm 44:27; Psalm 48:10; Psalm 51:3; Psalm 52:3,10; Psalm 56:11; Psalm 57:4,11; Psalm 59:11,17,18; Psalm 62:13; Psalm 63:4; Psalm 66:20; Psalm 69:14,17; Psalm 77:9; Psalm 85:8; Psalm 86:5,13,15; Psalm 88:12; Psalm 89: 2,15,25,29,34,50; Psalm 90:14; Psalm 92:3; Psalm 94:18; Psalm 98:3; Psalm 100:5; Psalm 101:1; Psalm 103:4,8,11,17; Psalm 106:1,7,45; Psalm 107:1,8,15,21,31; Psalm 108:5; Psalm 109:21,26; Psalm 115:1; Psalm 117:2; Psalm 118:1,2,3,4,29; Psalm 119:17,41,64,76,88,124,149,159; Psalm 130:7; Psalm 138:2,8; Psalm 143:8,12; Psalm 144:2; Psalm 145:8; Psalm 147:11; Lamentations 3:22,32; Daniel 9:4; Ezra 3:11; Ezra 7:28; Ezra 9:9; Nehemiah 1:5; Nehemiah 9:17,32; Nehemiah 13:22; 1 Chronicles 16:34,41; 1 Chronicles 17:13; 2 Chronicles 1:8; 2 Chronicles 5:13; 2 Chronicles 6:14; 2 Chronicles 7:3,6; 2 Chronicles 20:21.

6. Genesis 18:24; Leviticus 4:20,26,31,35; Leviticus 5:10,13,16,18,26; Leviticus 10:17; Leviticus 19:22; Numbers 14:18,20; Numbers 15:25,26,28; Numbers 30:6,9,13; 1 Kings 8:30,34,36,39; Isaiah 55:7; Jeremiah 5:1; Jeremiah 33:8; Jeremiah 36:3; Jeremiah 50:20; Ezekiel 16:63; Micah 7:18; Psalm 25:11; Psalm 32:1; Psalm 85:3; Psalm 86:5; Psalm 99:8; Psalm 103:3; Daniel 9:9; Nehemiah 9:17; 2 Chronicles 6:21,25,27,30,39; 2 Chronicles 7:14.

the 40 days-period of repentance is the waking call to become aware of one's transgressions and to repent. The first ritual blowing is done one month before Rosh Hashanah and the last one on the conclusion of the fast at Yom Kippur. Maimonides said it with these words: 'It is as if the shofar's call is saying: Wake up sleepy ones from your sleep and you who slumber, arise. Inspect your deeds, repent, remember your Creator. Those who forget the truth in the vanities of time and throughout the entire year, devote their energies to vanity and emptiness which will not benefit nor save. Look at your souls. Improve your ways and your deeds and let every one of you abandon his evil path and thoughts.'[7]

Christian churches have the liturgical period of Lent that commemorates the 40 days Jesus Christ spent fasting in the desert before beginning his public ministry. It is a period in preparation of Easter during which fastening, giving alms and a simple lifestyle are required. Fastening is regarded as an exercise in self-control which is necessary to control the evil inclination of men. Lent is a time for introspection and self-examination and the imposition of ashes at the beginning of Lent is a call to return to our true self. The season of Lent is inspired by the Old Testament when the prophet Moses went into the hills for 40 days and nights to pray and fast before receiving the Ten Commandments.

The two stone tablets are frequently called the 'Ten Commandments'. However, Exodus 34:28 calls them 'Aseret ha-D'varim' which is better translated as the 'Ten Sayings'. The 'Ten Sayings' are not understood as specific commandments but rather as ten categories of commandments. The 'Ten Sayings' of Exodus 20:3-14 are: (1) You shall have no other gods besides Me, (2) you shall not make for yourself a sculptured image, or any likeness of what is in the heavens above, or on the earth below, or in the waters, and worship them, (3) you shall not swear falsely by the name of the LORD, (4) remember the Shabbat as a day of rest and keep it holy, (5) honor your father and your mother, (6) you shall not murder, (7) you shall not commit adultery, (8) you shall not steal, (9) you shall not bear false witness against your neighbor, and (10) you shall not covet your neighbor's house, his wife or his property.

Verse 7 is a difficult one when God says that He will visit the iniquity of parents upon children and children's children, upon the third and fourth generation. It is a repetition of God's words in Exodus 20:5 when God gave the 'Ten Sayings' to Moses.[8] The word 'visit' is not the same as 'punish'. Four

---

7. Moshe Maimonides, Mishneh Torah, Sefer Madda, Hilchot Teshuva, Chapter Three, Halacha 4.

8. Exodus 20:5 'You shall not bow down to them (false gods) or serve them. For I, the LORD, your God am a jealous God, visiting the iniquity of the parents upon the

generations are the usual length of time that people remember their direct ancestors without need of written records. God teaches that the iniquities of parents influence the immediate circle around them, their children, and grandchildren. Hence parents have the duty to show how to live a righteous life and avoid transgression. If parents are wicked, their children may experience great difficulties in life to find out how to live a righteous life. For this reason, many countries have adopted laws to address bad parenting, even by denying such parents the right to educate their own children who are placed in other families by a decision of judicial authorities. It is a protective measure against the immediate and corruptive effects of wicked parental behavior. Finally, verse 7 draws our attention to the possible outcome of actual behavior on future generations, the intergenerational effects.

---

children, upon the third and the fourth generations of those who reject Me'. It is also mentioned in Deuteronomy 5:9.

Leviticus

Reading 5   Individual confession

Leviticus 1:4

4. And he shall lay his hand forcefully upon the head of the burnt offering, and that it may be accepted as atonement for him.

THESE ARE THE WORDS of the LORD when He called Moses and spoke to him from the Tent of Meeting at the base of Mount Sinai, saying 'Speak to the Israelite people, and say to them …' Every time God communicated with Moses, it was always preceded by God calling Moses by name as an expression of affection. In Leviticus 1, God spoke to Moses while the rest of Israel did not hear it. It also excluded Aaron, the brother of Moses. Thirteen times in the Torah, God spoke to both Moses and Aaron together, and, corresponding to them were thirteen other occasions when God spoke only to Moses who was ordered to communicate God's message. God spoke from the Tent of Meeting, meaning that God's voice stopped and could not be heard beyond the Tent of Meeting. The Book of Leviticus rests on the belief that the world was created as a paradise and retains the capacity to achieve that state although it is prone to transgression and defilement. In Leviticus, ritual practices are a reminder of God's presence on earth and make God's presence and dwelling place available in the middle of the people, while violation of ritual rules compromises the harmony between God and the world.

Leviticus 1:4 makes no reference to any specific sin, guilt, or transgression for which one needs to repent and be forgiven. 'Semicha' literally means 'to place upon'. In Temple times, confession was accompanied by the laying of the hands on the head of the burnt offering, a bull, a ram or male goat, a turtle dove, or a pigeon. If carried out according to the ritual rules of Leviticus, the offering was accepted and the sin, guilt or transgression forgiven. Pressing firmly the hands on the head of the sacrificial animal was symbolically transmitting sin or guilt onto the animal. When the person placed his hands on the head of the sacrificial animal, he confessed his transgressions saying, "I sinned, I transgressed, I committed iniquity, and I did this-and-this, and I have repented before You and this is my atonement". The confession is necessary, for without regret and change, a sacrifice will not bring atonement to the person. The 'laws of repentance' contain only one commandment, namely that a sinner should regret his transgression before God and confess. This commandment is essential, in the past times and for all times to come. It is so important that Leviticus is dedicated to regret, change and forgiveness as well as cleansing ('kipper').

Reading 6   *Atonement for the community*

Leviticus 4:20-21

20. He shall do to the bull just as he did to the bull of sin offering, thus he shall do to it. Thus the kohen shall make atonement for the community, and they will be forgiven.

21. And he shall take the bull outside the camp and burn it, just as he burned the first bull. It is the sin offering for the community.

THE TWO VERSES DEAL with the transgressions of a society and how to expiate them. In present-day time there is a clear theological tendency to regard transgression as attributable only to individuals. This view is reinforced by the human rights doctrine which puts emphasis on the rights of the individual.[1] However, the Book of Leviticus maintains that a society can be liable and therefore needs collective repentance and purification. It merely confirms God's many sayings that He will punish an entire society, either the Israelite people or other peoples. In such cases, the community is called upon to repent, to confess transgression and to reconcile with God. Leviticus lays out a way for atonement or cleansing ('kipper') of the community through a priestly ritual centered on sacrificial animals in the Holy Temple of Jerusalem. The book prescribes the precise rituals that restore normalcy and reconciliation with God. The rituals are instrumental in improving the spiritual mindset of the people and recognizing everyone's obligation to be sensitive towards others.

The influence of one person or a group is a subtle process of transmission of thoughts, emotions, and perceptions. If we fail to stop and correct transgressive behavior, the community is contaminated and becomes impure, prone to more sins and transgressions. Allowing negative dynamics,

---

1. Exceptional communal rights of the human rights doctrine are the right to self-determination and the right to self-defense of a country or population.

uncorrected behavior can morph into a community's wrongdoing of great proportion. We may even say that a community's insensitivity regarding transgressions makes the community itself guilty. For present-day practice regarding the cleansing of community transgressions we refer to the communal repentance and prayers for atonement on Yom Kippur. The opinion that a community, a country or even the world can be liable to sin and wickedness is confirmed by Maimonides: 'Each and every person has merits and sins. A person whose merits exceed his sins is termed righteous. A person whose sins exceed his merits is termed wicked. If his sins and merits are equal, he is termed *a Beinoni*. The same applies to an entire country. If the merits of all its inhabitants exceed their sins, it is termed righteous. If their sins are greater, it is termed wicked. The same applies to the entire world.'[2]

---

2. Moshe Maimonides, Mishneh Torah, Sefer Madda, Hilchot Teshuva, Chapter Three, Halacha 1.

Reading 7   *Sending away the transgressions*

Leviticus 16:1-2

1. The LORD spoke to Moses after the two sons of Aaron died when they drew too close to the presence of the LORD.

2. The LORD said to Moses:

Tell your brother Aaron that he is not to come whenever he pleases into the Shrine behind the screen, in front of the cover that is upon the Ark, so that he does not die; for I appear in the cloud over the cover.

...

Leviticus 16:9-10

9. Aaron shall present the goat designated by lot for the LORD, which he is to offer as a sin offering;

10. while the goat designated by lot to Azazel shall be set standing alive before the LORD, to make atonement for him and to send it away for Azazel into the wilderness.

...

Leviticus 16:20-22

20. When Aaron has finished purging the Shrine, the Tent of Meeting, and the altar, he shall bring forward the live goat.

21. Aaron shall lay both his hands on the head of the live goat and confess over it all the iniquities and transgressions of the Israelites—all their transgressions—putting them on the goat's head; and it shall be sent away to the wilderness through a designated man.

22. The goat shall carry all their iniquities to an inaccessible place; and the goat shall be set free in the wilderness.

Leviticus 8 instituted the Israelite priestly theology when God commanded Moses to take Aaron, his brother, and Aaron's sons before the assembled community at the entrance of the Tent of Meeting. There Moses consecrated Aaron as the first high priest and his sons as priests by performing a lengthy ritual as God had commanded. After Aaron and his sons were first bathed in water, Aaron took on the priestly garments and was anointed with oil on his head. The sons of Aaron were also clothed with white tunics. In the next stage, a sacrificial ram was brought forward. Aaron and his sons leaned their hands forcefully on the head of the ram before sacrificing it. A second ram was brought, the ram of ordination, and Aaron and his sons leaned again their hands forcefully on the ram's head. Then the ram was slaughtered, and Moses took some of its blood and placed it on the cartilage of Aaron's right ear, on the thumb of his right hand and on the big toe of his right foot. The ritual was again performed with Aaron's sons. The ritual proceeded with Moses taking one loaf of unleavened bread, and one loaf of oily bread, and one wafer, and he placed them on top of the fats and the right thigh of the slaughtered ram. Moses placed it all on Aaron's palms and on his sons' palms, and Moses waved them as a waving before the LORD. He then took some of the anointing oil and some of the blood that was on the altar and sprinkled it on Aaron and his garments, and on his sons and their garments, and he sanctified Aaron, his garments, his sons, and his sons' garments. Aaron and his sons were commanded not to leave the entrance of the Tent of Meeting for seven days, until the day of the completion of their ordination days. God had commanded this to effect atonement for Aaron and his sons. The seven-day period became the basis of the later priestly ritual of the service of Yom Kippur. Just as there were seven days of the ordination, so too the high priest ('Kohen Gadol'), who performed the service of Yom Kippur, was required to separate from his home seven days before Yom Kippur. The primary temporal category of a seven-day period of ritual enactment parallels the seven days of the creation of the cosmic order.[1] On the eight day, Moses summoned Aaron and his sons and the elders of Israel and said to Aaron: 'Take yourself a bull calf as a sin offering, and a ram as a burnt offering, both unblemished, and bring them near before the LORD.' God had commanded to take a bull-calf to inform Aaron that God had granted him atonement through this calf for the incident involving the golden calf, which Aaron had made at Mount Sinai. Moses told Aaron to speak to the children of Israel, saying that the sacrificial animals shall be a burnt offering and a peace offering. After having performed the ritual, Aaron lifted his hands towards the people and blessed them. And the glory

---

1. Genesis 1:3-31 and 2:1-3.

of the LORD appeared to all the people. At this point the tabernacle cult was established, and the priests were set apart from the people of Israel because they were in the service of God.[2]

A great priestly drama occurred shortly afterwards when Aaron's sons, Nadab and Abihu, took their pan, put fire in them, and placed incense on it. Then they brought before the LORD 'foreign fire', which God had not commanded them.[3] Suddenly, a fire went forth from before the LORD and consumed them, and they died before the LORD. The 'Holy of Holies' ('Kodesh Kodashim') was crucial in the one ritual moment of the year when the high priest entered this categorically distinct area. Concern for the integrity of the 'Holy of Holies' was at the heart of the ritual. For this reason, the sacred and the profane should always be distinguished and separated.[4] Violation of the distinction is a consideration in God's judgment on the destruction of the first Temple by the Babylonians: 'Your priests have violated My instructions. They have profaned what is sacred to Me, they have not distinguished between the sacred and the secular, they have not taught the difference between the unclean and the clean …' (Ezekiel 22: 26)

In the yearly purification ritual on Yom Kippur, Aaron placed two lots on the two goats: one lot "For the LORD", and the other lot "For Azazel". These lots were mixed up, and Aaron, with both hands inside the urn, took one lot in his right hand and the other in his left hand. The goat upon which he would place the lot with the inscription "For the LORD" would be for God and sacrificed. The goat upon which he placed the lot "For Azazel" would be sent off to Azazel, which is a strong and hard mountain, cut-off from cultivated land—see Rashi comment on 16:8. Before the goat for Azazel was sent away, it was placed before the LORD to initiate atonement upon it. This ritual took place once a year in the Temple service of Yom Kippur or

---

2. The Tabernacle ('mishkan') was the divinely ordained structure and portable dwelling place of God's Presence (the 'Shekinah'), from Mount Sinai to Canaan and later Jerusalem. The portable tent structure was replaced by the First Temple built by King Solomon around 1000 BC but ended by the destruction of the Second Temple in 70 AD.

3. Leviticus 16:12-13 contains the instructions given to Aaron and his sons on how to enter safely before the LORD. He is to take fire from the coals of fire on the altar before the LORD since only this fire is holy. Any other fire is foreign and leads to death. The grave transgression of Aaron's sons is the creation of confusion by denying the separation between sacred and non-sacred categories and acts. Fire from outside the sacred area had been brought into the sacred area and caused impurity of the 'Holy of Holies' ('Kodesh Kodashim'), the innermost sanctuary of the Tabernacle and later the Temple in Jerusalem. God had told Moses to say to Aaron that any violation would result in death.

4. In general, any order is based on divisions and separations with clear demarcations. Violations may lead to a possible breakdown of the entire system.

the Day of Atonement.[5] The goat for Azazel was sent away into the wilderness to carry the sins of the Israelites into the wilderness[6] and to avoid transfer of the sins placed on its head to anyone who might encounter it. The contagious nature of transgression is underlined here.

The ritual is communal in nature and deals with sin and defilement in the context of the Israelite community. It serves to restore the nation to its prescribed and founded state, a return to the founded order of creation. The act cleansed the Israelites of their sins. However, Talmudic sages rightly emphasize that, at the individual level, the atonement of the goat for Azazel was only effective for him who repented, for the Day of Atonement only atones when accompanied by repentance.

After the destruction of the Temple of Jerusalem, there is no altar of atonement, only repentance remains. Yet, Azazel still has a meaning today. Anyone who repents sincerely in heart and mind is liberated from all sins so that he can continue his life fully, enjoy life as much as possible without becoming torn down by remorse and guilt for the rest of his life. As Psalm 32:1 proclaims: 'How happy is he whose transgression is forgiven.' Thus, repentance sends away the transgressions and the feelings of guilt and restores life as if one is reborn. But regret is more than confessing transgression and making the decision not to commit the transgressions again. It always involves the firm determination to return to God because He guides us on rights paths as befits His name. Therefore, even when the repentant walks through the valley of deepest darkness, he fears no harm, for God is with him. His rod and His staff, they comfort him. He may hope to dwell in the house of the LORD forever (Psalm 23:3-6).

---

5. See also Numbers 29:7-11.

6. The wilderness was the place where the Jews wandered for 40 years after their flight from Egypt to the promised land of Canaan. It is considered as a place of disorder and evil. In Numbers 20:5 the people ask, 'Why have you (Moses) led us out of Egypt to bring us to this barren place; it is not a place for seeds, or for fig trees, grapevines, or pomegranate trees, and there is no water.'

Reading 8   *Day of Atonement: Yom Kippur*

Leviticus 23:26-32

26. The LORD spoke to Moses, saying:

27. On exactly the tenth day of this seventh month is the Day of Atonement. It shall be a holy occasion for you: you shall humble your souls and you shall bring an offering by fire to the LORD;

28. you shall do no work ton this day that is consecrated as a Day of Atonement, on which atonement is made on your behalf before the LORD your God.

29. If there is any person who does not humble himself throughout that day, he shall be cut off from his kin;

30. and whoever does any work on that day, I will cause that person to disappear from among his people.

31. You shall not work at all, it is a rule for all time, throughout the ages wherever you live.

32. It is a sabbath of rest for you, and you shall abstain from work; on the ninth day of the month at evening, from evening to evening, you shall observe this your sabbath.

GOD DEDICATED YOM KIPPUR or Day of Atonement to repentance, atonement, and abstinence on the tenth day of the seventh month. It was on this day that the high priest performed the sacred rites as explained in Reading 7. After the destruction of the Temple of Jerusalem, the rabbis shifted focus from the Temple ritual to the trial period. They called to examine individual sin and transgression by means of self-examination. The ten days following Rosh Hashanah (Jewish New Year) are the 'Ten Days of Repentance' or the Days of Awe and a time for appeals—see also Reading 4. Every Jew is required to take stock and account of one's life and to make the necessary corrections. The opening session begins in the synagogue just before sunset on the evening of Yom Kippur. The Ark is opened and two people take the Torah scrolls while the cantor or 'chazzan' and the two people, placed on each side of the cantor, recite in Hebrew: 'In the tribunal of Heaven and the tribunal of earth, by the permission of God—praised be He—and by permission of this holy congregation, we hold it lawful to pray with transgressors.' The cantor then chants the 'Kol Nidre' ('All Vows') declaration in Aramaic: 'All personal vows we are likely to make, all personal oaths and pledges we are likely to take between this Yom Kippur and the next Yom Kippur, we publicly renounce. Let them all be relinquished and abandoned, null and void, neither firm nor established. Let our personal vows, pledges and oaths be considered neither vows nor pledges nor oaths.'[1] The congregation says three times: 'May all the people of Israel be forgiven, including all the strangers who live in their midst, for all the people are in fault.'[2] The rabbi then says 'O pardon the iniquities of this people, according to Your abundant mercy, just as You forgave this people ever since they left Egypt.' Finally, the rabbi and the congregation say together three times 'The LORD said, "I pardon them according to your words".'[3] The Torah scrolls are then replaced, and the evening service begins.

Yom Kippur, which begins at sundown of the previous day, is the climax when the verdict is handed down by God, the true judge, who decides the fate of the Israelite community and every Jewish person, with the hope that God inscribes them in the Book of Life. According to Jewish tradition, repentance is the prerequisite of atonement on Yom Kippur, although every man ought to repent every day. However, the ten-day period is special because it obliges more than on other days to consider one's life, deeds, and thoughts. The return to God, which is part of the process of self-examination during these ten days, is made easier and more desirable as Isaiah 55:6 states 'Seek God when He is to be found.' The confessional prayer customarily recited is: 'For we have all sinned ...' The eve of Yom Kippur (called 'Erev Yom Kippur') is a day of festive meal, charity and asking others for forgiveness. Self-examination, repentance or 'teshuvah' at Yom Kippur only atones for transgressions between man and God, and a person who wronged another person should ask the other person to forgive him or her.

---

1. The 'Kol Nidrei' invalidates only the vows that one undertakes on his own volition. It does not make null and void the vows or oaths which have a legal force, such as a legally binding contract or on oath imposed by a tribunal.

2. These are the words in Numbers 15:26.

3. These are the words in Numbers 14:20.

Yom Kippur is the holiest and most solemn day of the year in the Jewish calendar during which Jews fast, pray, and attend synagogue services. It is forbidden to work on this day.[4] At the end of Yom Kippur, one considers oneself forgiven by God. As it is written 'For on this day you will be cleansed of all your iniquities; you shall be clean before the LORD.' (Leviticus 16:30). According to Maimonides, the essence of Yom Kippur atones for those who repent, underlining the individual nature of repentance based on self-examination.[5] A basic characteristic of the prayers for forgiveness is the repeated recitation of the 'Thirteen Attributes of God' because of emphasis on God's forgiving nature (Reading 4).

Christian doctrine views atonement as the satisfaction of Christ, whereby God and the world are reconciled and made to be at one. Reference is made to 2 Corinthians 5:19, saying, "For God indeed was in Christ, reconciling the world to himself." The Catholic Council of Trent (1518) commented that the Heavenly Father sent unto men Jesus Christ, His own Son who had been, both before the Law and during the time of the Law, to many of the holy fathers announced and promised, that He might both redeem the Jews, who were under the Law and that the Gentiles who followed not after justice might attain to justice and that all men might receive the adoption of sons." The same dogma was proclaimed by the Nicene Creed, ". . . who for us men and for our salvation, came down, took flesh, was made man, and suffered." This view on atonement is based on the New Testament.[6] According to the Church, atonement is thus founded on the Divine Incarnation.

---

4. Yom Kippur is in present-day Israel an official holiday, with no radio or television broadcasts, no transportation services and the shops are closed.

5. Moshe Maimonides, Mishneh Torah, Sefer Madda, Hilchot Teshuva, Chapter One, Halacha 3.

6. New Advent, www.newadvent.org/cathen/02055a.htm

Reading 9   *Upholding the Covenant and restoring the relationship with God*

Leviticus 26:3-5

3. If you walk in My laws and faithfully observe My commandments,

4. I will give your rains in their season, so that the earth shall yield a harvest and the trees of the field their fruit.

5. Your threshing shall last to the time of the vintage, and your vintage last to the time of sowing; you shall eat your daily bread and dwell securely in your land.

…

Leviticus 26:14-17

14. But if you do not obey Me and do not observe all these commandments,

15. if you refuse to follow My laws and have broken My rules, so that you do not observe all My commandments and you break My covenant,

16. I in turn will do this to you: I will bring misery on you—consumption and fever, which cause eyes pain and the body to weaken; you shall sow your seed in vain, for your enemies shall eat it.

17. And I will set My face against you: you shall be routed by your enemies, and your foes shall rule over you. You shall flee though none pursues you.

…

Leviticus 26:39-42

39. Those of you who survive shall regret in anguish their iniquity in the land of your enemies; more, they shall feel remorse for the iniquities of their fathers;

40. but if they shall confess their iniquity and the iniquity of their fathers, in that they disobeyed Me, ay, were hostile to Me.

41. when I, in turn, have been hostile to them and have sent them to the land of their enemies, then at last shall their stubborn heart humble itself, and they shall make atonement for their iniquity.

42. Then I will remember My covenant with Jacob; I will also remember My covenant with Isaac, and also My covenant with Abraham; and I will remember the land.

THIS MOVING QUOTATION DESCRIBES God's great anger after the people had abandoned Him and His commandments. At the same time, it reconfirms the conditions of God's favor. God's commandments are written down in the Torah and the message is to learn the Torah and keep them in your heart and to perform them. Not obeying the LORD and not observing His commandments is seen as an act of intentional rebellion against God. By not learning the Torah, one cannot fulfill its commandments. Breaking the covenant with God means that one denies the main tenet of the Torah, namely that God is the Creator of all existence. Hence, verse 15 implicitly refers to several inter-related transgressions. The first leads to the second, and so on, setting in motion a process of degeneration. First, a person does not learn the teachings of the Bible. Then, he does not fulfill the commandments. He then despises others who do fulfill them. Then he hates the Bible and discourages others from fulfilling the commandments. In a further step, he denies the authenticity of the commandments and, finally, denies the very existence and omnipotence of God. 'I will set My face against you' means that God will punish severely, even to the point of causing massive death and allowing your enemies to rule over you, including the enemies in your own ranks. Fleeing without pursuers evokes the suffering of psychological damage, blurring the distinction of what is real and imaginary, and losing his mind, and making errors of judgment. The survivors, aware of their great errors, will grieve about their iniquities and will show regret and confess to God and to their fellow citizens their iniquities. The cycle of severe punishments will lead to 'teshuvah' and redemption because the heart is no longer hard and closed but open to humility and awareness of God's existence, forgiveness, and mercy. Return to God is realized and the nurturing and benevolent power of God is felt again. The process calls us to teach others the greatness and righteousness of God's judgment. This was in the mind of the remorseful King David when he sang 'I will teach transgressors Your ways, that sinners may return to You.' (Psalm 51:15).

The three patriarchs are mentioned in reverse order. God explains here that the youngest patriarch, Jacob, is alone worthy for the redemption of the Israelites through his merit alone. But if this is not enough, then Isaac is together with him, and if this is not enough, then Abraham is with him. God's remembrance of the land is the promise that He will restore Israel as a country so that the Israelites are no longer oppressed and ruled by their enemies. It is the protective power of God that ultimately saves His people, even after terrible events such as the destruction of the First Temple and the Babylonian captivity: 'But the LORD is with me like a great warrior. My persecutors shall stumble before Him; they shall not overwhelm me and shall not succeed. They shall be utterly shamed with a humiliation forever, which shall not be forgotten.' (Jeremiah 20:11).

The covenantal relationship between God and His people is a fundamental element of the Old Testament. The word covenant or solemn agreement in Hebrew is 'berith' (תִּירְבּ).[1] God's covenant with Abraham was unilateral because the conditions were set by God alone and God selected Abraham and his offspring. The preparatory step of God was the LORD's saying to Abraham to leave his ancestral land of Ur of the Chaldeans and move to Canaan. The covenant between God and Abraham was made when God promised the land of Canaan to Abraham as his possession and that of his offspring (Genesis 12:1-7, 14-15). Another part of the covenant declared that Abraham would become the father of a multitude of nations, and kings would come from Abraham. God said that His covenant with Abraham was '. . . an everlasting covenant throughout the ages, to be God to you, from generation to generation.' (Genesis 17:7). God ordered that from this moment Abram changed his name in Abraham, a new name for him as a believer. The only condition God set for His covenant with Abraham and his offspring was an unquestionable obedience to the rules God would reveal in the future because no such rules were revealed to Abraham at that time. It implies a firm belief in God's plans, even when one does not know His plans. The Bible rests on the deep conviction that God's will, in the end, will prevail. This was dramatically demonstrated by Abraham when he was willing to sacrifice his son Isaac as a burnt offering, a deed which God prevented in the end: 'And Abraham picked up the knife to kill his son. Then an angel of the LORD called him: "Abraham! Abraham!" and he answered, "Here I am". And the angel said, "Do not hurt the boy, or do anything to him. For now, I know that you fear God, since you have not spared your son, your favored one, from Me." (Genesis 22: 10-12). God's covenant was renewed on Mount

---

1. The Greek word for covenant is 'diatheke' ('διαθήκη'), as used in the Septuagint or the Greek translation of the Bible, and the Latin word is 'testamentum', as used in the Vulgate or the Latin translation of the Bible.

Sinai when the Israelite people pledged to keep God's covenant (Exodus 19:8). The 'Ten Sayings' are regarded as the words of the covenant (Exodus 34:28) and from this the 'Ark of the Covenant' is a physical manifestation of it (Numbers 10:33; Deuteronomy 10:8, 21:26).

There is a social nature in God's covenant because it is made in relationship with His people and for this reason God judges not only individuals but also a people.[2] We refer to Reading 8 which deals with the Day of Atonement addressed both at individuals and the community. A universal interpretation is given to the covenant by referring to the covenant of God with the first man and woman in Paradise, and later with Noah which is interpreted by Rabbis to include humanity.[3] God's covenant with the Jewish people is to set an example for the religious and moral education of humanity.

---

2. God concluded a covenant, not only with His people but later also with the priestly tribe of Levi, especially with the house of Aaron (Numbers 18:19, 25:12; Deuteronomy 33:9; Jeremiah 33:21; Malachi 2:4). God granted a 'pact of friendship' with Pinehas, son of Eleazar son of Aaron, the priest (Numbers 25:10-13). God concluded a covenant with the house of King David (2 Samuel 23:5; Jeremiah 33:21; Psalm 89:4, 35; Psalm 132:12; 2 Chronicles 13:5).

3. Rabbi Jonathan Sacks, Righteousness is not leadership, October 19, 2020 (hhttps://rab bisacks.org/noach-5781/): 'Noah is the classic case of someone who is righteous, but who is not a leader. In a disastrous age, when all has been corrupted, when the world is filled with violence, when even God Himself—in the most poignant line in the whole Torah—"regretted that He had made man on earth, and was pained to His very core," Noah alone justifies God's faith in humanity, the faith that led Him to create humankind in the first place. That is an immense achievement, and nothing should detract from it. Noah is, after all, the man through whom God makes a covenant with all humanity. Noah is to humanity what Abraham is to the Jewish people.'

Numbers

Reading 10 *Individual confession and forgiveness*

Numbers 5:5-7

5. The LORD spoke to Moses:

6. Say to the Israelites: When a man or woman commits any wrong toward a fellow man, thus breaking faith with the LORD, and that person regrets his guilt,

7. he shall confess the wrong that he has done. He shall make compensation for the principal amount and add a fifth of the value to it, giving it to the person he has wronged.

THE BOOK OF NUMBERS or 'Bamidbar' in Hebrew stands for 'in the desert' and covers the period of Israelite history known as the wilderness wanderings which came to an end with the entry into the Promised Land. It contains the census of all the Israelite males (the total count is 603,550), the institution of the Levitical priesthood, the community as a priestly theocracy, the holy feasts, some detailed rules of law, and blessings. The wilderness became not only a place of purification of the mind, the reduction of daily life to the most essential elements for survival, but also a spiritual setting for shaping the law. Quite appropriate the Book of Numbers (36:13) ends with the verse: 'These are the commandments and regulations that the LORD gave to the Israelites, through Moses, on the steppes of Moab, at the Jordan river near Jericho.' Moreover, the Old Testament views the desert as a place of the forces of evil making the 40 years of wanderings through the desert a very testing period both physically and spiritually. Not surprisingly, the Book of Numbers is also the story of betrayal, rebellion, and bitter complaints.

In time of hardship and distress one may expect the people to blame the leadership as if it can protect the people in any circumstances; sometimes these complaints are unreasonable because a government does not have full control of everything that happens. Moses' leadership was challenged, although forcefully confirmed by God. He had to plead before God not to destroy the Israelite people because of their complaints and rebellion (Numbers 17:8-10) after which God changed His mind. The underlying message of Numbers 5:1-14 is that God loves the Israelites notwithstanding their transgressions. Sin makes the Israelite community unclean, and uncleanness must be removed because of the sanctity of the camp by God's dwelling inside it.

Transgression of the commandments requires confession before God. The Bible tells us that God will not accept confession without a sincere change of heart and mind. 'Teshuvah' involves the clear intent not to commit the transgression again, to be careful on other similar occasions in order not to stumble again. The duty to make restitution or compensation to the wronged person has two purposes. First, it is a confession to the wronged person that one acted wrongly against him, and a question for forgiveness. The wronged person has the moral duty to forgive, and if not, the wronged person commits a transgression. His act of forgiveness should be sincere in heart and mind. A person who forgives verbally, but holds a grudge, is a transgressor. Secondly, restitution or compensation should be made according to the law which is now the law of the country. Maimonides made these comments on Numbers 5:6-7: 'If a person transgresses any of the mitzvoth of the Torah, whether a positive command or a negative command—whether willingly or inadvertently—when he repents, and returns from his sin, he must confess before God, blessed be, He as Numbers 5:6-7 states: 'If a man or a woman commit any of the sins of man… they must confess the sin that they committed.' How does one confess? Maimonides states: "I implore You, God, I sinned, I transgressed, I committed iniquity before You by doing the following. Behold, I regret and am embarrassed for my deeds. I promise never to repeat this act again." These are the essential elements of the confessional prayer. Whoever confesses profusely and elaborates on these matters is worthy of praise.'[1]

---

1. Moshe Maimonides, Mishneh Torah, Sefer Madda, Hilchot Teshuva, Chapter One, Halacha 1.

Reading 11 *Moses prays to spare God's unfaithful people*

Numbers 14:19-20

19. "Pardon, I pray, the iniquity of this people according to Your great kindness, as You have forgiven this people from the time since they have left Egypt."

20. And the LORD answered, "I have forgiven them, as you have asked."

…

Numbers 14:26-30

26. The LORD spoke further to Moses and Aaron,

27. "How much longer shall this wicked people grumble against Me? Yea, I have heard the ceaseless muttering of the Israelites against Me.

28. So tell them, 'As surely as I live', says the LORD, 'I will do to you just as you have urged Me.

29. In this wilderness your carcasses shall drop. Of all of you who were recorded in your various lists from the age of twenty years up, you who have muttered against Me,

30. not one shall enter the land in which I promised to you—save Caleb son of Jephunneh and Joshua son of Nun.

…

Numbers 14:39-45

39. When Moses reported these words to all the Israelites, the people mourned bitterly.

40. Early the next morning they set out toward the highest top of the hill country, saying, "We are ready to go up to the land that the LORD promised, for we were wrong."

41. But Moses said, "Why do you transgress by disobeying the LORD's command? This will not succeed!

42. Do not go up, so that you be routed by your enemies, for the LORD is not with you.

43. For the Amalekites and the Canaanites lay there in ambush, and you will fall by the sword, because you have turned away from the LORD and the LORD will not be with you."

BEFORE THE CONQUEST OF the promised land of Canaan, God commanded Moses to send men to scout the land, one man from each of the 12 ancestral tribes, each one a chieftain among them.[1] After 40 days they returned and reported about the land which indeed flowed 'with milk and honey'. Except for Caleb, the other men spread calumnies among the Israelites saying that the people of Canaan were stronger and could not be overpowered. The whole community broke out in loud cries, wept that night and railed against Moses and Aaron. They claimed 'If only we had died in the land of Egypt, or if only we might die in the wilderness' (Numbers 14:2). God became angry because the Israelite people did not belief His promise to give them possession of the Land of Canaan. He told Moses that He would strike them with pestilence and disown them while making of Moses a nation far more numerous than the Israelite tribes. But Moses pleaded for the Israelite people by remembering God's 13 attributes which God had revealed earlier (see Reading 4). Moses ended his plea with the words 'Please pardon the iniquity of this people according to Your great kindness, as You have forgiven this people ever since they left Egypt.' On his own initiative and for the sake of the Israelite people, Moses repented and asked for forgiveness to God. In this verse Moses shows himself as a humble man, wanting only to serve God and his people. Not his own name and glory were important, notwithstanding God's promise to choose him as the ancestral father of a new people, but deep concern about the Israelites.[2] For this reason alone, Moses deserves to be regarded as the greatest prophet: 'Never again did there arise

---

1. The Old Testament almost always mentions the names of the persons in the narrative instead of giving mere numbers. These are the names of the scouting spies: Shammua son of Zaccur; Shaphat son of Hori; Caleb son of Jephunneh; Igal son of Joseph; Hosea son of Nun; Palti son of Rafu; Gaddiel son of Sodi; Gaddi son of Susi; Ammiel son of Gemalli; Sethur son of Michael; Nahbi son of Vophsi; and Geuel son of Machi (Numbers 13:4-15).

2. 'And the LORD said to Moses, "How long will this people spurn Me, and how long will they have no faith in Me despite all the signs that I have performed in their midst? I will strike them with pestilence and disown them, and I will make of you a nation far more numerous than they!" (Numbers 14:11-12).

in Israel a prophet like Moses—whom the LORD singled out, face to face …' (Deuteronomy 34:10). God answered his call for mercy and spared the Israelite people.

The number 40 has a special meaning in the Old Testament. Moses was on Mount Sinai for 40 days and nights before receiving the 'Ten Sayings' (Reading 4). The Israelites wandered for 40 days in the wilderness before entering the Land of Canaan, and the Israelite spies scouted for 40 days. A period of 40 units (days or years) is always a period of testing, trial, purification and ends with a revival or a renewal.[3] Here the 40 days served to cleanse the Israelite people from the transgression of the ten Israelite spies (chieftains) and their followers who doubted God's promise of the Land of Canaan by believing that they were not strong enough to conquer the land and to defeat the Canaanites. The purification continues with God's judgment that nobody of the generation which left Egypt, would settle in Canaan, except Caleb, son of Jephuneh, and Joshua, son of Nun.[4]

Moses and Aaron, the two leaders of the Israelites, would never set foot in Canaan. Aaron died at Moserah, on Mount Hor, and was buried there (Deuteronomy 10:6 and 32:50) while Moses died in the land of Moab, near Mount Nebo, and was buried in a valley near Beth-peor (Deuteronomy 34:5-6).[5] Verse 14:28 'I will do to you just as you have urged Me' refers to verse 14:2 regarding the complaints of the Israelites. God punished them by letting to die those who had left Egypt while their descendants would enter the Land of Canaan. God punished the Israelite people again when they went into battle without the Ark of the Covenant, or God's presence. They were defeated by the Amalekites and the Canaanites when they marched defiantly toward the crest of the hill country which is the route leading directly

---

3. There are other instances. In the story of Noah and the Great Flood, 'The rain fell on the earth 40 days and 40 nights.' (Genesis 7:12). 'The length of David's reign over Israel was 40 years: he reigned seven years in Hebron, and he reigned 33 years in Jerusalem.' (1 Kings 2:11); 'The length of Solomon's reign in Jerusalem, over all Israel, was 40 years.' (1 Kings 11:42); 'He (Elijah) arose and ate and drank; and with the strength from that meal, he walked 40 days and 40 nights as far as the mountain of God at Horeb.' (1 Kings 19:8); 'Jonah started out and made his way into the city the distance of one day's walk, and proclaimed: "40 days more, and Nineveh shall be overthrown!" (Jonah 3:4).

4. Of the 12 Israelite spies, only Caleb and Hosea did not take part in spreading false rumors and believed in final victory—see also Deuteronomy 1:35. Moses changed the name of Hosea to Joshua (Numbers 13:16). Joshua would become the leader after the death of Moses and lead the conquest of Canaan—see Book of Joshua.

5. Moses and Aaron were punished because both had broken faith with God among the Israelite people, at the waters of Meribath-kadesh in the wilderness of Zin, by failing to uphold God's sanctity among and in sight of the Israelite people. Moses could see the Promised Land from a distance, but he would not enter it (Numbers 20:12-13 and Deuteronomy 32:51-52).

from Kadesh-Barnea up to the Land of Israel. The lost battle took place near Hormah, a Canaanite royal city on the border of the Negev, close to Arad.[6] Ever since the name Hormah stands for destruction.

---

6. The Canaanite king of Arad, when he was informed that the Israelites were coming by the way of Atharim, attacked the Israelites and took some of them captive. (Numbers 21:1-2).

Reading 12   *Idolatry and a return to God*

Numbers 21:4-9

4. They traveled from Mount Hor by way of the Sea of Reeds to go around the land of Edom. But the people grew restive on the way,

5. and the people spoke against God and against Moses, "Why did you order us to leave Egypt to die in the wilderness? There is no bread! There is no water! and we detest this miserable food!"

6. The LORD sent venomous serpents among the people. They bit the people and many of the Israelites died.

7. The people came to Moses and said, "We sinned when we spoke against the LORD and against you. Intercede with the LORD that He take away the serpents from us!" And Moses interceded for the people.

8. Then the LORD said to Moses, "Make a snake figurine and mount it on a standard. And if anyone who is bitten looks at it, he shall recover."

9. Moses made a bronze serpent and mounted it on a standard; and when anyone was bitten by a serpent, he would look at the bronze serpent and recover.

BEFORE THE ISRAELITES SET out from Mount Hor, the LORD heeded their plea so that they defeated the Canaanite king of Arad at Hormah. The Canaanites and their cities were proscribed by divine order. On their journey, the Israelites circled the land of Edom because they did not allow them to pass through their land. It is probable that the Israelites traveled through a desolate, nearly waterless sand desert and salt pans and became disheartened because of the hardship of traveling. They were so close to the Promised Land but were turning back. Because the people kept complaining about God and Moses, God sent poisonous snakes as a symbol of speaking evil, implicitly referring to the snake that spoke to Eve in the Garden of Eden. The Israelite people repented by admitting their slander against God and Moses. Again, Moses was asked to act as their spokesperson and ask for God's forgiveness which was granted. Moses asked God's forgiveness although he himself was the victim of the people's slander. From this we learn that someone, who is asked to forgive, should not be so cruel as not to forgive.

The copper snake mounted on a standard was kept by the Israelites for its healing powers. However, they erred and became idolatrous because not the copper snake was the real healing power but God's mercy. The copper snake resembles the golden calf of Exodus 32, a case of idolatry. Thus, worship of relics is forbidden and amounts to idolatry. Later, around 700 BC, King Hezekiah broke into pieces the copper snake that Moses had made so that the Israelites no longer could make sacrificial offerings to it. Hence it is written that 'He (King Hezekiah) trusted only in the LORD the God of Israel; there was none like him among all the kings of Judah after him, or among those before him.' (2 Kings 18:4).

Reading 13   *Balaam keeps up appearances, but his true character is revealed.*

Numbers 22:4-6

4. Balak son of Zippor, who was king of Moab at that time,

5. sent messengers to Balaam son of Beor in Pethor, near the Euphrates, tin the land of his kinsfolk, to invite him, saying "There is a people that arrived from Egypt; it is like a swarm covering the earth, and it is settled next to me.

6. Come here to curse this people for me, since they are too numerous for me; perhaps I can thus defeat them and drive them out of the land. For I know that he whom you bless is blessed indeed, and he whom you curse is cursed."

...

Numbers 22:21-36

21. The next morning, Balaam saddled his ass and set out with the Moabite dignitaries.

22. But God was angry with his mission; so an angel of the LORD placed himself in his way as an adversary. Balaam was riding on his donkey, with his two servants alongside,

23. when the donkey caught sight of the angel of the LORD standing in the way, with a drawn sword in his hand. The got off course and went into the fields; and Balaam beat the donkey to turn her back onto the road.

24. However, the angel of the LORD then placed himself at a narrow passage between the vineyards, with walls on either side.

25. The donkey saw the angel of the LORD, pressed herself against the wall and squeezed Balaam's foot against the wall; so he beat her again.

26. Once more the angel of the LORD moved forward and stood on a spot so narrow that there was no room to veer right or left.

27. This time, when the donkey saw the angel of the LORD, she lay down under Balaam; and Balaam was outraged and beat the donkey with his stick.

28. Then the LORD opened the donkey' mouth, and she asked Balaam, "What have I done to you that you have beaten me these three times?"

29. Balaam shouted to the donkey, "You have made me look like a fool! If I had a sword with me, I'd kill you!"

30. But the donkey said to Balaam, "Look, I am the donkey that you have been all along until this day! Is this my manner of doing thus to you?" And he answered, "No."

31. Then the LORD opened Balaam's eyes, and he saw the angel of the LORD standing in the way, with a drawn sword in his hand; then he bowed to the ground.

32. The angel of the LORD asked him, "Why have you beaten your donkey three times? It's me who came out as an adversary because you were resisting me.

33. And when the donkey saw me, she shied away because of me those three times. If not, you are the one I should have killed, while sparing her."

34. Balaam confessed to the angel of the LORD, "I erred because I did not know that you were standing in my way. If you still disapprove, I will turn back home."

35. But the angel of the LORD told Balaam, "Go with these men but ay nothing except what I tell you." So Balaam went on with Balak's dignitaries.

THE BALAAM STORY IS a distinct literary unit or pericope within the Book of Numbers. The Israelites encamped in the desert of Moab on their way to conquer the land of Canaan, causing great fear in Moab. Balak, son of Zippor, is the first king of Moab whose name is known thanks to the Balaam story. After the Israelite victories over the Amorites, Balak hired Balaam to curse the Israelites so that he could defeat them in battle. Balaam was a seer of a distant Babylonian region near the Euphrates with the recognized power of cursing or blessing. He was perceived as a spiritual man with the ability to foretell future events by means of an alleged supernatural power. When the messengers of Balak, elders of Moab and Midian, asked Balaam to curse Israel, Balaam asked them to stay with him and promised them to reply as the LORD would instruct him. At night God said to Balaam 'Do not go with them. You must not curse that people, for they are blessed.' The next morning, he sent the messengers away saying that the LORD would not let him go with them. After having received Balaam's answer, Balak sent again messengers, more distinguished dignitaries than the first, with the same petition. This time God said to Balaam 'If these men have come to invite you, you may go with them. But whatever I command you, that you shall do.' On his way to Balak, the angel of the LORD appeared as an adversary. This well-known incident describes that the donkey of Balaam could perceive the angel of God and is given the power to speak to reprove Balaam for his cruel behavior.

Since the first revelation of God, Balaam knew that the Israelite people were blessed, so he had no reason to go to Balak, knowing the words of God. However, he goes with the messengers to Balak for the reward with riches because of his divination. After the incident with the angel, Balaam said that he had erred and showed regret. But his expression of regret was insincere, just as the Pharaoh's insincere regret (Reading 3) because the real Balaam was a man driven by greed. At first sight, he had an appearance of respectability but in time his true character would be revealed. The great sin of Balaam was his attempt of cursing the Israelites at the request of Balak. After his return Balaam explained to Balak that he could not curse the Israelite people; on the contrary, he blessed the Israelites four times. His inability to curse the Israelite people was not his free choice since God had put the words of blessing in his mouth. God explained how He had used Balaam to bless the Israelites, instead of cursing it: '. . . Balak, son of Zippor, the king of Moab, started to attack Israel. He sent Balaam son of Beor to curse you, but I refused to listen to Balaam; he had to bless you, and thus I saved you from Balak.' (Joshua 24:9). The real Balaam taught the Moabites how to defile the people of Israel for he knew that introducing prostitution would cause the Israelites to break the covenant with God and with it came Babylonian paganism and various deities. Numbers 31:16 gives the reason, namely the Midianite women, at the bidding of Balaam, had induced the Israelites to trespass the LORD in the matter of Peor (namely the Babylonian way), so that the LORD's community was struck by the plague. Balaam will be remembered for his greed, spiritual blindness, and treason. He used religion to make money, which was his real intention, and covered up his deception. Numbers 31:8 mentions that the Israelites put Balaam to the sword.

The pericope explains the difference between reputation and true character. Balaam was good in hiding his own interests and keeping up appearances. His reputation and social standing were excellent although God knew his true colors. Examination and revelation of his true character were put to the test when he had to make a choice under pressure. He failed to show personal integrity, honesty, and courage which he could have developed by self-examination during his life. By keeping up appearances he could no longer repent with a sincere heart.

In an unexpected twist of the events, the words put in Balaam's mouth by God represent some of the most beautiful examples of early Hebrew poetry.[1] The description of the Israelite tent camp became part of Jewish liturgy as a prayer to be recited on entering the synagogue. Here are some of the best-known verses:

> 9. Looking at them from the mountain tops,
> watching them from the heights,
> there is a people that lives apart,
> not reckoned among the nations.
> 10. Who can count Jacob's descendants,
> number the grains of sand of Israel?
> May I die the death of the righteous,
> may my fate be like theirs!
> - Numbers 23:9-10
>
> 21. No danger is in sight for Jacob,
> no trouble in view for Israel.
> The LORD their God is with them,
> and their King's acclaim among his people.
> 22. God set them free from Egypt and
> is for them strong like the wild ox.
> 23. No, there is no curse that can touch Jacob,
> no magic power against Israel:
> to Jacob is revealed,
> you, Israel, what God has in His mind.
> - Numbers 23:21-23
>
> 5. How fair are your tents, O Jacob,
> your homes, O Israel!
> 6. Like palm-groves that line out to the horizon,
> like gardens by the riverside,
> like tall trees planted by the LORD,
> like cedars alongside the water;
> 7. their tree branches drip with moisture,
> their sprouts have abundant water.
> Their king shall be more powerful than Agag,

---

1. The ancient poetry of the Old Testament is limited to seven songs/prayers, namely the 'Song of the Sea' by Moses and the Israelites (Exodus 15:1-18), the 'Song of the Ark' by Moses (Numbers 10:35-36), the 'Oracles of Balaam' (Numbers 23 and 24), the 'Song of Moses' (Deuteronomy 32:1-43), the 'Blessing of Moses (Deuteronomy 33), the 'Song of Deborah' (Judges 5), and the 'Song of Hannah' (1 Samuel 2:1-10).

Their kingdom shall be exalted.
- Numbers 24:5-7

Deuteronomy

Reading 14 — *God shall be among His exiled people who return to Him.*

Deuteronomy 4:27-31

27. The LORD will scatter you among the nations, and only a handful of you shall be left among the nations to which the LORD will banish you.

28. There you will serve man-made idols of wood and stone, that cannot see or hear or eat or smell.

29. But from there you will search again for the LORD your God, you will find Him, if only you seek Him with all your heart and soul.

30. When you are in distress because all these bad things have befallen you and, in the end, you will return to the LORD your God and listen to His words.

31. For the LORD your God is a compassionate God: He will not fail you nor will He let you perish; He will not forget the unbreakable covenant which He made with your fathers.

THESE ARE THE WORDS Moses spoke to the Israelites in the valley near Beth-peor located across the Jordan river in present-day Jordan. The quotation begins with a warning that the Israelite people will be scattered among the nations as a punishment if they abandon the LORD. It is an implicit prophecy about possible destruction and exile, even before they would settle in Canaan and establish there a sovereign Jewish nation. The enforced exile not only refers to the exile policy of the Assyrians and Babylonians, later described in the Old Testament, but to all enforced exiles in the future.

The expression 'wood and stone' is used here to compare the God of the Israelites with 'other gods', human-made idols which are the subject of ridicule. The God of the Israelite people is not material but spiritual and can neither be comprehended nor represented by materials such as wood or stone. In the places of exile, the Jewish people will be confronted with worship of wood and stone. Moreover, in these places of exile, the Jewish people will decrease in number because many will lose their life or faith. Moses immediately warns not to despair when such calamities happen. One of the most important expressions of hope in the Old Testament is the promise that personal and communal contact with the God remains possible, also in foreign lands: if you search there for the LORD your God, you will find Him, if only you seek Him with all your heart and soul … Even before the Temple of Jerusalem was built, which would become the most sacred dwelling place of God, Moses revealed that God shall always be with His people if they search for the LORD and seek Him with all their heart and soul.[1] The return to the LORD your God is the change of heart and mind which is answered by God through His compassion. Moses' prophecy gains an even deeper meaning when he said that the most important duty is to follow God's commandments and laws. Thus, the Bible is the most trustworthy path, more important than the Tabernacle or the Temple, built with stone and wood. By keeping the teachings of the Bible, and by seeking God with heart and soul, the exiles will not succumb to worshiping 'other gods' in foreign places. This promise was essential to let survive the people of God and to preserve His presence among them. The worship of God would not disappear, for it needed no more than sincere prayer and obedience to His words. Sincerity of prayer and following God's commandments are the most important elements, not the outward appearances of devotion and worship. Isaiah re-emphasized the most essential condition of the heart and soul with these verses.

> 11. "Do you really think that I need all your sacrifices?"
> asked the LORD.
> "I am sated with burnt offerings of rams,
> and the fat of fattened cattle,
> and blood of bulls;
> and I have no delight
> in lambs and goats.
> …
> 16. Wash yourselves clean;
> put your transgressions
> away from My sight.
> Cease to do evil;
> 17. learn to do good.

---

1. See also Micah 5:6.

Seek to do justice;
aid the wronged.
Uphold the rights of the orphan;
defend the cause of the widow.
- Isaiah 1:11 and 1:16-17

ered in the very heavens themselves. Their vast panoramas are grand and evocative, and their narratives of the end of the world are as brilliantly compelling today as ever.

Joshua

Reading 15 *Achan transgresses and confesses but is executed under emergency powers.*

Joshua 6:18-19

18. "But you may not take the spoil that is proscribed, or else you will be sanctioned: if you take anything from that which is proscribed, you will cause the camp of Israel to be proscribed; you will bring catastrophe upon it.

19. All the silver and gold and objects made of copper and iron are consecrated to the LORD; they must be brought into the treasury of the LORD."

…

Joshua 7:1

1. But the Israelites violated the proscription: Achan son of Carmi son of Zabdi son of Zerah, of the tribe of Judah, took of that which was proscribed, and the LORD was infuriated with the Israelites.

…

Joshua 7:19-26

19. Then Joshua said to Achan, "My son, honor the LORD, the God of Israel, and make confession to Him. Tell me the truth about what you have done; do not hold anything back from me."

20. Achan answered Joshua, "It is true! I have sinned against the LORD, the God of Israel. This is what I did:

21. I saw among the spoil a fine Babylonian robe, two hundred shekels of silver, and a bar of gold weighing fifty shekels, and I had an eye on them and

took them. They are buried in the ground beneath my tent, with the silver under it."

22. Joshua sent some men who hurried to the tent; and, buried in his tent, they found it with the silver underneath.

23. They took them from the tent and brought them to Joshua and all the Israelites. Then they displayed them before the LORD.

24. Then Joshua, and all Israel with him, took Achan son of Zerah—and the silver, the mantle, and the bar of gold—his sons and daughters, and his cattle, his donkey and his sheep, and his tent, and all his belongings, and brought them to the Valley of Achor.

25. And Joshua said to Achan, "What misfortune you have brought upon us! The LORD will bring calamity upon you this day." And all Israel stoned Achan and his family and put them to the fire and burned them.

26. They piled a huge mound of stones over him, which is still there. Then the anger of the LORD subsided. That is why that place was named the Valley of Achor ever since.

THE BOOK OF JOSHUA is the sixth book of the Old Testament and tells the conquest of Canaan under the leadership of Joshua. It begins with the destructions of Jericho and the small city of Ai in central Canaan. Joshua was the son of Nun of the tribe of Ephraim. Moses renamed him Yehoshua which means 'Yahweh is salvation' (Numbers 13:16). Joshua and Caleb were the only ones, born in Egypt, who entered the Promised Land, a privilege granted by God because they were the only ones of the 12 spies who had reported positively about the possible conquest of Canaan, and thus had shown trust in the LORD (Reading 11). Joshua is portrayed as the military leader and prophet in the style of Moses who had appointed him as his successor on the instruction of God (Numbers 27:18-20). The battle of Jericho is the first battle of the Israelites in the conquest of Canaan. God commanded Joshua to let march the Israelite army around Jericho once every day for six consecutive days with seven priests carrying seven ram's horns preceding the Ark. On the seventh day, they had to march around Jericho seven times, with the priests blowing the horns. When a long blast was sounded on the horn, all the people gave a mighty shout after which the city walls collapsed (Joshua 2:2-5). The Israelites burned down the city and exterminated its population. When they went up to the city of Ai, the Israelites lost their first battle with 36 Israelite deaths. Ai is mentioned together with Beth-El as near the site where Abraham pitched his tent and built an altar to the LORD after he had left his native land in Ur of the Chaldeans (Genesis 11:31, 12:8 and 13:3).

Joshua's leadership was questioned because of this unexpected defeat against a small city. Joshua rented his clothes and he and the elders of Israel laid until evening with their faces to the ground in front of the Ark of the LORD. They strewed earth on their heads. Joshua cried 'O LORD, what can I say after Israel has run away before its enemies? When the Canaanites and all the inhabitants of the land hear of this, they will turn upon us and wipe out our name off the face of the earth.' (Joshua 7:8-9). God answered by saying that the Israelite people had transgressed because of the violation of the proscription that all the silver and gold and objects of copper and iron of Jericho were consecrated to the LORD; instead, the Israelites plundered it for their own gain. Because any violation would bring calamity on the Israelites (Joshua 6:18-19), God said to Joshua 'I will not be with you anymore unless you destroy the things that were proscribed.' (Joshua 7:12). In the end, Achan confessed that he had stolen the spoil consisting of a fine Babylonian mantle, 200 shekels of silver, and a bar of gold weighing 50 shekels. In a second battle the king of Ai was defeated in an ambush and the city was left in ruins (Joshua 12:9).

The Israelite defeat at Ai was attributed to Achan who had violated the proscription about the sack of Jericho. A proscription is called 'herem' in Hebrew, meaning the status of separation from common use or contact either because it is proscribed as an abomination to God or because it is consecrated to God. The 'herem' was applicable in the last-mentioned sense and equals the status of 'qodesh' or sanctity. Things in the 'herem' are also called 'herem'. The 'herem' of Jericho was the severest possible: animals as well as humans were put to death by the sword, the city burned down, its spoliation banned, and its riches (gold, silver and copper) dedicated to the Israelite sanctuary treasure. The severest degree of 'herem' is deemed to be contagious, and an individual who incurs the severest degree of 'herem' contaminates everything and everyone who encountered him. Achan's sacrilegious transgression caused the communal responsibility of the Israelites who were punished for the transgression, namely their defeat at Ai with the loss of 36 soldiers. Thus, Achan's transgression was ascribed to the people: 'The Israelites, however, violated the proscription: Achan son of Carmi son of Zabdi son of Zerah, of the tribe of Judah, took of that which was proscribed, and the LORD was infuriated with the Israelites' (Joshua 7:1); 'But the LORD answered Joshua: "Arise! Why do you lie prostrated? Israel has sinned! They have broken the covenant by which I bound them. They have stolen of the proscribed and put it in their vessels; they have stolen; they have broken faith!' (Joshua 7:10-11). The Israelite people reacted by stoning Achan with all his family to death in the valley of Achor where the stolen things were burned, and a great mound of stones was raised over him and the burned things. They raised a huge mound of stones over him, which is still there. Then the anger of the LORD subsided. Note that the death penalty was not carried out before Achan had admitted having done the wrongdoings. It is an element of judicial fairness because the Israelites feared to punish an innocent man. The defendant was given an opportunity of clearing himself or of making a confession.

Confession of sin is an essential prerequisite for expiation and atonement according to the Bible—see Introduction. Such confession is often followed by divine pardon. According to the old Israelite legal traditions, theft did not warrant capital punishment but compensation. In addition, an execution was only legitimate when the offense was seen by two eyewitnesses who warned the sinner, before he acted, that his intended act was illegal, and that punishment was death. In the case of Achan, no one knew what Achan had done, thus capital punishment was not provided for. However, the execution could be carried out legally under the provisions of 'emergency measures' which require that the usual law is ignored to save the people.

Judges

Reading 16   *The Israelites are rebuked by an angel and weep.*

Judges 2:1-5

1. An angel of the LORD came up from Gilgal to Bochim and said to the Israelites, "I brought you out of Egypt and I took you into the land which I had solemnly promised to your forefathers. And I said, 'I will never break My covenant with you.

2. For your part, must make no covenant with the people of this land; you must tear down their altars.' But you have not listened to Me—look what you have done!

3. Therefore, I have decided not to drive them out before you but they shall become your oppressors, and their gods shall be a temptation to you."

4. As the angel of the LORD spoke these words to all the Israelites, the people broke into weeping.

5. So they called that place Bochim, and they offered sacrifices there to the LORD.

THE BOOK OF JUDGES is the second book after the Book of Joshua in the second part of the Old Testament, called Prophets. Along with the first chapters of 1 Samuel, it covers the period from the death of Joshua to the first Israelite King Saul.[1] The completion of the conquest of Canaan was lengthy and only achieved by David when he captured Jerusalem in the 10th century

---

1. The story of the judges is preceded by a short account of the settlement of the Israelites in Canaan (Judges 2 to 5) and is closed by two appendices concerning Micah's sanctuary and the crime of Gibeah and its punishment (Judges 17 to 21). The Book of Judges places the tribe of Judah in a prominent role.

BC—more details in the Book of Deuteronomy. Meanwhile the conquered land of Canaan was divided among the Israelite tribes.

The twelve judges were not judges in the legal sense but divinely inspired leaders. None of the names mentioned in the Book of Judges is a prophet except Deborah, one of the seven female prophets of the Old Testament according to the Jewish Sages. Angels were sent as spokespersons of God to announce and appoint a new judge. The Book of Judges follows a repetitive pattern. The Israelite people were unfaithful to God and started to worship gods of the conquered Canaanites or neighboring peoples. As punishment, God delivered them in the hand of their enemies after which the people repented and asked for God's mercy. God answered their petition for forgiveness by sending a judge who liberated the Israelites. After the death of the judge, the people abandoned God again and started worshipping other gods, after which God punished them. The cycle of transgression, regret, and God's forgiveness by sending another judge is repeated.[2] The first judge was Othniel, a transitional figure.[3] The next is Ehud who rescued the Israelites from a long time of oppression by the Moabites.[4] Shamgar succeeded Ehud and restored peace after defeating the Philistines: 'After him (Ehud) came Shamgar son of Anath, who slew six hundred Philistines with an ox goad. He too was a champion of Israel' (Judges 3:31).

The Israelite people were punished again after they had sinned, this time the punishment was enslavement to the Canaanite King Jabin. Deborah, the wife of Lappidoth, became a judge and prophetess (Judges 4:4). She is the only prophet in the Book of Judges. Deborah called for a war of liberation against King Jabin, claiming that King Jabin would be defeated by a woman (Judges 4:9). She succeeded in assembling troops under the skillful military commander Barak on Mount Tabor from where they struck and defeated Jabin's army of 900 iron chariots near the Kishon River. The fourth major judge is Gideon, a young man, who was called to be a judge by the appearance of an angel of God who sat under the oak in Ophra.[5] He was successful in defeating the more numerous Midianites by a coordinated

---

2. See for example Judges 3:7-11 and 10:6-16; 1 Samuel 7:3-6.

3. He is the first judge and the only judge who came from the tribe of Judah. He captured Debir, a Canaanite royal city in Judah and later a Levitical city, and married Achsah, the daughter of Caleb, as a reward.

4. Ehud, son of Gera the Benjaminite, ended the Moabite rule over Israel for generations. He was left-handed and killed the Moabite King Eglon with his sword during an audience with the king (Judges 3:15-30).

5. 'Then Gideon realized that it was an angel of the LORD; and Gideon said "Alas, O LORD GOD! For I have seen an angel of the LORD". But the LORD said to him "Have no fear, you shall not die." (Judges 6:22-23).

night attack. Gideon was succeeded by his son Abimelech who reigned only three years. In a rebellion, he was mortally wounded by a woman who dropped an upper millstone on Abimelech's head and cracked his skull. 'The LORD repaid Abimelech for the evil he had done to his father by slaying his seventy brothers' (Judges 10:56). The next judges were Tola and Jair, who judged Israel 23 and 22 years respectively. Both had a minor role.

Israel sinned again by worshipping other gods and fell in the hands of the Philistines and the Ammonites. Israel repented, removed the alien gods from among them and served the LORD, '. . . and He could not bear the miseries of Israel' (Judges 10:16). Jephtah was the next judge for six years and defeated the Ammonites. When the Israelites of Ephraim rebelled against him, Jephtah mobilized the men of Gilead who defeated Ephraim.[6] After him came Ibzan of Bethlehem who was a judge for seven years. Then came Elon the Zebulunite who judged Israel for ten years. After him came Abdon, the son of Hillel, who judged for eight years. The Israelites continued to do what displeased the LORD and were delivered in the hands of the Philistines for 40 years. Again, an angel of the LORD was sent, this time to the barren wife of Manoah, and the angel predicted that she would give birth to a son.[7] Upon his birth, the son was called Samson who judged Israel in the days of the Philistines for 20 years (Judges 16:31).

The Book of Judges ends with a sentence that prepares the ground for a kingdom: 'In those days there was no king in Israel; every man did what was right in his eyes' (Judges 21:25), implying that chaos reigned among the tribes and that a kingdom was necessary to establish peace in Israel. The twelve judges were temporary leaders without a national political order and a defined process of power transfer from one leader to the next one. The Book of Judges pictures the Israelites as a people who had not the same loyalty to God as the generation of Joshua.[8] As a result, they were not only

6. The Gileadites held the fords of the Jordan against the Ephraimites. When any fugitive from Ephraim said, "Let me cross", the men of Gilead would ask him "Are you an Ephraimite?"; if he said "No" they would say to him, "Then say shibboleth"; but he would say "sibboleth", not being able to pronounce it correctly. Then the men of Gilead would seize him and slay him by the fords of the Jordan (Judges 12:5-6).

7. 'Manoah said to his wife, "We shall surely die, because we have seen God". But his wife said to him "If the LORD meant to take our lives, He would not have accepted a burnt offering and a meal offering from us, nor would He have shown us these things; nor would He have made such an announcement to us." (Judges 13:22-23).

8. In the period of the judges, the worship of the LORD was not limited to the place of the Ark but occurred also at local sanctuaries provided that a Levite priest was present. The appendix concerning Micah deals with Micah's private sanctuary. He invites a young travelling Levite priest to stay with him '. . . and be a father and a priest to me'. The Levite agreed to stay with Micah and he became like one of Micah's sons. The Levite priest remained in Micah's shrine. 'Now I know', Micah told himself, '. . . that the

repeatedly punished by God but the complete conquest of Canaan became unattainable. Only in sincere regret and change would the Israelites be able to live a secure life in the Promised Land.

Judges 5 is called 'The Song of Deborah', one of the earliest pieces of Hebrew poetry and a rare biblical event when a woman speaks directly and as a leader. Here is an appealing excerpt which contrasts the idolatrous and careless people with those few who stand up and are dedicated to God and the nation.

> 6. In the days of Shamgar son of Anath,
> in the days of Jael, travelers avoided the main roads,
> and they went
> on winding paths.
> 7. Few people live in the land of Israel,
> till you arose, O Deborah,
> arose, O mother, in Israel!
> 8. When they chose new gods,
> was there a guardian then in the gates?
> No shield or spear was seen
> among forty thousand in Israel!
>
> 9. My heart is with Israel's leaders,
> with the dedicated of the people –
> Praise the LORD!
> - Judges 5:6-9

At a fundamental level, reflection on Judges 2 reveals that neither national feelings nor the political leadership will determine the fate of the people but adherence to the spiritual world created by God. Faith doesn't deny the importance of national questions or policies but subordinates them to ideology, a set of ideas and beliefs that justify the social order. This interpretation is how we understand verse 9 in 'The Song of Deborah' in which the government symbolizes the uniting ideology.

LORD will favor me, since the Levite has become my priest.' (Judges 17:7-13).

1 Samuel

Reading 17 *Samuel calls for a return to God—Israel confesses its idolatry and returns to God.*

1 Samuel 7:2-6

2. For a long time the Ark was housed in Kiriath-jearim, twenty years in all; and all the House of Israel began to seek the LORD.

3. Then Samuel said to all the people of Israel, "If you yearn for a return to the LORD, you must remove the foreign gods and the Ashtaroth from your midst and direct your heart to the LORD and serve Him alone. He will rescue you from the hands of the Philistines."

4. And the Israelites removed the Baalim and Ashtaroth and they served the LORD alone.

5. Samuel said, "Assemble all Israel at Mizpah, and I will pray to the LORD for you."

6. They gathered at Mizpah, drew water, and poured it out before the LORD; they fasted that day, and there they confessed that they had sinned before the LORD. And Samuel acted as judge and leader of the Israelites at Mizpah.

THE TWO BOOKS OF Samuel record the history from the end of the period of the judges to the establishment of the Israelite kingdom around 1000 BC. Already as a boy, Samuel was in the service of the LORD under the care and instruction of the high priest Eli in Shiloh, although Samuel was not a priest because he was not of the family of Aaron. His mother Hannah, one of the seven prophetesses in the Old Testament, had trusted him to Eli because she had asked God for a child when she was barren. Samuel means 'I asked the

LORD for him.'[1] The boy grew up and the LORD was with him: He did not leave any of Samuel's predictions unfulfilled. The LORD revealed Himself to Samuel and all Israel acknowledged that Samuel was a trustworthy prophet. He became one of the most influential prophets and anointed the first two Israelite kings, Saul, and David. Chapters 4 and 5 narrate how the Israelites were routed by the Philistines, that the two lewd and impious sons of Eli, Hophni and Phinehas, were killed in battle, and that the Ark of the Covenant was captured by the Philistines. When the 98-year-old Eli heard that the Ark had been captured, he fell backward off the seat, broke his neck, and died. He had been a judge of Israel for 40 years.

The Ark remained in the land of the Philistines for seven months where they kept the Ark in Ashdod, beside the temple of Dagonbut, but were punished by God when its population was struck with hemorrhoids.[2] Then the Ark was moved from Ashdod to Gath and from there to Ekron but also in that place the population was struck by deadly hemorrhoids. Finally, after seven months, the elders of the Philistines decided to let the Ark return to the Israelites and pay an indemnity. The Philistines took two cows and harnessed them to a cart upon which the Ark was placed. Five elders of the Philistines went to the border of the Israelite place Beth-shemesh where they left the cart with the Ark and the indemnity (a chest, golden mice and the golden figures of their hemorrhoids) and returned to Ekron. The people of Beth-shemesh were reaping their wheat harvest in the valley when they noticed the Ark, and they rejoiced. But the LORD struck 70 elders and 50,000 men of the common people in Beth-shemesh because they had investigated the Ark. Ever since the construction of the Ark at Mount Sinai, it was forbidden to look at the inside of the Ark with the Covenant, and even the high priest might not look upon it but once a year on Yom Kippur through a cloud of incense.[3] The familiarity with which the people of Beth-

---

1. After giving birth, Hannah's prayer is one of the most moving prayers of the Old Testament. Her prayer proclaims that God is the source of victory, justice, fertility, and legitimacy, as well as the source of humility for the proud and exaltation for the meek. Hannah's prayer is recited in the first day service of Rosh Hashanah.

2. The Sumerian and Canaanite god of Dagon was the god of seed, vegetation, and crops. Temples to Dagon were built in Gaza and Ashdod. The reference to Dagon alluded to the fact that the Ark would be found by the Israelites of Beth-shemesh when they were reaping their wheat harvest. It asserts that God alone is the source of the earth and its crops. 'Baalim' is the plural of Baal and refers in this context to city gods, local fertility, and nature gods. Literally, 'baal' means lord or master and is not necessarily related to religion.

3. For the same reason, two sons of Aaron died when they drew too close to the presence of the LORD (Reading 7). Only the priests could carry the Ark which was covered with several layers of cloth, a dolphin skin and on top of it a cloth of pure blue wool to protect it from being seen. (Numbers 4:5-6, and 15).

shemesh handled the Ark was an affront to God and degraded the Holy Ark to a piece of curiosity and irreverence. After having sent messengers to another Israelite place, Kiriath-jearim, the Ark was housed with Abinadab on a hill and the people consecrated his son Eleazar to take charge of the Ark. There the Ark stayed for 20 years.

By letting the Ark captured for seven months, God wanted to humble the Israelites because of their idolatry which is the greatest transgression of the Ten Sayings written on the two Tablets of the Covenant. The capture of the Ark meant that God was no longer among His people and this time was one of the darkest moments in the history of the Israelites. Only after 20 years that the Ark was in Kiriath-jearim, the Israelites yearned more than ever for the LORD. It is probable that Samuel travelled from city to city during these 20 years consistently calling upon the people to return to God. The Old Testament mentions that 'Each year he (Samuel) made the rounds of Bethel, Gilgal, and Mizpah, and acted as a judge over Israel at all those places. Then he would return to Ramah, for his home was there; and there too he would judge Israel.' (1 Samuel 7:16-17). When Samuel saw that the people returned to God and repented for their worship of other gods, he was deeply moved.[4] To cleanse away their moral impurity, namely idolatry, the Israelites purified themselves by 'living water' or streaming water—worded here as pouring of water—before the LORD. Moreover, the people fasted that day which was part of the self-examination process. Once this was done, the people confessed their sin openly and as a community. Samuel acted as judge and leader for the last time before anointing Saul as the first Israelite king.

In our time, idolatry is not limited to worshipping other gods, but also includes the denial of the existence of one God. Idolatry originally means 'image' or 'fantasy' worship. The use of images or fantasies is equated with the service of other gods or the denial of God. Denial of God is a fantasy worship of the material world and violates the first commandment or mitzvah: to know that God exists. The second mitzvah adds the duty to be aware of the oneness of God. The 'Shema Yisrael' are the first two words of Deuteronomy 6:4 and are the title of the prayer that is the centerpiece in weekly service prayers, expressing the monotheistic essence of the Jewish belief, starting with the two mentioned mitzvoth.

---

4. Ashtaroth (plural) was the generic term in the Old Testament for goddesses. It is derived from the Phoenician goddess Astarte and the Babylonian goddess Ishtar. The Old Testament mentions that King Solomon, in his later years, worshipped Ashtoreth, the goddess of the Phoenicians (1 Kings 11:5).

'Hear, o Israel! The LORD is our God, the LORD is One. (Sh'ma Yisrael, Adonai Eloheinu, Adonai Echad)[5]

And you shall love the LORD your God with all your heart and with all your soul and with all your might.

And these words that I command you today shall be in your heart.

And you shall teach them diligently to your children, and you shall speak of them when you sit at home, and when you walk along the way, and when you lie down and when you rise up.

And you shall bind them as a sign on your hand, and they shall be for frontlets between your eyes.

And you shall write them on the doorposts of your house and on your gates.'

Deuteronomy 6:4-9

And because the 'Shema Yisrael' is the central tenet of the Old Testament, these words are holy. Rabbinic Judaism teaches that the Tetragrammaton (ה-ו-ה-י), YHWH, is the ineffable and actual name of God, and as such is not read aloud in the Shema but is traditionally replaced with יְנדא, Adonai ('LORD'). Maimonides wrote that we are to recite the 'Shema Yisrael' twice daily (when you lie down and when you rise) and that the one who recites the 'Shema Yisrael' should wash his hands with water before reciting it.[6] This is done by using a vessel or flowing water.

In the New Testament, the cleansing with water has a fundamental meaning. Baptism ,derived from the Greek word 'βάπτισμα' or baptisma, is the immersion in water and signifies purification and conversion to Jesus Christ, the Savior of mankind. As is written in John 3:5, Jesus said, "Truly, truly, I say to you, unless one is born of water and the Spirit, he cannot enter the kingdom of God." Jesus himself was baptized by John the Baptist. According to the various practices of Christian churches, baptism takes place at the age of newborns, infants or later in adult life after a confession of faith. According to the oldest Christian tradition, it signifies the

---

5. This is repeated in Isaiah 44:6 'Thus said the LORD, the King of Israel, their Savior, the LORD of Hosts: I am the first and I am the last, and there is no god but Me.'

6. Moshe Maimonides, Mishneh Torah, Sefer Ahavah, Hilchot, Kri'at Shema, Chapter One, Halacha 1 and Chapter Three, Halacha 1.

sacramental washing by which the soul is cleansed from the sin while water is poured on the body. It takes away the sin inherited since the fall of man in paradise when Adam and Eve sinned and lost their innocence. It is called original sin or ancestral sin. In English, the term 'christen' is familiarly used for 'baptize.'[7]

---

7. www.newadvent.org/cathen/02258b.htm

Reading 18   *Saul disobeys God and loses his kingship.*

1 Samuel 15:1-3

1. Samuel said to Saul, 'I am the one the LORD commanded to anoint you king of His people Israel. Therefore, listen to the LORD's command!

2. "Thus said the LORD of Hosts: I am punishing Amalek for what it did to Israel, for the assault Amalek made upon them on the road, when they came from Egypt.

3. Now go, attack Amalek, and completely destroy all that belongs to him. Spare no one, but kill alike men and women, infants and sucklings, cattle and sheep, camels and donkeys!"

...

1 Samuel 15:7-35

7. Saul slaughtered the Amalekites from Havilah all the way to Shur, east of Egypt,

8. and he captured King Agag of Amalek. He killed all the people, putting them to the sword;

9. but Saul and the troops spared Agag and the best of the sheep, cattle, the fat calves, the lambs, and all else that was of value. They would not destroy them; they destroyed only what was cheap and worthless.

10. Then the LORD came to Samuel and said:

11. "I regret that I ever made Saul king, for he has turned away from Me and has not carried out My commands." Samuel was tormented and he cried out to the LORD all night long.

12. Early the next morning Samuel went to meet Saul when someone was told him, "Saul went to Carmel, where he set up a monument for himself; then he went on to Gilgal."

13. When Samuel finally found Saul, Saul said to him, "May the LORD bless you! I have fulfilled the LORD's commandment."

14. "Then what", demanded Samuel, "is this bleating of sheep in my ears, and the lowing of cattle?"

15. Saul admitted, "The troops spared the choicest of the sheep and cattle for sacrificing to the LORD your God. And we destroyed the rest."

16. Then Samuel said to Saul, "Stop! Let me reveal what the LORD said to me last night!" "Speak!", he replied.

17. And Samuel said, "You may think little of yourself, but you are the leader of the tribes of Israel. The LORD anointed you king of Israel,

18. and the LORD sent you on a mission, saying, 'Go and destroy the sinful Amalekites; make war on them until you have exterminated them.'

19. Why did you disobey the LORD? Why did you rush for the plunder of the spoil in defiance of the LORD's commandment?"

20. Saul muttered, "But I did obey the LORD! I carried out the mission on which the LORD sent me: I took King Agag of Amalek as prisoner, and I destroyed Amalek, and the troops took from the spoil the best of the sheep and cattle to sacrifice to the LORD your God at Gilgal."

22. But Samuel replied:

> "Does the LORD delight in burnt offerings and sacrifices
> as much as in obedience to His will and commandment?
> For sure, obedience is better than sacrifice,
> compliance better than the offering of fat rams.
> 23. For rebellion is like the sin of witchcraft,
> defiance, like the iniquity of worshipping idols.
> Because you rejected the LORD's command,
> He has rejected you as king."

24. At once Saul admitted to Samuel, "I did wrong to transgress the LORD's commandment and your instructions; but I was afraid of the troops and I gave in to them.

25. Please, forgive my transgression and come back with me, and I will worship the LORD."

26. But Samuel replied, "I will not go back with you! You have rejected the LORD's command, and the LORD has rejected you as king of Israel."

27. As Samuel turned away, Saul seized the corner of his robe, and it tore.

28. And Samuel said to him, "This day the LORD has torn the kingship over Israel away from you and has given it to another who is worthier than you.

29. Moreover, God, the Glory of Israel, does neither deceive nor change His mind, for He is not human that He should change His mind."

30. But Saul pleaded again, "I know I did wrong. But please, at least honor me in the presence of the elders and before Israel, and come back with me so that I may worship the LORD your God."

31. So Samuel followed Saul back, and Saul worshipped the LORD.

32. Samuel said, "Bring King Agag of Amalek to me." Agag stepped forward to him with trembling knees and said, "Ah, the bitterness of death is at hand!"

33. But Samuel said:

> "As your sword have made women childless,
> so shall your mother be childless among women."

And Samuel cut Agag down before the LORD at Gilgal.

34. Samuel then went home to Ramah, and Saul returned home at Gibeah.

35. Samuel never saw Saul again to the day of his death. But Samuel grieved over Saul, and the LORD regretted that He had made Saul king of Israel.

ALTHOUGH SAMUEL HIMSELF WAS opposed to appointing a king because in his view the LORD was the true king and leader of the Jewish people. He anointed the first two kings of the Israelites at the command of God. The LORD replied to Samuel: 'Do as the people ask; but warn them about the practices of any king who will rule over them.' (1 Samuel 8:9). After Samuel's warning, the people would not listen. 'No,' they said. 'We must have a king over us, that we may be like all the other nations.' (1 Samuel 8:19-20). Maimonides explained that the appointment of a king should precede a war against Amalek. This is evident from Samuel's words to King Saul 'God sent me to anoint you as king … Now, go and proscribe Amalek.' (1 Samuel 15:1-3).

Why was God displeased with the people's request of a king from Samuel? Because the people made their request in a spirit of complaint, as the story tells us. Rather than seeking to appoint a king, they were simply intent on rejecting the prophet Samuel as implied by God's reply to him: 'It is not you, but Me they have rejected.' (1 Samuel 8:7) God then revealed to Samuel that he should anoint Saul, a Benjamite, as king because Saul is described as an excellent young man. No one among the Israelites was handsomer than he. He was a head taller than any of the people (1 Samuel 9:2). When Samuel told Saul about his future anointment as king, Saul was hesitant and protested: 'But I am only a Benjamite, from the smallest of the tribes of Israel, and my clan is the least of all the clans of the tribe of Benjamin! Why do you say such things to me?' (1 Samuel 9:21).[1] Silently, Samuel took a flask of oil and poured some on Saul's head and kissed him and said: 'The LORD anoints you ruler over His own people.' As Saul turned around to leave Samuel, God gave him another heart. The spirit of God gripped him, and he spoke in ecstasy (1 Samuel 10:9-10). When Saul was acclaimed king in front of the people, he was a humble man who had hidden himself among the baggage of the camp. As a king he became a charismatic leader characterized by great courage and boldness in battle against Moab, the Ammonites, Edom, the kings of Zobah and the Philistines. The Old Testament tells us how Saul gradually behaved more and more like the other kings of the region forgetting to follow God's instructions.

A first incident in Saul's relationship with God occurred when the Israelites gathered at Gilgal and fled after seeing the combat strength of their enemies. Samuel had ordered Saul to wait for him before going into battle. Saul waited seven days, the time that Samuel had set. When Samuel failed to come to Gilgal, and the people began to scatter, Saul himself presented the burnt offering, assuming the office of the priest. He had just finished presenting the burnt offering when Samuel arrived and said: 'You acted foolishly in not keeping the commandments that the LORD your God gave you! Otherwise, the LORD would have established your dynasty over Israel forever. But now your dynasty will not endure. The LORD will seek out a man after His own heart, and the LORD will appoint him ruler over His people, because you did not keep the LORD's command.' (1 Samuel 13:13-14). At Gilgal Saul did not wait for Samuel but began the burnt offerings assuming the office of the priest. This was not only a transgression of the LORD's command but also usurpation of power since Saul was not a priest. He invaded the sacred sphere without permission. For this disobedience alone, the punishment was that Saul's dynasty would not endure. The LORD made it clear that no high position, not even the king's authority, could justify disobedience. He makes no distinction between men when His commandments are violated. This lesson was extraordinary in ancient times because kings and princes were above the law; they could act according to their own will and their gods were used to confirm their deeds. That the God of Israel is totally different is expressly stated in the story on Saul's disobedience. However, it was not the first time that the LORD punished a disobedient king. The Pharaoh's denial of God's command to let the people of Israel go and his repeated

---

1. Also, Moses had protested to become the agent of God when he was told to become the leader of the Israelites, up to the point that God became angry with Moses: Exodus 4:13.

insincere expressions of regret had brought great calamities on the house of the Pharaoh and his people (Reading 3 on Pharaoh's insincere repentance).

One day Samuel asked Saul to listen to the LORD's command and exact the penalty for what Amalek had done to Israel, for the assault Amalek had made upon the Israelites on the road, on their way up from Egypt. Saul was ordered to attack Amalek and proscribe all that belonged to him. The order was also given not to spare anyone, but to kill alike men and women, infants and sucklings, oxen and sheep, camels, and donkeys (1 Samuel 15:2-3). Hundred years before, the LORD had said that He wanted to destroy Amalek: 'Then the LORD said to Moses, "Inscribe this in a document as a reminder, and read it aloud to Joshua: I will utterly blot out the memory of Amalek from under heaven!" And Moses built an altar and named it Adonai-nissi. He said, "It means, 'Hand upon the throne of the LORD!' The LORD will be at war with Amalek throughout the ages." (Exodus 17:14-16).[2] The great sin of Amalek was that they had attacked the weakest parts of the Israelite people for reasons of random violence and greed. The Old Testament explains that time does not erase transgression before the LORD, only true regret and change can achieve this. Another point made here is the possible inter-generational character of transgression. The people of Amalek transgressed and neither they nor their descendants ever repented for it although they could have done so, even when they were never utterly defeated by the Israelites. It was the reason why God's judgment was passed over from generation to generation. According to the Old Testament, a society as such can be sinful and has the option to repent and be forgiven—as the Israelite people did on many occasions—or be judged by God, now or in the future. Societies and nations come and go into oblivion because of their own wicked deeds. For the first time, God's judgment against the entire humanity was revealed with the Great Flood, except for the righteous Noah and his family. The second time of God's war against a society was the destruction of the cities of Sodom and Gomorrah: '. . . the LORD completely destroyed those cities and the entire Plain, and all the inhabitants of the cities and the vegetation on the ground' (Genesis 19:25).

King Saul disobeyed again when he spared the life of the captured King Agag of Amalek notwithstanding the LORD's command to kill him and not to appropriate 'the choicest of the sheep and oxen.'[3] This time Samuel is

---

2. Deuteronomy 25:17-19 repeats God's judgment but with more detailed reasons. The great sin of Amalek was aggravated because it had attacked the weakest and the hungry among His people. As a matter of fact, Amalek would be destroyed and disappeared from history by the wars of Saul and David.

3. During the siege of Jericho, the LORD had proscribed to take away its treasures (Joshua 6:18 and 7:1)—see Reading 15.

even more explicit on Saul's destiny when he prophesizes 'The LORD has this day torn the kingship over Israel away from you and has given it to another who is worthier than you.' Samuel told Saul that his kingship was already lost, and a new king was already anointed. To underline the finality of this divine decision, Samuel went home and never saw Saul again to the day of his death. Saul must have felt a strong feeling of abandonment and despair. His spiritual estrangement from God, his benefactor, can also be read in Saul's plea. He does not say 'my God' but '. . . come back with me until I have bowed low to the LORD your God.' Saul speaks in terms of the God of Samuel, not his own God. Compare Saul's words and spiritual estrangement with the words of Moses who always walked in the awareness of his God's presence: 'The LORD is my strength and might; He is my Savior. This is my God and I will enshrine Him.' (Exodus 15:2). The tragedy of Saul teaches the importance of a daily awareness of God's presence and the personal relationship true believers maintain with God. Without it, a spiritual estrangement becomes inevitable and leads to sorrow, distress, and drama. Good intentions alone cannot replace the regular contact with 'my God'.

Reading 19   *Saul asks David for forgiveness.*

1 Samuel 24:17-23

17. When David had finished speaking, Saul said, "Is that your voice, my son David?" And Saul broke down and wept.

18. He said to David, "You are more righteous than I; for you have treated me kindly, but I have treated you badly.

19. Yes, you have just shown how generously you treated me, for the LORD delivered me into your hands and you did not kill me.

20. If a man meets his enemy, does he let him go unharmed? Surely, the LORD will reward you generously for what you have done for me this day.

21. I know now that you will become king, and that the kingship over Israel will be in your hands.

22. So swear to me by the LORD that you will not destroy my descendants or wipe out my name from my father's house."

23. David swore to Saul, and Saul went home, but David and his men went up to the strongholds.

THE RELATIONSHIP BETWEEN SAUL and David is one of the most complex relations between men recorded in the Old Testament. It even exceeds the personal bonds and involves two family members of Saul, namely Saul's son Jonathan and daughter Michal. It soon develops into antagonism, regret, conciliation and again antagonism. Although David is steadfastly loyal to his king, Saul loses his emotional stability and ability to maintain friendship and begins to persecute David. Saul's state of mind develops further into a mixture of depression, paranoia, and violent outbursts. Soon he became an ineffectual leader while David proved his valor in leading battles against the enemies of the Israelites. The passage of King Saul and David in the cave in the wilderness of En-gedi happened shortly before the death of Samuel while Saul pursued David with troops to kill him. Saul went into the cave to relieve himself, but he didn't know that David and his men were hiding in the back of the cave. Although this was an easy opportunity for David to kill Saul, David respected his anointed king, the first king of the Israelites, and instead stealthily cut off the corner of Saul's cloak. However, David immediately regretted this because Saul was the LORD's anointed, he rebuked his men and did not permit them to attack Saul. When Saul left the cave David also went out and called after Saul 'My lord king!' Saul looked around and David bowed low in homage, with his face to the ground. Then Saul realized that David had spared his life and had respected him as king. Saul experienced an emotional breakdown and wept while he confessed to David that he had transgressed by persecuting a most loyal citizen and servant.[1]

Notwithstanding his regret at that time, King Saul would later resume the persecution of David. The Old Testament gives the impression that Saul was aware of his unstable thoughts and emotions and feared that this would lead to his downfall and that of his relatives. He knew that he had become mentally unstable and thus unfit to lead the country. Therefore, he asked David to swear that he would not destroy his descendants after David would have become the new king. The killing of the descendants of the former king was the usual measure taken when a new king of a new dynastic family was crowned to save his throne from attempts of members of the old royal house to regain power. Such brutal practices were not uncommon in ancient and early medieval times, for example among relatives in the Merovingian dynasty and the succession tragedies of the Byzantine Empire. The harmful conduct of Saul was rooted in his persistent estrangement from God over many years. He sought no strength and help from God in the face of adversities but relied only on his royal power and pride. As a matter of fact, Saul had lost his faith. This caused all other problems such as uncertainty, false promises, deceit, lies and erratic behavior. Although Saul might have suffered from a mental illness, as many modern writers suggest, there is still a spiritual weakness by losing his faith.[2] A return to God was always

---

1. The same scene was later repeated in the wilderness of Ziph when David and his lieutenant Abishai were able to approach Saul while he was asleep in his camp, and they stole his spear and a jar but David did not kill Saul because no one can lay hands on the LORD's anointed with impunity. When Saul heard about this event, he answered David how foolish he had been. (1 Samuel 26:21).

2. Regarding the possible mental illness, see for example, George Stein, The Case of King Saul: Did He Have Recurrent Unipolar Depression or Bipolar Affective Disorder?, in: The British Journal of Psychiatry, March 2011, p. 212; Liubov Ben-Noun, What Was the Mental Disease That Afflicted King Saul?, in: Clinical Case Studies, 2003, pp. 270-282.

possible and in the many years of estrangement Saul had enough time to return to God but he didn't. God gives time and opportunities to return to Him but if we do not take a step towards Him, the end will be lonely, bitter, and disgraced. When the Philistines attacked Israel on Mount Gilboa, they pursued Saul and his three sons and struck down Jonathan, Abinadab and Malchi-shua, sons of Saul. The battle raged around Saul and some Philistine archers hit him. Severely wounded and isolated, Saul grasped his sword and fell upon it. When his arm-bearer saw that Saul was dead, he too fell on his sword and died with him.

The story about Saul underlines that a remorseless transgressor is doomed to repeat his mistakes. In contrast, the loyal David exercised faith and patience. Although he was already God's chosen new king, anointed by Samuel, he did not order to kill King Saul but left his fate in the hands of God and the events to come. David's mental strength was that he overcame evil by doing good instead of allowing to be dragged down in a cycle of evil. Yet there is another reason for David's compassionate attitude. David had a sharp mind and a feeling for diplomacy and timing. He understood that killing the king would discredit his own claim to the throne in the eyes of many Israelites who would consider it an act of high treason. He would be regarded as a rebel, an image which Saul had already used against him. Tragically, King David would suffer rebellion and treason by his son Absalom who lost his life because of it (Reading 40). David's character was able to exercise self-control which is understood as the ability to regulate one's emotions, thoughts and behavior when tested by temptations and impulses.

Reading 20   Abigail begs David for mercy for her foolish husband Nabal.

1 Samuel 25:23-35

23. When Abigail saw David, she quickly dismounted from the donkey and bowed low before David.

24. Laying before his feet, she pleaded, "Blame me, my lord, but let your handmaid speak to you; hear your maid's plea.

25. Please, my lord, pay no attention to that wicked and ill-tempered man Nabal. For he is just what is name says: His name means 'boor' and he is a boor.

...

32. David replied to Abigail, "Praised be the LORD, the God of Israel, who sent you to meet me this day!

33. And blessed be your common sense, and blessed be you yourself for restraining me from seeking vengeance in blood by my own hands.

34. For as sure as the LORD, the God of Israel, lives—who has kept me from harming you—had you not hurried to meet me, not a single male of Nabal's line would have been left tomorrow morning."

35. David then accepted from her gift, and he said to her, "Return to your home safely. See, I have heeded your plea and we will not kill your husband."

DAVID WAS ON THE run for Saul and camped in the wilderness with his followers, a band of destitute men and outlaws. In need of supplies, he sent ten men to seek provisions from Nabal, a wealthy man in Maon whose land was in Carmel in the north of Israel. David instructed his men to remind Nabal that his band had protected Nabal's shepherds in the wilderness.

Thus, David sought food and other supplies for his men in exchange for the protection they had provided. The Old Testament describes Nabal as 'a hard man and an evildoer'. Instead of giving David's men the supplies they needed, Nabal insulted David and denied any assistance. He implied that David was a rebel and compared him with a runaway slave: 'Who is David? Who is the son of Jesse? There are many slaves nowadays who run away from their masters.' David became angry and ordered his men to gird their swords, a clear indication that he was intent on attacking Nabal and his servants and to take revenge. When Abigail, wife of Nabal, was informed by her servants about her husband's rude words, she immediately realized the danger. Abigail is portrayed as a beautiful and intelligent woman with leadership qualities. In her encounter with David, she predicted that David would one day become king of the Israelites: 'And when the LORD has accomplished for my lord all the good He has promised you, and has appointed you ruler of Israel …' (1 Samuel 25:30). David was overwhelmed by the lucid and bold action of Abigail, accepted her gifts of food and wine and, more importantly, promised not to avenge himself. Abigail's claim for mercy for her foolish husband is not the same as 'teshuvah' which can only be done by the transgressor himself. Although David promised not to take revenge, Nabal himself remained unrepentant and beyond redemption.

Nabal was drunk when Abigail told him what she had done to spare his life, '. . . and his heart died within him, and he became like a stone.' It was just ten days later that the LORD inflicted a stroke on Nabal, and he died. For ten days the LORD waited for Nabal to repent. After hearing the news that Nabal had died, David said 'Blessed is the LORD Who has judged the cause of my reproach from the hand of Nabal, and restrained His bondsman from evil, and returned Nabal's evil upon his own head.' David's servants came to Abigail, to Carmel, and told her that David had sent them to take her to him for a wife. Abigail arose, prostrated herself on her face to the ground, and said 'Behold, your bondswoman is a slave to wash the feet of my lord's servants.' She hastened and mounted the donkey with her five maidens who went with her, and she went after David's messengers, and became his wife. Around the same time King Saul gave his daughter Michal, who was married to David, to Palti the son of Lashi from Gallim.

David's judgment regarding Nabal shows his steady self-examination and self-control while he was in power. He faced the question whether vengeance should be pursued like many tyrants of that time would have chosen. Yet, David grounded his judgment on God's attention for human actions and was convinced that Nabal would face judgment in one way or another. The incident with Nabal shows an important and enduring aspect of David's character during his entire life. He spared the life of King Saul while Saul was in search of him to kill him (see Reading 19) and later in life he begged his followers to pardon his rebellious son Absalom although his call was not heeded (see Reading 40). David's restrained attitude prevented him becoming a despot, set him apart from most leaders of his time. One may also view David as a precursor of humanitarian thinking according to which victory over an enemy is the justified purpose, not bloodshed or vengeance.

2 Samuel

Reading 21 *David transgresses, seeks God's forgiveness and is forgiven but there is divine justice.*

2 Samuel 12:1

1. But the LORD was displeased with what David had done, and the LORD sent Nathan to David.

...

2 Samuel 12:7-14

7. And Nathan said to David, "You are that man! Thus said the LORD, the God of Israel: "I anointed you king of Israel and it was I who saved you from the hand of Saul.

8. I gave you your master's house and his wives and the House of Israel and Judah; and if that were not enough, I would have given you much more.

9. Why then have you despised the command of the LORD and done what displeases Him? You have set up the murder of Uriah the Hittite; you took his wife and made her your wife and had him killed by the sword of the Ammonites.

10. Therefore the sword shall never depart from your House—because you despised Me by taking the wife of Uriah the Hittite."

11. Thus said the LORD: "I will make a calamity rise against you from within your own house; I will take your wives and give them to another man before your very eyes and he shall sleep with your wives in plain sight.

12. You acted in secret, but I will make this happen in the sight of all Israel and in broad daylight."

13. David confessed to Nathan: "I have sinned against the LORD!" And Nathan replied to David, "The LORD has forgiven your transgression; you shall not die.

14. However, since you have shown contempt to the LORD by your deed, your child about to be born shall die."

KING DAVID WAS THE powerful and uncontested leader of the Israelites when he transgressed by committing adultery with Bathsheba and then arranging for her husband soldier, Uriah, to be killed in battle so that David could take her as his wife.[1] Confronted with his felony by the prophet Nathan, David immediately repented instead of providing an excuse as Saul had done when he did wrong. God spared the life of David as an act of divine mercy. It was at this moment in life that David composed Psalm 51, the greatest penitentiary text ever written (Reading 43).

Throughout his long life, David cared for his personal relationship with God, regardless of his social position, and therefore remained a humble man. The bottom line is David's fundamental trust in God's mercy and loving kindness if there is sincere regret. David is composed, intensely self-examining and convinced that God would not let him down in his darkest moment, even if the whole world would condemn him for his crime. Although he has been told by the prophet Nathan, and he knows, that he will be punished for his crime—there will be a calamity in his family against David and his new-born child with Bathsheba will die—his ultimate intention is to be reconciled with God. For this reason alone, David deserved to be called a man after God's own heart (1 Samuel 13:14) and God said about David 'I will be a father to him, and he shall be a son to Me.' (2 Samuel 7:14). David regretted sincerely, confessed directly to God and God forgave him.

---

1. In a similar scenario, King Saul wanted David dead and threw his javelin at him twice but missed him. Then Saul hoped that David would be killed in battle and appointed him commander with the order to march at the head of the troops. But David survived it and won general approval with the troops—1 Samuel 18:13-16.

1 Kings

Reading 22 *Solomon, when he Dedicated the Temple, prayed for forgiveness for the mistakes of future generations.*

1 Kings 8:27-30

27. But will God really dwell on earth? Even the heavens to their greatest expanse cannot contain You, how much less this Temple that I have built!

28. Yet turn, O LORD my God, to the prayer and appeal of Your servant, and hear the cry and prayer which Your servant offers before You this day.

29. May Your eyes be upon this House day and night, toward the place of which You have said "My name shall always be there; may You always answer the prayers which Your servant will offer toward this place.

30. And when You hear the pleas which Your servant and Your people Israel offer toward this place, answer them favorably in Your heavenly abode—consider and forgive.

...

1 Kings 8:33-40

33. Should Your people Israel be defeated by an enemy because they have transgressed against You, and then turn back to You and acknowledge Your name, and they offer prayer and pleas to You in this Temple,

34. oh, hear in heaven and forgive the transgressions of Your people Israel and restore them to the land that You gave to their forefathers.

35. Should the heavens be shut up and there be no rain, because they have transgressed against You, and then pray toward this Temple and acknowledge Your name and turn from their sins, when You punished them,

36. oh, hear in heaven and forgive the transgressions of Your servants, Your people Israel, then teach them Your ways; and send down rain upon the land which You gave to Your people as their ancestral heritage.

37. So, too, if there is famine in the land, if there is plague, crop disease, mildew, locusts or caterpillars, or if an enemy oppresses them in any of the towns of the land.

"In any plague and in any disease,

38. in any prayer or plea offered by any person among Your people Israel— each with his own affliction—when he raises his hands towards this Temple,

39. oh, hear in Your heavenly abode, and forgive! Render to each man according to his righteous ways as You know his heart

40. so that they may glorify You all the days of their life on the land that You gave to our forefathers.

…

1 Kings 8:46-53

46. When they transgress against You—for there is no man without sin— and You are angry with them and deliver them in the hands of the enemy, and their captors carry them off to an enemy land, near or far;

47. and then they regret and return to You and make a plea to You in the land of their captors, saying "We have transgressed, we have acted perversely, we have acted wickedly",

48. and they turn back to You with all their heart and soul, in the land of the enemies who have carried them off, and they pray to You in the direction of their land which You gave to their forefathers, of the city which You have chosen, and of the Temple which I have built to Your name –

49. oh, hear their prayers and pleas in Your heavenly place, uphold their cause,

50. and forgive Your people who have transgressed against You for all the iniquities that they have committed against You. Make their captors merciful to them

51. for they are Your very own people that You liberated from Egypt, from the hot iron furnace of Egypt.

52. May Your eyes be open to the entreaties of Your servant and the entreaties of Your people Israel, and may You grant them wherever they call upon You.

53. For You, O Lord GOD, have set them apart for Yourself from all the peoples of the earth as Your very own, as You promised through Moses Your servant when You freed our forefathers from Egypt.

THIS SOLEMN AND PROFOUND text is known as Solomon's speech at the dedication of the Temple around 960 BC. Shortly before his death David had appointed Solomon, son with Bathsheba, as his successor. The ritual confirmation of his enthronement was Solomon's anointment in Gihon by the priest Zadok and the prophet Nathan. The new king became famous because of his wisdom and several psalms and proverbs as well of the Book of Kohelet attributed to him. Although David wanted to build a Temple for the LORD and made plans for its construction, God ordered that his son build the Temple by letting it know 'Your son, whom I will set on your throne in your place, shall build the house for My name.' (1 Kings 5:19) King Hiram of Tyre, who had always been a friend of David, provided the cedars and sent several masons. 1 Kings 6 and 7 mention the exact measurements of the Temple, its layout, and furnishings. It took Solomon seven years to build the Temple, a work that became the most important architectural achievement of Solomon's reign. Shortly before Solomon delivered his speech at the dedication of the Temple, the Ark of the Covenant was brought to the Temple. When all the elders of Israel had come, the priests lifted the Ark and carried it to the Tent of Meeting along with all the holy vessels.

Meanwhile King Solomon, and the whole community of Israel, who were assembled with him before the Ark, were sacrificing sheep and oxen. The priests brought the Ark of the LORD's Covenant to its place underneath the wings of the cherubim, in the Shrine of the House, in the Holy of Holies where the tablets were safeguarded. The cherubim had their wings spread over the place of the Ark for its protection. Inside the Ark were placed the two tablets of stone which Moses had put there at Horeb, when the LORD made a covenant with the Israelites after their departure from the land of Egypt. It suggests that King Solomon, while building the Temple, was aware that it would ultimately be destroyed.[1] For this reason, he constructed a chamber in which the Ark could be entombed below the Temple building in deep, maze-like vaults. The later King Josiah, one of the kings of Judah

---

1. The Babylonian King Nebuchadnezzar II destroyed the First Temple after the siege of Jerusalem of 587 BC.

(641-609 BC), commanded that the Ark be entombed in the chamber built by King Solomon.

Solomon delivered his speech standing before the altar LORD of the LORD in the presence of the whole community of Israel with the palms of his hands spread toward heaven. His speech is not only a dedication prayer but also a prayer of repentance. At this most joyful and historic moment of the Temple's dedication, the words of regret and spiritual change on behalf of the Israelites are remarkable. How are they connected to the House of the LORD, also called the Beit YHWH, the Beit Ha-Elohim, or the Beit HaMikdash? King Solomon knew the history of his people and was aware of the close connection between the House of the LORD, transgression and 'teshuvah'. In the Book of Exodus Moses came down from Mount Sinai with the incised tablets and with the order of God to keep them in a temporary dwelling place, the Ark of the Covenant. The first scene Moses saw was the people worshipping a golden calf. He became so enraged that he hurled the tablets from his hands and shattered them at the foot of the mountain. He then took the golden calf and burned it. When Moses asked his brother Aaron why the people did this, Aaron answered 'You know that this people is inclined to evil.' (Exodus 32:22). King Solomon, in his wisdom, knew that human nature would always be prone to corruption, even close to the place of God's permanent House. In his speech, Solomon acknowledged that transgressive and criminal things were likely to happen due to man's evil inclination, notwithstanding the joyful dedication of the Temple. Anticipating it, he begged for pardon and confessed '. . . for there is no man without sin'. After acknowledging man's failures Solomon expressed the only possible remedy in the name of all: 'We have transgressed, we have acted perversely, we have acted wickedly' and we want to turn back to You with all our heart and soul. This longing for a return to God is always in the mind of the believer who is pleading for mercy and forgiveness. Transgressive conduct happens because man forgets God, his Creator, and strays. Therefore, it is said that 'teshuvah' is the deliberate process of returning to God with heart and soul. The Temple service can never replace this inner process which transpires deep in the heart and mind. In this sense, the true Temple is within our heart and soul.

A test of the people's sincere change is spoken by King Solomon in 1 Kings 8:33-34: 'Should Your people Israel be defeated by an enemy because they have sinned against You, and then turn back to You and acknowledge Your name, and they offer prayer and supplication to You in this Temple, oh, hear in heaven and forgive the sin of Your people Israel and restore them to the land that You gave to their fathers'. Rashi refers to the Sages who said that a person is obliged to bless God for the bad as well as the good. King

Solomon prayed already for future transgressions and asked for forgiveness if the people are regretful. He had the wisdom to foresee future transgressions because of man's evil inclination, and he sought God's reassurance of forgiveness. King Solomon's prayer for forgiveness for future transgressions refers to God's saying in Genesis 8:21, namely that God would never again doom the earth because of man, since the devisings of man's mind are evil from his youth. (Reading 1).

Reading 23 *After being rebuked by Elijah, king Ahab rends his clothes and puts sackcloth on his body.*

1 Kings 21:17-29

17. Then the LORD said to Elijah the Tishbite:

18. "Go down and confront King Ahab of Israel who rules in Samaria. He is now in Naboth's vineyard; he has gone down there to confiscate it.

19. Say this to him, "Thus said the LORD: Was the murder of Naboth not enough? Will you also take possession of his vineyard? Thus said the LORD: In the very place where the dogs licked Naboth's blood, the dogs will lick your blood too."

20. Ahab sneered to Elijah, "So you have found me, my enemy?" "Yes, I have found you" he replied. "Because you have done what is evil in the sight of the LORD,

21. I will bring disaster upon you. I will make a clean sweep of you, I will cut off from Israel every male belonging to Ahab, slave and free alike. And I will make your family like the family of Jeroboam son of Nebat and like the family of Baasha son of Ahijah, because of the stirring you have caused by leading Israel to transgress.

23. And concerning Jezebel the LORD has said: "The dogs shall devour Jezebel in the field of Jezreel.

24. All of Ahab's line who die in the town shall be devoured by the vultures."

25. Indeed, there never was anyone like Ahab, who committed himself to doing what was displeasing to the LORD, under the influence of his wife Jezebel.

26. He acted most despicably, straying after the fetishes just like the Amorites, whom the LORD had driven out the land before the Israelites.

27. When Ahab heard these words, he rent his clothes and put sackcloth on his body. He fasted and lay in sackcloth and walked about in mourning.

28. Then the LORD spoke to Elijah the Tishbite:

29. "Have you seen how Ahab has humbled himself before Me? Because he has humbled himself before Me, I will not bring the disaster in his lifetime; I will bring the disaster upon his family in his son's time."

ISRAEL AND JUDAH WERE already separate political entities in the Iron Age of ancient Canaan, a region comprising present-day Lebanon, Syria, Jordan, and Israel. Sometimes the name Phoenicia was used instead of Canaan, a fertile region at the crossroads of important trade routes. Over time the trade routes became an important military road for neighboring empires such as ancient Egypt, the Hittite empire, Babylon, and Assyria. The indigenous peoples of Canaan worshipped many gods, but the goddess Astarte and her consort Baal were the major gods symbolizing fertility. Moses had led the Jewish people out of Egypt toward the promised land of Canaan, a land 'flowing with milk and honey' (Exodus 3:8). When Saul was anointed king by Samuel, the tribes of Israel and Judah united into one kingdom that lasted until the death of King Solomon. Soon after Solomon's death the ten northern Israelite tribes revolted against Rehoboam, a son of Solomon, which put an end to the united kingdom. It fell again apart into two separate kingdoms, the Northern Kingdom of Israel, and the Southern Kingdom of Judah. Rehoboam became the first king of the Kingdom of Judah while Jeroboam I became the first king of the Kingdom of Israel.[1] Ahab became the seventh king of the Kingdom of Israel in the period around 870 BC and was married to Jezebel of Sidon, the daughter of Ethbaal, King of Tyre. According to the above-mentioned excerpt, '. . . there never was anyone like Ahab, who committed himself to doing what was displeasing to the LORD, at the instigation of his wife Jezebel. He acted most abominably, straying after the fetishes just like the Amorites.' The Book of 1 Kings tells the story

---

1. The Israelite Kingdom of Israel comprised the ten northern tribes and was ruled by 19 successive kings: Jeroboam I, Nadab, Baasha, Elah, Zimri, Omri, Ahab, Ahaziah, Joram, Jehu, Jehoahaz, Jehoash, Jeroboam II, Zechariah, Shallum, Menahem, Pekahiah, Pekah, and Hoshea. In 722 BC Israel fell to Assyria. The Assyrian king Sargon II deported the citizens of Israel beyond the river Euphrates. The Kingdom of Judah had more than 20 successive kings until the destruction of Jerusalem by the Babylonians in 588 BC which led to the Babylonian captivity by order of the Babylonian King Nebuchadnezzar.

of an ever-worsening idolatry in the northern kingdom since the first king Jeroboam I, who installed two golden calves at Bethel and Dan, made cult places and appointed priests from the ranks of the people who were not of Levite descent (1 Kings 13:28-31). Under the reign of Ahab, and influenced by his Phoenician wife Jezebel, idolatry reached another dimension with the worship of Baal.

The prophet Elijah, defender of God and Ahab's major antagonist, performed several miracles to proof that God, Yahweh, is the LORD. In a first encounter Ahab called Elijah 'the troubler of Israel' (1 Kings 18:17). In a second encounter Elijah confronted Ahab over his execution of Naboth so that Ahab could usurp Naboth's ancestral vineyard.[2] Murder and greed were the grave transgressions of Ahab, charges brought against him by Elijah. When Elijah rebuked Ahab he was greeted by Ahab with the words 'my enemy'. But after Elijah had revealed the LORD's punishment for Ahab, his wife Jezebel and their offspring, Ahab repented publicly. He knew that Elijah was a man of great integrity and always loyal to God, even when his life was threatened. Ahab had threatened Elijah in a first encounter when Elijah had predicted that, because of the sins of Ahab, there would be no dew or rain except at his bidding. The LORD then warned Elijah to go into hiding by the Wadi Cherith which is east of the river Jordan (1 Kings 17:2). Later, after Elijah had killed the prophets of Baal at the Wadi Kishon, Jezebel sent a messenger to Elijah with the words that his fate would be the same as that of the prophets of Baal. Frightened, Elijah fled at once for his life and came to Beer-sheba, into the wilderness. Sitting there under a broom bush he prayed that he might die. 'Enough!, he cried. Now, O LORD, take my life, for I am no better than my fathers.' (1 Kings 19:4).

The prophet Elijah always acted when he was called upon by God, despite his mortal fears and Ahab knew that Elijah had the quality of integrity because of his honesty. Another great quality of Elijah was his spirituality. What was important to the LORD was important to Elijah, he never doubted the words from God and acted accordingly. Ahab knew this and realized that Elijah's words came from God. Over many years, Elijah had distinguished himself as a true prophet in a time of many false prophets. God asked Elijah if he saw that Ahab repented. Perhaps Elijah did not notice it or he noticed it but was convinced that a most wicked man could never be regarded as a true repentant. However, God's question confirms that even the most wicked man can become a true repentant. Further evidence comes from God's change of the punishment. God would not bring disaster

---

2. According to 2 Kings 9:26 Naboth and his sons were probably killed to prevent that their sons would claim the vineyard as their inheritance.

in Ahab's lifetime, but upon his house in his son's time.³ God's question to Elijah is also an encouragement for the prophet who could witness that his actions had led to Ahab's return to God.

As the story continues, Ahab is put again in a bad light. Three years later Ahab and the king of Judah, Jehoshaphat, considered war against Aram for the reconquest of Ramoth-gilead, a Hebrew city east of the river Jordan and in the territory of the tribe of Gad. On advice of Jehoshaphat, Ahab gathered around 400 prophets to question whether to go in battle for the conquest of Ramoth-gilead. After the 400 prophets unanimously predicted a victory for Israel and Judah, King Jehoshaphat asked if there was another prophet of the LORD through whom the kings could inquire. Ahab answered Jehoshaphat 'There is one more man through whom we can inquire the LORD; but I hate him, because he never prophesies anything good for me, but only misfortune—Micaiah son of Imlah.' (1 Kings 22:8). When the prophet Micaiah was led before the two kings, he prophesied that Israel and Judah would be victorious although Ahab would die on the battlefield. Then Ahab ordered Micaiah to be put in prison with scant bread and scant water until Ahab would come home safely. The two kings went into battle and Ahab disguised himself as a common soldier riding in a chariot. A man of the army of the king of Aram drew his bow at random and hit Ahab between the plates of armor. Wounded, Ahab remained propped up in the chariot and the blood of the wound ran down into the hollow of the chariot until he died at dusk.⁴ His body was brought to Samaria where he was buried. 'The soldiers flushed out his chariot at the pool of Samaria, the dogs licked his blood and the whores bathed in it, in accordance with the word that the LORD had spoken' (1 Kings 22:38). The story about the battle of Ramoth-gilead suggests that Ahab had relapsed into wickedness, seeking advice from false prophets who were always willing to tell the king whatever he wanted to hear. In the end, God decreed disaster upon Ahab.

According to this story, the most wicked persons can become true repentants although it is much harder for them to continue following the

---

3. In a similar decision of God, King Solomon was punished for turning away from God although, for the sake of his father King David and for the sake of Jerusalem, the punishment was not carried out during Solomon's lifetime but postponed to the reign of his son—see 1 Kings 9-13. And King Josiah was told by the prophetess Hulda that the destruction of the Temple of Jerusalem and the Babylonian captivity would not happen during Josiah's lifetime because he had been repentful—see Reading 24.

4. Rashi comment on 1 Kings 22:35 regarding the expression that Ahab was propped up in his chariot during the rest of the battle: 'He exerted himself to remain standing so that the Israelites would not become aware of his wound and flee, for flight is the beginning of defeat.'

right path for the rest of their lives. However, 'more hard' does not mean impossible.

2 Kings

Reading 24 *Josiah rends his clothes when he hears that the scroll of the teaching has been discovered in the Temple by the high priest Hilkiah.*

2 Kings 22:11-20

11. When the king heard the words of the scroll of the Teaching, he rent his clothes.

12. And the king ordered the priest Hilkiah, and to Ahikam son of Shaphan, Achbor son of Michaiah, the scribe Shaphan, and Asaiah the king's servant:

13. "Go, inquire of the LORD on my behalf, and on behalf of the people, and on behalf of Judah, concerning the words of this scroll that has been found. For great indeed must be the anger of the LORD that has been kindled against us, because your fathers did not obey the words of this scroll to do all that has been laid down for us."

14. So the priest Hilkiah, and Ahikam, Achbor, Shaphan, and Asaiah went to the prophetess Huldah—the wife of Shallum son of Tikvah son of Harhas, the keeper of the wardrobe—who was living in Jerusalem in the Mishneh, and they spoke to her.

15. She said to them: "The LORD, the God of Israel has spoken. Return and say to the man who sent you:

16. This said the LORD: I am going to bring a catastrophe on this place and its inhabitants. All the words of the scroll which the king of Judah has heard will become true.

17. Because they have abandoned Me and have made offerings to other gods and angered Me with all their deeds, My anger is kindled against this place and it shall not be quenched.

18. But say this to the king, who sent you to inquire of the LORD: Thus said the LORD, the God of Israel: As for the words which you have heard –

19. because your heart was softened and you humbled yourself before the LORD when you heard what I decreed against this place and its inhabitants—that it will become desolate and cursed—and because you rent your clothes and wept before Me in regret, I for My part have listened—declares the LORD.

20. Assuredly, I will gather you to your fathers and you will be laid in your tomb in peace. Your eyes shall not see the disaster which I will bring upon this place." So they brought back the reply to the king.

JOSIAH BECAME KING OF Judah after his father Amon, described as a bad king displeasing the LORD, had been murdered by his courtiers. The citizens of Jerusalem and Judah slew the murderers and made Josiah king at the age of eight years. He would reign for 31 years from 639 to 608 BC when he died at the Battle of Meggido against Pharaoh Necho II. In the early years of Josiah's reign, the prophet Jeremiah started his preachings and prophecies which gave the impetus to religious reform. An important element of the religious revival was the reparation of the Temple, a work that was supervised by the high priest Hilkiah. This undertaking required the silver, that was deposited in the Temple, to be melted and used for paying the workmen and the purchase of wood and quarried stones. One day the high priest discovered a scroll of the Teaching in the Temple that was hidden under a layer of stones where the priests had concealed it when Ahaz burned the Torah—Rashi comment on 2 Kings 22:8 According to rabbinical tradition, when the scroll was found it fell open at the verses 'The LORD will drive you, and the king you have set over you, to a nation unknown to you or your fathers, where you shall serve other gods, of wood and stone. You shall be a consternation, a proverb, and a byword among all the peoples to which the LORD will drive you.' (Deuteronomy 28:36-37).

When King Josiah heard of it, he rent his clothes because he knew that his forefathers and the people had not followed the commands of the LORD. The king sent messengers to inquire the prophetess Huldah what this meant. She prophesied the destruction of the Temple of Jerusalem and the Babylonian captivity because of the idolatry in the country. However, since King Josiah was repentant, she also prophesied that this disaster would not happen during his life. Because the whole people were sinful by abandoning God, the whole people would be punished. The subsequent Babylonian exile is sometimes explained as a necessary condition for self-examination by the people because exile creates the conditions to gain a contrite mind and do self-examination. Maimonides wrote on exile as a way of self-examination with the following words: 'Among the paths of repentance is for the penitent to travel in exile from his home. Exile atones for sin because it causes a person to be submissive, humble, and meek of spirit.'[1]

The fall of Jerusalem was in the short reign of King Jehoiachin who died at the end of the siege in 598 BC. The citizens of Jerusalem were exiled to Babylonia; only the poorest people in the land were left (2 Kings 24:14). The Babylonian King Nebuchadnezzar II appointed Zedekiah as the new king of Judah. However, the newly appointed king rebelled against the Babylonians who sent again an army to Jerusalem. This time the Temple, once built by King Solomon, was destroyed and a second deportation followed in 586 BC. King Zedekiah stood trial. His sons were slaughtered before his eyes and his eyes were put out. He was then chained in bronze fetters and brought to Babylon (2 Kings 25:7). The Northern Kingdom of Israel had already undergone a similar fate. The Assyrians had conquered the country and deported its citizens to the Assyrian places of Halah, at the river Habor, at the river Gozan, and in the towns of Media (2 Kings 17:6). The Bible explains that the deportations of the citizens of both the northern kingdom and the southern kingdom were a clear signal that God had cast them out of His presence.[2] However, the estrangement from God is not absolute because 'Wherever they were exiled, the Shekinah went with them' (Talmud, Megillah 29a). God's spirit would be among the exiled people if they returned to the LORD with heart and soul.

2 Kings 22 signifies that contrition or remorse is a necessary condition to seek pardon for transgression. It is based on an awareness that transgression is not without consequences and should be corrected to restore personal integrity and a good relationship with God. Sometimes transgression or widespread transgression in a people can result in great drama such as exile. An exiled flees his homeland to live in a foreign place by necessity. The shock it creates may trigger self-examination and the hope for a better future if the heart and mind are opened and pave the way for a change. One

---

1. Moshe Maimonides, Mishneh Torah, Sefer Madda, Hilchot Teshuva, Chapter Two, Halacha 4.

2. Regarding the Northern Kingdom, 2 Kings 17:23 mentions that in the end, the LORD removed Israel from His presence. The Israelites were deported from their land to Assyria. And after the deportation of Judah, 2 Kings 24:20 states 'Indeed, Jerusalem and Judah were a cause of anger for the LORD, so that He cast them out of His presence.'

may also regard a prison sentence as an exile from society and a place for self-examination. In short, self-examination and a humble heart—a symbolic retreat in exile—create a place to come to peace with yourself in your unique circumstances, and to restore good standing with God.

Isaiah

Reading 25 *Angels prepare Isaiah for his prophetic mission and the Lord promises forgiveness.*

Isaiah 6:1-13

1. In the year that King Uzziah died, I beheld my LORD seated on a high and lofty throne; and the skirts of His robe filled the Temple.

2. Seraphim stood in attendance around Him. Each of them had six wings: with two he covered his face, with two he covered his legs, and with two he would fly.

> 3. And one would call to the other,
> "Holy, holy, holy!
> The LORD of Hosts!
> His presence fills all the earth!"

4. The foundations would shake at the sound of the one who called, and the House kept filling with smoke. 5. I cried,

> "Woe is me! I am doomed!
> for I am a man of unclean lips
> and I live among a people
> of unclean lips;
> yet my own eyes have beheld
> The King LORD of Hosts."

6. Then one of the seraphim flew over me with a red-glowing coal, which he had taken from the altar with a pair of tongs.

7. He touched it to my lips and declared,

> "Now that this has touched your lips,

> your guilt is over
and your sin be cleansed away."

8. Then I heard the voice of my LORD asking, "Whom shall I send? Who will go for us as messenger?" And I said, "Here am I, send me."

9. And He said, "Go, say to that people:

> "Hear, indeed, but do not understand;
> see, indeed, but do not grasp.'
> 10. Harden that people's mind,
> plug its ears,
> and shut its eyes –
> Lest, seeing with its eyes
> and hearing with its ears,
> it also grasps with its mind,
> and repent and ask Me to save it."

11. I asked, "How long, my LORD?" And He replied:

> "Till towns lie waste without inhabitants
> and houses without people,
> and the countryside lies waste and desolate –
> 12. For the LORD will banish the population –
> and the land has become a wasteland.

13. Even if a tenth part yet remains in it and repents, it shall be ravaged like the terebinth and the oak, of which the stumps are left even when they are felled: its stump shall be a holy seed.

ISAIAH WAS STILL A young man of the well-educated elite in Jerusalem when King Uzziah of Judah died around 740 BC. The death of the king was the key event that started Isaiah's prophetic mission with a heavenly vision. Isaiah was in ecstasy and saw God as the Heavenly King on His throne, surrounded by seraphim or angels. Isaiah frequently called God the 'LORD of Hosts' to underline that He is the all-powerful God on earth and in the universe. He felt himself unworthy and imperfect in the view of God's holiness and omnipotence. The angels acted like a chorus—not unlike the chorus in ancient Greek tragedies—to encourage Isaiah and prepare him for his mission. Isaiah immediately admitted his transgressions by saying that he had unclean lips. After admission of guilt, he said that the people had unclean lips too. Thus Isaiah, by spontaneously confessing his own transgressions before mentioning those of others, gave the example of a humble heart. He had the strong feeling of being lost because of his transgressions. An angel flied over Isaiah with a red-glowing coal which he had taken from the altar with a pair of tongs and so hot that even an angel could not touch it. The angel took Isaiah's feelings of unworthiness away by touching his lips with the glowing coal, the symbol of purification and forgiveness.

The expression 'unclean lips' has a double meaning in the vision. First, lips are like swords, ready to hurt somebody, or they are used to flatter or speak with deceit. Hurtful speech is the most common transgression in daily life, often not sanctioned by other men or authorities. Today one is saddened to read daily newspapers, media and social media publishing slander and false accusations to gain attention by a gleeful public. Unopposed, malicious, and harmful speech often becomes addictive. During the Yom Kippur services two of the confessed sins (the Text of Al Chet) are 'the sin which we have committed before You with an utterance of the lips' and 'the sin which we have committed before You through speech'.

The Old Testament repeatedly warns against slander, deceitful or hateful speech.

> 'Your lips speak lies, your tongue utters treachery.' (Isaiah 59:3)
>
> 'May the LORD cut off all flattering lips, the tongue that speaks arrogance.' (Psalm 12:4)
>
> 'Let lying lips become mute, those that speak against a righteous man falsely, with pride and contempt.' (Psalm 31:19)
>
> 'Keep your tongue from evil and your lips from speaking with deceit.' (Psalm 34:14)
>
> 'They rant with their mouths, sharp words are on their lips.' (Psalm 59:8)
>
> 'O LORD, deliver me from treacherous lips, from a deceitful tongue!' (Psalm 120:2)
>
> 'They sharpen their tongues like a serpent; spiders' poison is under their lips.' (Psalm 140:4)
>
> 'O LORD, set a guard over my mouth, a watch at the door of my lips;' (Psalm 141:3)

'Keep crooked speech away from you; keep perverse talk far from you.' (Proverbs 4:24)

'A scoundrel, an evil man lives by crooked speech' (Proverbs 6:12)

'He who conceals hatred has lying lips' (Proverbs 10:18)

'The lips of the righteous know what is acceptable; the mouth of the wicked knows duplicity.' (Proverbs 10:32)

'Sinful speech is a trap for the evil man, but the righteous escapes from trouble.' (Proverbs 12:13)

'Lying speech is an abomination to the LORD, but those who act faithfully are His delight.' (Proverbs 12:22)

'The words of a fool lead to strife; his speech invites fights.' (Proverbs 18:6)

'A wise man's talking brings him favor, but a fool's lips are his undoing.' (Ecclesiastes 10:12)

In a second meaning purification of the lips is the precondition for becoming a prophet who conveys God's message. The Hebrew word for prophet is 'navi' and derived from the term 'niv sefatayim' or 'fruit of the lips' meaning a prophet's speech is blameless and pure. Although other great leaders of the Israelites had humbled themselves before God when they first encountered the LORD, Isaiah was the first to seek cleansing of his mistakes before anything else ('Ai me!'). The process of sincere regret and receiving God's forgiveness is the central theme of Isaiah's mission.

Isaiah is a prophet of consolation and hope, even in the darkest of times. The name Isaiah means 'the LORD is salvation', a proper name for his prophetic mission. As a boy, he had witnessed the destruction of the Northern Kingdom of Israel and the exile of its people in Assyria. In the first part of his life the prophet Isaiah conveyed a message of judgment against the Southern Kingdom of Judah and made a call to repentance and purification although the people and the king of Judah ignored his warnings. Finally, Isaiah prophesized the destruction of Judah and the Temple of Jerusalem as well as the exile of its people in Babylonia. In the Book of Isaiah, we read that Assyria and Babylon will be used by God as His instruments to punish an ungodly people who had abandoned Him. 'Ha! Assyria, rod of My anger, in whose hand, as a staff, is My fury!' (Isaiah 10:5). But amidst the many future afflictions brought on the Israelites, Isaiah brings a message of hope and consolation by prophesizing that a purified remnant of the people will be saved. In the quotation above the remorseful remnant is compared to a ravaged terebinth and oak, the two mightiest trees in the Middle East.[1] They are felled but out of their stumps grows a holy seed. The terebinth and the oak represent the Kingdom of Israel and the kingdom of Judah. Only a remnant shall return from exile in Assyria and Babylonia.

Ultimately, the country shall be saved because of her repentant ones: 'Zion shall be saved in the judgment; her repentant ones, in the retribution.' (Isaiah 1:27). Isaiah's consolation is read out in the synagogues during the seven consecutive sabbaths leading up to Rosh Hashanah which is also a period of repentance or 'teshuvah' in the Jewish calendar (Reading 4). The consolation offered by Isaiah is a promised recovery from mistakes and tragedies, either communal or personal, and the empowerment to persevere and to live with a renewed spirit. Like David, Isaiah is one of the great personalities of the Old Testament. He held no official position, and his calls were not always welcome because they criticized the policies of Judah. Yet, his words were not forgotten because they had revealed the truth. The Fathers of the Church confirmed that Isaiah was the greatest of the literary prophets. His powerful words, his poetic talent and industrious character became a great inspiration for later literary works and Gregorian chant. Isaiah's prophecies are read in the liturgies of all Christian churches. According to Christian theology, Isaiah 7:14 is a key verse because it is understood as a prediction of the coming of Jesus Christ, the Son of God, "Therefore the LORD Himself will give you a sign: behold, a virgin will be with child and bear a son, and she will call His name Immanuel." It is quoted in Matthew 1:23. Because of his prediction of the coming of the Savior, Isaiah is read on the first Sunday of the Advent in the catholic church and at Christmas time in the orthodox church. Moreover, Luke 4:16-19 reports that Jesus started his public ministry by going to the synagogue. He stood up to read, and the scroll of the prophet Isaiah was handed to him. Unrolling it, he found the place where it is written:

> "The Spirit of the LORD is on me,
> because he has anointed me

---

1. The terebinth tree or 'genus Pistacia' is mentioned in sixteen instances in the Old Testament and serves well to symbolize the tenacity and survival of the Israelite people, even in the hardest circumstances. The terebinth can live up to a thousand years and is solitary, rooted deeply on mountainous slopes. Because of its deep roots it can produce green leaves even in times of drought and heatwaves. Moreover, the terebinth is special in that it can regenerate when fell, a result of its ever-living nature.

to proclaim good news to the poor.
He has sent me to proclaim freedom for the prisoners
and recovery of sight for the blind,
to set the oppressed free,
to proclaim the year of the LORD's favor."

Jeremiah

Reading 26 *God does not look in anger for He is compassionate.*

Jeremiah 3:11-15

11. And the LORD said to me: Faithless Israel has shown herself more in the right than Treacherous Judah.

12. Go, make bring this message to the north, and say: Turn back, O Faithless Israel—declares the LORD. I will not look on you in anger forever, for I am compassionate—declares the LORD; I do not bear a grudge for all time.

13. Only accept responsibility for your misdeeds; for you have transgressed against the LORD, and squandered your favors among strangers under every green tree, and you have not listened to Me—declares the LORD.

14. Turn back, rebellious children—declares the LORD. Though I have rejected you, I will take you back, one from a town and two from a family, and bring you to Zion.

15. And I will give you shepherds after My own heart, who will pasture you with knowledge and understanding.

...

Jeremiah 33:7-9

7. And I will restore the good fortunes of Judah and Israel, and I will rebuild them as of old.

8. And I will cleanse them of all their transgressions which they committed against Me, and I will forgive all the transgressions which they committed against Me, by which they rebelled against Me.

9. And this city shall gain through Me renown, joy, fame, and glory above all the nations on earth, when they hear of all the good fortune I grant them.

They will fear and tremble because of all the good fortune and all the prosperity that I grant her.

A PROPHET DOES NOT choose to become a prophet but is chosen by God, and often it is against his own will. Jeremiah is an example of a man reluctant to answer the burdensome call of God. When the LORD told he was appointed as a prophet concerning the nations, he replied 'Ah, LORD GOD! I don't know how to speak, for I am still a boy'. But the LORD assured him 'Have no fear of them, for I am with you to deliver you.' (Jeremiah 1:6-8). And again, God promised Jeremiah that, despite the many personal attacks because of his prophecies, he would be protected: 'Attack you they will, overcome you they can't.' (Jeremiah 1:19). He was born into a priestly family in the small village of Anathoth, approximately six miles northeast of Jerusalem, and started his prophetic ministry around 626 BC with the firm conviction that his fellow Jewish citizens were under God's punishing judgment. It was a time of great dangers and hostility against the Jewish people that greatly impacted the religious beliefs in Judah, especially the preaching prophets. The northern Israelite Kingdom had already been destroyed, many of its people sent into exile in Assyria, and Judah was on the target list of Assyria and later also Babylon.

In his early years, he had warned for the 'Foe from the North'—'For I bring evil from the north, and great disaster.' (Jeremiah 4:6). After the battle of Carchemish in 605 BC in which the allied forces of Egypt and Assyria were destroyed by the Babylonians, Jeremiah realized that the 'Foe from the North' was Babylon. The Babylonian victory at Carchemish came seven years after they had captured and destroyed the Assyrian capital Nineveh (Reading 32). Jeremiah was above all concerned about the moral and spiritual degradation of his fellow citizens. He preached against the idolatrous practices in the country even after the religious reform of King Josiah, the last pious king (2 Kings 23). He accused the people of being dishonest, selfish and immoral: 'Run up and down the streets of Jerusalem, search its squares, look about and take note: you will not find a man, there is none who is just and honest.' (Jeremiah 5:1). Throughout his life, Jeremiah's words were never accepted by the people and the king of Judah. They resented his lamentations and his perceived offensive language, rejecting him because he was a detestable man in their eyes.[1] While the Babylonian army was approaching, Jeremiah advised King Zedekiah to surrender to the king of Babylon so that his life would be spared, and the city of Jerusalem not destroyed.

---

1. Jeremiah was not the only prophet who was rejected. The prophet Micaiah was hated by King Ahab—see Reading 23.

After hearing this advice King Zedekiah put Jeremiah in prison where he remained until the day Jerusalem was captured by the Babylonians. The victorious Babylonian King Nebuchadnezzar put King Zedekiah on trial while his children and the nobles of Judah were slaughtered at Riblah before his eyes. Then the eyes of Zedekiah were put out and he was chained in bronze fetters and brought to Babylon (Jeremiah 39:5-7) where he died.

Jeremiah found favor with King Nebuchadnezzar because of Jeremiah's open call to surrender the city to him and ordered his immediate release. Jeremiah went to Gedaliah at Mizpah, who had been appointed governor of Judah, and stayed with him among the Jewish remnant in the land. Shortly after Gedaliah was murdered by Ishmael, a Judean nationalist, he was succeeded by Johanan. When asked by the people whether to stay in Judah or to flee to Egypt, Jeremiah gave his last prophecy to stay in Judah or perish in Egypt. For the last time, the people and their leader rejected his prophecy and departed to Egypt, forcibly taking Jeremiah with them. The LORD said 'Of the remnant of Judah who came to sojourn here in the land of Egypt, no survivor or fugitive shall be left to return to the land of Judah. Though they all long to return and dwell there, none shall return except a few survivors.' (Jeremiah 44:14). According to legend, Jeremiah and the scribe Baruch were among the few survivors who returned to Judah.

Jeremiah's never-ending call to return to God, to trust in Him instead of one's own talents, good fortunes or capabilities is strongly expressed by these verses.

> 22. This said the LORD:
> let not the wise man glory in his wisdom;
> let not the strong man glory in his strength;
> let not the rich man glory in his riches.
> 23. But only in this should one glory:
> in his love to Me.
> For I the LORD act with kindness,
> justice, and equity in the world.
> For in these I delight.
> Declares the LORD

Jeremiah 9:22-23

Jeremiah's message to trust always in the LORD is a beacon for all times.

> 5. This said the LORD:
> cursed is he who put his trust in man,
> who relies on human strength,

and turns his thoughts from the LORD.
6. He shall be like a bush in the desert,
he does not sense the coming of good.
He will live in the scorched places of the wilderness,
in a desolate land without inhabitants.
7. Blessed is he who trusts in the LORD,
whose trust is the LORD alone.

Jeremiah 17:5-7

Notwithstanding the clear warning by the loss of the northern kingdom and the many calls of Jeremiah and other prophets, the unashamed people of the southern kingdom continued their corruption and denial of God's presence in their midst. Their spiritual poverty and final downfall were caused by a rejection of the LORD as the ultimate source of kindness, justice, and equity. Instead, they relied only on political leaders, their city walls, and their ever-shifting alliances with other powers, such as Egypt. The hardheaded people rationalized and justified their feckless mind by branding Jeremiah as a traitor who would surrender to Babylon, another illustration that they trusted only political calculations and second-guessing. Although the priests and prophets and all the people had seized him and shouted, 'You shall die!' (Jeremiah 26:8), his life was spared because some elders arose and said to the entire assembly that the prophet Micah too had prophesized against Judah but was not put to death.

Chapter 3 is unusual in that God addresses Himself to the Northern Kingdom of Israel which had ceased to exist for over one hundred years, its citizens led into Assyrian captivity. However, the true audience is Judah. God declared that 'Rebel Israel has shown herself more in the right than Faithless Judah' because Judah had even more reasons than Israel to embrace God. David became king of the tribe of Judah before he united Israel and Judah. It established an eternal link between Judah and the Davidic dynasty. Moreover, the Temple of Jerusalem was God's dwelling place on earth and was in Judah. God refers to the dilapidated mental state of Judah after it saw that Israel had gone into captivity for its persistent transgressions and inequities. Rashi comments about verse 11: 'Israel has been cleared and she has freed herself from an unfavorable verdict, for Israel had no one to learn from'. At least Judah had seen the consequences of abandoning God and could have avoided the fate of the northern kingdom. Israel and Judah failed to understand that they had a Heavenly Father who cared about them.[2] It would have encouraged them to remain calm and composed, even in harsh

---

2. Jeremiah portrays God as a loving father—see Jeremiah 31:20

times. Instead, the peoples of both kingdoms became entangled in a web of doom and despair, a cycle of chaos and destruction.

Jeremiah 3 is unusual for another reason. It implicitly refers to the divorce law of Deuteronomy 24:1-4 which states that a husband should not remarry his divorced wife if she had remarried another man who divorced her or had died. In this metaphor Israel had left God, her husband, and remarried 'another' in the form of false gods or idolatry. God breaks the law by taking back Israel because the law makes a reconciliation between God and Israel impossible. Thus, a return to God is the overriding principle in the Old Testament even if it means that the law must be broken, or in other words, God's loving kindness is stronger than any legalistic interpretation of the Old Testament. The LORD will take back any sincerely shamefaced person even when society rejects and punishes him for any detestable deed. The metaphor of the divorce laws was a clear message to Judah. If God was willing to remarry Israel, He would undoubtedly take back Judah who had not yet been divorced from God and gone into exile.

God promised the restoration of the good fortunes of Judah and Israel, the rebuilding of them as of old. It will happen after He will have purged them of all their transgressions and pardoned them because they had rebelled against Him. Of all books of the Old Testament, the promise of forgiveness and restoration is most often repeated in the Book of Jeremiah.[3] Because of this repeated promise, the prophet Jeremiah is above all a prophet of hope and deliverance notwithstanding that he is commonly represented as a prophet of doom and gloom.

Like Isaiah, Jeremiah rejected the formal rituals and the outward appearances of Jewish life, although he himself was a priest. For this reason, he clashed with other priests and other prophets, especially the false prophet Hananiah.[4] However, the divine spirit allowed Jeremiah to foresee and weigh the consequences of the destruction of the Temple and its localized cult as well as to predict the deportation of the people of Judah to Babylon. Jeremiah's message gave already a solution for the question how the bond with God could be maintained in exile after the foreseeable destruction of the Temple. In the Book of Jeremiah God announces a new era in which a New Covenant will rule the relationship between God and mankind. The Temple cult will be replaced by a personal relationship with God, an inner bond

---

3. Jeremiah 23:3-6, 24:6, 29:14, 30:3, 30:18, 30:20, 31:4, 31:28, 32:44, 33:11, 33:26, and 42:10.

4. Jeremiah 23:11: 'Even the prophet and the priest are godless; even in My House I find their iniquities—declares the LORD.' Concerning the false prophet Hananiah, see Jeremiah 28.

inscribed in the heart and mind of man.⁵ Having this in mind Jeremiah 31:31-33 prophesized 'See, the day is coming—declares the LORD—when I will make a new covenant with the House of Israel and the House of Judah. It will not be like the covenant I made with their forefathers, when I took them by the hand and brought them out of the land of Egypt, a covenant which they broke, so that I rejected them—declares the LORD... But such is the covenant I will make with the House of Israel on that day—declares the LORD: I will put My Teaching into their innermost being and inscribe it upon their hearts. Then I will be their God, and they shall be My people.'

The prophetic mission of Jeremiah reveals another dimension of self-examination. It warns against merely considering power relations and the advancement of self-interest, often relying on second-guessing. Fateful events can unfold unexpectedly and take away our calculated advantages, guarantees and insurances. Vulnerability and unpredictability remind us that the true protector of life and existence is our Heavenly Father. At the same time Jeremiah's judgments refer to the importance of individual conscience and upholding a code of kindness, justice, and equity, even in the face of great danger like this prophet witnessed and endured. It has been said that God gave Jeremiah the most precious gift that He can bestow, namely knowledge of his own calling, and thus intimate relationship with his own conscience.⁶

---

5. Emphasis on a person's relationship with God in heart and mind, rather than outward appearances, is also made in 1 Samuel 16:7 (Reading 3), Deuteronomy 4:27-31 (Reading 14), Deuteronomy 6:4-9 (Reading 17), and 1 Kings 8:33-40 (Reading 22).

6. Jonathan Zasloff, Calling and Conscience: Haftarat Mattot, Jeremiah 1-1-2—https://jewishjournal.com/culture/food/130834/calling-and-conscience-haftarat-mattot-jeremiah-11-23/

Ezekiel

Reading 27 Individual responsibility and salvation

Ezekiel 18:1-4

1. And the word of the LORD came to me;

2. What do you mean by using the proverb in Israel, "Parents eat sour grapes and their children's teeth are blunted?"

3. As I live—declares the Lord GOD—this proverb shall no longer be used among you in Israel.

4. Consider this: all lives are Mine; the life of the parent and the life of the child are both Mine. The person who transgresses, only he shall die.

…

Ezekiel 18:20-32

20. The person who transgresses, he alone shall die. A child shall not share the burden of a parent's guilt, nor shall a parent share the burden of a child's guilt; the righteousness of the righteous shall be accounted to him alone, and the wickedness of the wicked shall be accounted to him alone.

21. Moreover, if the wicked one repents of all the transgressions that he committed and keeps all My commandments and does what is just and right, he shall live; he shall not die.

22. None of the transgressions he committed shall be remembered against him; for his righteousness, he shall live.

23. Is it in My thoughts that a wicked person shall die?—says the Lord GOD. It is rather that he shall turn back from his ways, and live.

24. Even so, if a righteous person turns away from his righteousness and acts wrongly, doing the very abominations that the wicked person is practicing, shall he live? None of the righteous deeds that he did shall be remembered; because of the trespass he has done and the transgressions he has committed—because of these, he shall die.

25. Yet you say, "The way of the LORD is unfair." Listen, O House of Israel: Is My way unfair? It is your ways that are unfair!

26. When a righteous person turns away from his righteousness and commits iniquity, he shall die for it; he shall die for the wrong he has done.

27. And if a wicked person turns back from the wickedness that he has done and does what is just and right, such a person shall save his life.

28. Because he did self-examination and turned back from all the transgressions that he committed, he shall live; he shall not die.

29. Yet the House of Israel said, "The way of the LORD is unfair." Are My ways unfair, O House of Israel? It is your ways that are unfair!

30. Therefore, O House of Israel, I will judge each one of you according to his ways—declares the Lord GOD. Return and turn back from your transgressions; let them not be a stumbling block of guilt for you.

31. Cast away all the transgressions by which you have offended, and get yourselves a new heart and a new spirit, that you may not die, O House of Israel.

32. For it is not My desire that anyone shall die—declares the Lord GOD. Return, therefore, and live!

EZEKIEL WAS A YOUNGER contemporary of Jeremiah. Like Jeremiah, he was born in a priestly family in Anathoth and prophesized the destruction of Judah and the Temple of Jerusalem by Babylon. At the age of 25 years, he was exiled to Babylonia in the first captivity wave and only the poorest people were left in the land of Judah to cultivate the land (Jeremiah 39:10). The Book of Ezekiel begins with proclaiming that Ezekiel was in the community of exiles that dwelt in Tel Aviv by the Chebar Canal in Babylonia when he saw a heavenly vision of four winged angels who had the figures of humans.[1] Next to each angel was a moving wheel, which made a great roaring sound, and above the angels was an expanse with an awe-inspiring

---

1. Since Tel Aviv was the place of the Jewish exiles in Babylonia, the name Tel Aviv was used at the time of establishment of Israel on 14 May 1948 with the message that the exiled Jews now had their own place in the new Israel as the reborn Jewish state.

gleam of crystal.[2] And above the expanse was the semblance of a throne with a semblance of the Presence of the LORD Ezekiel prophesized in exile and the Old Testament suggests that he was reluctant to be appointed as a prophet. After the first call of God, Ezekiel said '. . . I went in bitterness, in the heat of my spirit, with the hand of the LORD strong upon me.' He went to Tel Aviv by the Chebar Canal and for seven days he sat there stunned among his fellow exiled countrymen (Ezekiel 3: 14-15). Ezekiel got even an early warning by God not to be '. . . rebellious like that rebellious breed' (Ezekiel 2:8).

Like Jeremiah, Elijah, and Moses, he was reluctant to accept his prophetic mission. The reluctance of some prophets is caused by an intense apprehension of their transitory position between God and the people. Like priests he is a bridge between the people and God and, living among the people, he reminds, like priests in the Temple, that God is dwelling in the land and involved in human affairs. The prophet also compares to the set apart status of the priesthood, the Leviim. However, in contrast to the priesthood, the prophet's position in undefined and allows him to carry out his unusual mission. Being faithful to God is the most essential condition of any prophecy and, for this reason, a prophet faced a double danger. If he would fail to remain faithful to God, he would become a false prophet and be severely punished by God. The Old Testament makes mention of numerous false prophets, see for example Hananiah (Reading 26). But if the prophet would be faithful to God and rebuke the people for their wicked behavior, he could be ridiculed by the stubborn people. As is said in one of the closing verses of the Old Testament, "But they mocked the messengers of God and disdained His words and taunted His prophets until the wrath of the LORD against His people grew beyond remedy." (2 Chronicles 36:16).

The bitterest moment in Ezekiel's life in exile was the day when news reached him that Jerusalem was captured and the Temple destroyed and he realized that his prophecy on Jerusalem was confirmed: 'In the twelfth year of our exile, on the fifth day of the tenth month, a fugitive came to me from Jerusalem and reported, "The city has fallen!" (Ezekiel 33:21). It was also the moment that Babylonian Jews realized that Ezekiel was indeed a true prophet. Months later a new wave of Jewish deportees joined the Jews already in Babylonian exile.

---

2. Each giant wheel was made of two intersecting wheels and next to each wheel was an angel. Later, in a second vision, a fiery figure took Ezekiel by the hair of his head and lifted him up between heaven and earth and brought Ezekiel in visions of God to Jerusalem. Then Ezekiel saw again the 'wheelwork' that he had already seen in his first vision by the Chebar Canal (Ezekiel 10:9-15).

The LORD appointed Ezekiel as a 'watchman for the House of Israel'. From then onwards the name Israel means all Jews regardless of whether they were in exile or in Judah or in Israel. God's promise to restore and unify Israel under a renovated leadership is a consolation during the hard time of exile: 'Then I shall appoint a single shepherd over them to tend them—My servant David. He shall tend them; he shall be a shepherd to them.' (Ezekiel 34:23). This promise of unification is in sharp contrast with the pronounced judgment of God that He will scatter the Jews '. . . among the nations and disperse them through the lands' (Ezekiel 20:23). The paradox of dispersing and unifying the people stands for punishing and saving in one move, a promise that must have seemed impossible to understand by Ezekiel's audience. Even Ezekiel himself is not presumed to fully understand God's predictions for Ezekiel is a watchman who is standing as an eyewitness and messenger. Ezekiel was told by God not to worry whether his prophecies would be taken to heart. His mission is to convey a clear message of change, bearing in mind that his fellow countrymen are a rebellious people: '. . . but speak My words to them, whether they listen or not, for they are most rebellious.' (Ezekiel 2:7)

The Book of Ezekiel contains three explicit calls for regret, change and a return to God: Ezekiel 14: 6, 'Now say to the people of Israel: This said the Lord GOD: Return, and turn back from your fetishes and turn your minds away from all your abominations.', Ezekiel 18 (see above), and Ezekiel 33:1-21. In Chapter 18 Ezekiel counters the then popular belief that catastrophes were God's punishment for the transgressions of the ancestors.[3] Ezekiel teaches that God will judge each person for his transgressions alone, and that God is always willing to forgive a sincerely contrite heart, even a person who was corrupt his whole life and changed in his final moments, asking for forgiveness.[4]

In Ezekiel's view, self-examination and responsibility are the cornerstones of personal salvation as well as the prerequisite for the reconstruction of the Jewish people. Blaming the fathers for the calamities of the day is without a purpose and an easy excuse for failing to act. What is needed is correction of one's own life, an empowering act. If we do so, God will

---

3. This was a widely held belief and repeated in Lamentations 5:7 'Our fathers committed iniquities and are no more; and we must bear their guilt.'

4. Moshe Maimonides, Mishneh Torah, Sefer Madda, Chapter One, Halacha 3: 'At present the Temple does not exist and there is no altar of atonement, there remains nothing else aside from Teshuvah. Teshuvah atones for all sins. Even a person who was wicked his whole life and repented in his final moments will not be remembered of any aspect of his wickedness as Ezekiel 33:12 states ". . . the wickedness of the wicked one will not cause him to stumble on the day he regrets his wickedness."

not look at what we were but will reassure us of His enduring love. He will recognize that we became another person. Instead of wanting our spiritual death, God wants us to be alive and doing well. He wants us to acquire a new heart and a new spirit.[5] This hopeful promise is always subject to profound change, whenever it is needed. Thus, a righteous man with many good deeds but who seriously errs without regret will not be spared, as Ezekiel 18:26 states 'When a righteous person turns away from his righteousness and commits iniquity, he shall die for it; he shall die for the wrong he has done.'

Ezekiel's greatest message concerns the nature of God's forgiveness. God is not concerned about the mere administration of justice as humans do because He also shows mercy. The LORD considers the human weakness of a person from the day that he was born. Our flawed human nature makes us vulnerable to iniquity. This inherent condition of imperfection or weakness exists in every person and remains a challenge throughout life. The LORD knows this aspect of His creation and is willing to show mercy and compassion. Notwithstanding any marginalization or stigmatization by social convention or conviction by the administration of human justice, God has other more profound considerations when judging a person's life (see Reading 1 on the evil of man).

Ezekiel has a heavenly vision of the new Temple of Jerusalem which shall be built in the future (Ezekiel Chapters 40 to 48). He goes in detail to measure the proportions of the new Temple and its ornamental accoutrements. After the Persian King Cyrus the Great had permitted the Babylonian Jews to return to Judah and rebuild the Temple (Ezra 1:1-4), the Second Temple was rebuilt around 516 BC. Ezekiel's prophecy was thus confirmed. However, the Book of Ezekiel is also important for the message that God dwells among those who accept Him and follow His ways, wherever they are. This will prove to be even more important in history because the Second Temple too would be destroyed in 70 AD, this time by the legions of the Roman Empire. A Jewish life without the Temple reconnects to the time of the exodus out of Egypt when God dwelt among His people in their wanderings through the desert and in Canaan, which is called the Tabernacle period. With the building of the First Temple by King Solomon the period of the Temple as the dwelling-place of God began. When the first Temple was destroyed also the Ark of the Covenant was destroyed. It raised the question whether God was still dwelling among its people. Both Jeremiah and Ezekiel confirmed that God remained among His people.

---

5. 'And I will give you a new heart and blow a new spirit into you; I will remove the heart of stone from you and give you a heart of flesh.' (Ezekiel 36:26).

Ezekiel's message of individual responsibility builds further on Jeremiah's message of a personal bond with God (Reading 26). The end of the first Temple period emphasizes more than ever a personal relationship with God, an inner bond inscribed in the heart and mind of man. Ezekiel's life in exile testifies to God's presence based on a personal bond that needs no temple. However, Ezekiel is important for another important divine message, namely that destruction and disaster should not end in despair and feelings of total loss. Instead, the dramatic feelings of abandonment and the end of things are only the setting of a new heart and a new spirit, a rebirth as is written in Ezekiel 36:26, 'And I will give you a new heart and put a new spirit into you.'

The prophet Ezekiel died in exile and tradition tells us that his tomb is in Al Kifl, around 50 km south of Baghdad. It can still be visited today.

Hosea

Reading 28 — Return, O Israel, to the Lord, your God!

Hosea 14:2-10

2. Return, O Israel, to the LORD your God,
for you have stumbled because of your transgressions.
3. Take words with you
and return to the LORD.
Say to Him:
"Forgive all iniquity
and accept what is good;
instead of bulls we will pay
the offerings of our words.
4. Assyria shall not save us,
no more will we ride on horses.
Nor ever again will we call
the work of our hands our god,
since in You alone orphans find shelter!"
5. I will heal their backsliding,
generously will I take them back in love,
for My anger has turned away from them.
6. I will be to Israel like dew;
he shall blossom like the lily,

he shall spread its roots like a Lebanon tree.

7. His branches shall spread out far,

his beauty shall be like that of the olive tree,

his fragrance like that of Lebanon.

8. They who rest in his shade shall be revived:

they shall bring to life new seeds,

they shall blossom like the vine;

his scent shall be like the wine of Lebanon.

9. Ephraim shall say:

"What more have I to do with idols?

When I respond and look to Him,

I become like a leafy cypress."

Your fruit is served by Me.

10. He who is wise will consider these words,

he who is prudent will notice them.

For the paths of the LORD are easy;

the righteous can walk on them,

while transgressors stumble on them.

The Book of Hosea is the first book of the so-called twelve Minor Prophets. They are called 'minor' only because of the length of the books, between one and fourteen chapters which is shorter than the books of Isaiah, Jeremiah, and Ezekiel. However, the spiritual value and significance of the twelve Minor Prophets are not less than the three 'major' prophets.

Hosea lived in a turbulent time when Assyria's power was gradually expanding, and the Northern Kingdom of Israel became more and more entangled in Assyria's campaign of conquest. Shortly after Hosea's death in 722 BC, the Assyrian king Shalmaneser V captured Samaria (Shomron), the capital of the Northern Kingdom of Israel, and deported all remaining Israelites in captivity to Assyria.[1] The exiled population became known as the Ten Lost Tribes. Hosea was the son of Beeri and prophesized in the Northern Kingdom of Israel in the period 780 to 725 BC. His contemporary other prophets were Amos, Isaiah, and Micah. However, Hosea holds a

---

1. About ten years earlier, the then Assyrian king Tiglath-Pileser III had already deported a great number of Israelites to Assyria. According to Isaiah 7:9 Samaria was the capital of 'Ephraim' or the Northern Kingdom of Israel.

special place in the history of the Latter Prophets for several reasons. He is the only prophet of the Northern Kingdom of Israel with a written record. Secondly, according to rabbinical comments, he was the greatest prophet of his generation because he prophesized as the first.[2] Thirdly, he was the first prophet to announce publicly the paramount importance of regret, change and a return to God and he was the most articulate and persuasive on this.

The Book of Hosea is well structured and takes on the form of a legal proceeding against the Northern Kingdom of Israel. After an introduction into the wicked practices and idolatry in Ephraim, another word for the Northern Kingdom of Israel, Hosea proceeds with three distinct parts. The first part (Chapters 4 to 7) is an overview of the charges brought against the Northern Kingdom of Israel: 'For the LORD has a case against the people of this land', followed by a list of transgressions such as dishonesty, no goodness, no obedience to God, false swearing, murder, theft, and adultery (Hosea 4:1-2). The second part (Chapters 8 to 10) consists of the pronounced judgment and severe punishment of the northern kingdom. We quote some of the harsh pronouncements of the judgment.

> 'They sow wind, and they shall reap the whirlwind—without stalks and without buds and yielding no pollen.'
> Hosea 8:7

> 'They have now become among the nations like a worthless vessel, like a solitary wild donkey.'
> Hosea 8:8-9

> He will punish their transgressions: they shall be sent back to Egypt!'
> Hosea 8:13

> 'I will drive them out of My House. I will love them no more; all their officials are treacherous.'
> Hosea 9:15

---

2. Talmud, Pesachim 87a: 'The word of the LORD that came unto Hosea the son of Beeri, in the days of Uzziah, Jotham, Ahaz, and Hezekiah, kings of Judah. Four prophets prophesized in one age, and the greatest of all of them was Hosea. For it is said, the LORD spoke first with Hosea. Did He then speak first with Hosea? Were there not many prophets from Moses until Hosea? Said Rabbi Johanan. He was the first of four prophets who prophesized in that age, and these are Hosea, Isaiah, Amos and Micah.'

The third part (Chapters 11 to 14) is about God's promise of restoring Israel. Here are two of the most moving expressions of God's eternal love for Israel:

> 'When Israel was still a child I fell in love with Israel; and, ever since Egypt, I have called him My son.'
> Hosea 11:1

> 'I have a change of heart and My compassion is without end. I will not unlash My fierce anger, I will not turn to destroy Israel. For I am God, not man, the Hole One among you: I will not come in fury.'
> Hosea 11:8-9

The third part comprises Chapters 11 to 14 about the restoration of Israel. God's change of heart is also reflected in the book which starts with the portrayal of the northern kingdom as an unfaithful wife and a harlot but ends with God as the father of the child Israel. The prophet Hosea himself is commanded by God to marry the prostitute Gomer, daughter of Diblaim (Hosea 1:2-3). This strange story is an allegory of the relationship between God and unfaithful Israel. It is clearly intended to provoke a shock among the Israelites.

Chapter 14 is the most important one of the Book of Hosea. It is a consolation for the faithful, written in a poetic style and revealing the essentials of the Old Testament. Verses 2 to 4 state the precondition for personal restoration, namely regret and a return to God. God takes the initiative to restoration, but He expects a response in the form of a sincere desire to restore the relationship with Him. Verse 3 shows us how to repent and find the right words for expressing our desire, how to address God, as Hosea writes 'Say to Him …'. When we commit a transgression, we hope to be judged also based on our good deeds. Although regret and change are needed for all transgressions, we may express the hope that our good deeds will weigh more heavily in a final judgment, as Rashi offers this explanation of verse 3: 'Take the few good deeds in our hands in Your hand and judge us accordingly.' Verse 3 contains another important thought since the prophecy of Hosea. Instead of bull offerings or animal offerings, the believers offer their prayer and their clear intention never to repeat the same transgression again. It indicates a change of heart and mind. The prophets Isaiah and Jeremiah will repeat this thought (Readings 25 and 26). The ritual of animal offering will finally cease five centuries later with the destruction of the Second Temple in 70 CE.

Verse 4 of Chapter 14 begins with the firm conviction that man should not rely on other men but on God only: 'Assyria shall not save us, no more will we ride on horses'. As Rashi commented, riding on horses refers to '... the aid from Egypt, who would send them horses, as they said to Isaiah 30:16 "No, but on horses we will flee ... on swift horses will we ride."'[3] Notwithstanding our need for a secure political and social environment, our ultimate hope should rest on God, not men. Jeremiah repeats this thought—see Jeremiah 17:5-7 as quoted in Reading 26. Verse 4 continues with the statement 'Nor ever again will we call the work of our hands our god.' In Hosea's time the handiworks were the statues and figures of Baal, Astarte and other false gods made in the imagination of men. In our time the handiworks are man-made electronic devices, instruments, even our scientific instruments, or a house which give a false sense of security. It focuses our mind on the material world, not the world of God. Or if we focus on the material world, we forget who made the material world in the first place—see Book of Genesis.

Verse 5 and following verses are poetic references to the plentiful rewards we will receive once we have returned to God. The healing of afflictions is a consolation, repeated in Psalm 34:20 'Though the hardships of the righteous may be many, the LORD will save him from them all.' God will be to Israel like dew that shall strike the roots and let them prosper. 'Like the Lebanon' means like the roots of the trees of the Lebanon which are large. The repentant will say, 'I become like a verdant cypress.' (Verse 9).

---

3. Hosea uses the expression 'riding on horses' because neither Judah nor Israel had cavalry. In a battle with Assyria, only military aid from Egypt, consisting of chariots and horses, could make a difference. However, such military aid would mean that Israel would rely on Egypt. See for example Isaiah 36:9 'So how could you refuse anything, even to the deputy of one of my master's lesser officials, counting on Egypt for chariots and horsemen?'

Joel

Reading 29 *The Lord is gracious and compassionate, slow to anger, abounding in kindness.*

Joel 2:10-14
10. Before them the earth quakes,
heaven tremble,
sun and moon are darkened,
and the brightness of stars is fainting.
11. And the LORD shouts with a thundering voice
at the head of His army;
for immense indeed is His host,
countless are those that follow His orders.
for awesome is the day of the LORD,
most terrible—who can survive it?
12. "Yet even now"—says the LORD –
"Turn back to Me with all your heart,
and with fasting, weeping and regret."
13. Rend your hearts
instead of your garments,
and turn back to the LORD your God.
For He is gracious and compassionate,
slow to anger, abounding in kindness,
and renouncing punishment.
14. Whoever knows shall repent and regret,
and leave a blessing behind
and a meal offering and a drink offering
to the LORD your God.

THE BOOK OF JOEL begins with the statement that Joel is the son of Pethuel. No further information is provided regarding the life of Joel or the persons and kingdoms of his time. Because Assyria and Babylon are not mentioned, the best date estimate of the Book of is around 800 BC preceding Hosea and Isaiah. Because of his familiarity with many phrases in the Old Testament, Joel is considered as a learned prophet. The central theme of the book is the 'Day of the LORD' or the final judgment of humanity and every person at the end of time. It is the first book of the Bible that announces a final divine judgment.[1] Joel portrays that day as '. . . a day of darkness and gloom, a day of thick clouds as darkness spreads over the hills ... Nothing like this has ever happened, and it shall never happen again.' (Joel 2:2).

The book begins with a vivid description of a locust plague that ravages the country like a mighty army, destroying all crops, plants, and food. It is followed by an all-consuming fire. Amidst the description of complete devastation, two calls are made to change the heart and mind (Joel 1:13-20 and 2:12-17). The prophet's urgent message conveys the need to return to the LORD as the only way to survive the never-ending calamities. The locust plague and subsequent droughts only illustrate the dire mental condition of the people who strayed away from their covenantal bond with God. The last argument in Joel's discourse is the 'Day of the LORD' when God will judge the nations of the world and Judah. He tries to convince the people to return to God before it is too late, when time ends, and a final judgment will be delivered. As a matter of fact, every day can be the last day.

In his first call to return to God, Joel appeals to the priests and elders of the people to perform the traditional rites of lamentation. The loud call is addressed to the priests and political leaders who should give the example of regret, change and a return to God. Public fasting and sackcloth can create an atmosphere that inspires the arousal of a contrite spirit for we are not always in full control of our emotions.

> 13. Gird yourselves and lament, O priests,
> wail, O ministers of the altar;
> come, spend the night in sackcloth,
> O ministers of my God ...
> Joel 1:13

In the second call to change—see quotation above—the 'Day of the LORD' is assumed imminent and yet there is still time to change and return to God. Joel 2:13 is the most important verse of the Book of Joel. In it the

---

1. The final day of divine judgment is also mentioned by later prophets, namely Isaiah 17:7; Jeremiah 46:10; Ezekiel 13:5; Hosea 2:18; Amos 5:18; Obadiah 1:15; Zephaniah 1:14; Zechariah 14:1; Malachi 3:19.

prophet warns against hypocrisy by showing outward conduct of regret and sorrow without an inner experience of guilt and regret. Rending clothes was and still is a recognized expression of greatest grief and sorrow, for example the rending of the shirt at the burial of a spouse or a close relative.[2] The commandment 'Rend your heart' means that we repent with our thoughts and feelings since the heart was regarded in antiquity to be the place of the thoughts and feelings. Secondly, Verse 13 mentions the qualities of God in His relationship with humanity: gracious, compassionate, slow to anger, abounding in kindness, and renouncing punishment. Joel alludes to Exodus 34:6-7 where the same qualities are revealed by God when Moses carved the two tablets of stone on Mount Sinai (Reading 4). Regret, change and a return to God are the only conditions for the God's forgiveness, a message that is proclaimed by all prophets. Verse 2:14 starts with the words 'Whoever knows' which Rashi explains as 'whoever is aware of his responsibility for his iniquities.'[3] At the same time, such awareness is a recognition of one's transgressions according to Psalm 51:5 '… for I recognize my transgressions and am ever conscious of my sin.'

But how do we know what is right or wrong, or know when we committed a transgression? Life can be entangled in a web of actions and interactions among people, and it can be hard to maintain a righteous conduct, to stand firm among many uncertainties. The Bible is the first guide to consult and reflect upon. However, confusion and uncertainty can persist and mislead us into transgression. So, how do we know that we have transgressed? Or how do we know that we will not transgress in a particular instance? Throughout time many believers asked themselves such questions. King David also asked this question and in Psalm 25:4 he shows how he sought direct counsel from God by praying: 'Let me know Your paths, O LORD; teach me Your ways; guide me in Your true way and teach me, for You are God, my deliverer; it is You I look to at all times.' In the same sense, Micah 4:2 prays 'That He may instruct us in His ways, and that we may walk in His paths.' (Reading 28)

---

2. However, it was forbidden for priests to rend their garments—see Leviticus 10:6. The reason for this prohibition is given by Leviticus 21:10: 'The priest who is exalted above his fellows, on whose head the anointing oil has been poured and who has been ordained to wear the vestments, shall not bare his head or rend his vestments.'

3. Joel 2:14 is translated according to Rashi's comment: 'Whoever knows shall repent and regret …'

Amos

Reading 30   Seek the Lord and you will live.

Amos 5:4-7
4. This said the LORD
to the House of Israel:
Seek Me, and you will live!
5. Do not seek Bethel,
nor go to Gilgal,
nor visit Beer-sheba;
Gilgal shall go into exile,
and Bethel shall become a deception.
6. Seek the LORD, and you will live,
otherwise He will break out like fire upon the House of Joseph
and burn Bethel with none to quench it.
7. Ah, you who turn justice into wormwood
and smash righteousness to the ground!

ACCORDING TO AMOS 1:1, Amos prophesized in the reign of King Uzziah of the Kingdom of Judah and King Jeroboam of the Kingdom of Israel, two years before the big earthquake. The biblical information to the big earthquake allows scientists to date the Book of Amos around 750 BC.[1] He is

---

1. Geologists have found evidence of an earthquake with a magnitude of 8 on the scale of Richter around 750 BC. The epicenter was approximately 200 km in Lebanon from the present-day northern borders of Israel. It is the largest recorded earthquake on the Dead Sea transform fault zone of the last four millennia. Amos repeatedly refers to the terrible effects on the population. Amos 6:11 speaks of the 'great house' that shall be smashed to bits, and 'the little house to splinters'. Amos 8:8 mentions a great earthquake. In Amos 9:1 the prophet envisages that the temple of Bethel will be struck

the older contemporary of the prophet Hosea and a contemporary of the prophet Joel. Amos was a sheep breeder and a tender of sycamore figs from Tekoa, a village 15 km south of Jerusalem in Judah (Amos 1:1 and 7:14). In that time, the Northern Kingdom of Israel, far more powerful and richer than Judah. was enjoying great stability and wealth while its neighbors Syria and Assyria were weakened. Notwithstanding its prosperity, the northern kingdom experienced a decline in decent standards and religious practices, building shrines and altars to serve Baal and Astarte and shying away from the teaching of the Scriptures. The most important idolatrous shrine was the temple of Bethel for Golden Calf or bull worshipping on the southern border with Judah. The spiritual downfall of the northern kingdom was so great that no northerner was called by God to be his prophet.

Although from Judah, Amos became the prophet concerning the doom and fall of the Northern Kingdom of Israel. He was a humble man, although courageous and intense, who was called to deliver a terrible message, the end of the northern kingdom when it was at its height of power and prosperity. He went to the northern kingdom knowing that he would be despised and laughed at. In his heart Amos knew that his call for change would not be heeded by the people and the ruling elite of the north. Hence Amos's call for change is very short compared to his prophecies of condemnation and destruction. As always, God allows all transgressors time to change before His judgment strikes down. He gives an opportunity to return so that He can change His mind too. Because of this, God sent the prophet Amos so that He could revoke His judgment and avert catastrophe. And if the entire people could not be saved, perhaps a regretful remnant could be saved. Having this in mind, Amos proclaimed 'Hate evil and love good, and establish justice in the gate; perhaps the LORD, the God of Hosts, will be gracious to the remnant of Joseph' (Amos 5:15). The Book of Amos clearly confirms that the coming events are shaped by free choice, and by making the right choice God can always change His mind. The intensity of Amos's call for change is underlined by the fact that his message, the words of God, was reduced to one short sentence or command: 'Seek Me, and you will live!' The Talmud (Makkoth 24a) said about this one sentence or command: six hundred and thirteen precepts were communicated to Moses, but Amos reduced them to one principle: 'Seek Me, and you will live!' His call to seek the LORD refers to Moses' call to do this with heart and soul for the LORD is a compassionate God. He will not fail you nor will He let you perish (Deuteronomy 4:29-31). Christian theology refers to Amos as the prophet who

---

by an earthquake and reduced to rubble. 250 years later, the prophet Zechariah still refers to this earthquake in Zechariah 14:5 '... you shall flee, like you fled from before the earthquake in the days of King Uzziah of Judah.'

had bestowed the Israelites with favors and benefits in the past but they had abandoned God by their sinful acts. The same can happen today with the Western world that has gained so many improvements and material gains for the last one hundred years but is neglecting the plight of the poor in the world. The people and the church must never take God's favor for granted because His justice is universal.[2] Perhaps this message refers to our time when governments and their electorates choose their own advantages while neglecting neighborly love or global justice. Self-examination in international affairs is as necessary as for individual sanity.

The charges brought against the people of the Northern Kingdom of Israel had not only to do with abandoning the LORD but also with social injustice. Amos detested the great inequality between the wealthy ruling elite and the impoverished and heavily taxed population. He prophesized that the Northern Kingdom of Israel would be punished for the oppression of the poor and needy despite the root ritual performances of the wealthy at the shrines in Bethel and Gilgal. He sarcastically cried in front of the public shrine at Bethel: 'Come to Bethel and transgress; to Gilgal and transgress even more' (Amos 4:4). He takes up the plight of the poor by accusing the ruling elite of social indifference and greed.

> 6. Thus said the LORD:
> for three transgressions of Israel,
> yea, for four, I will not reverse it:
> because they have sold the righteous for silver
> and the needy for a pair of shoes.
> 7. Ah, you who trample on the head of the poor
> into the dust of the ground,
> and confuse the humble's paths!
> Amos 2:6-7

> ... who defraud the poor,
> who rob the needy
> Amos 4:1

> Assuredly,
> because you impose a heavy tax on the poor
> and exact from him levy of grain ...
> Amos 5:11

> ... you takers of ransom,

---

[2]. www.newadvent.org/cathen/01435a.htm; www.christianity.com/wiki/people/who-is-amos-in-the-bible-prophet-and-shepherd.html

you who subvert in the gate
the cause of the needy!
Amos 5:12

The final divine judgment on the Northern Kingdom of Israel is pronounced in Amos 5:1-2.

'Hear this word which I proclaim
as a lamentation over you, O House of Israel:
Maiden Israel is fallen
not to rise again!'
Amos 5:1-2

The northern kingdom's exile is pronounced in Amos 7:17

'And you yourself shall die on foreign soil; for Israel shall be exiled from its land.'
Amos 7:17

The priest Amaziah in Bethel accused Amos of conspiring against the king and the country.[3] He banned Amos out of the Northern Kingdom of Israel and sent him back to Judah. The Book of Amos ends with God's promise of the restoration of His people Israel, although be it through a faithful remnant: 'But I will not wholly wipe out the House of Jacob.' (Amos 9:8).

Justice after self-examination can be done 'in the gates', meaning that it may be necessary to do it in public since the gates of ancient towns were busy places where people constantly moved in and out and business dealings were sealed with nearby witnesses[4] Especially public personalities cannot escape 'justice in the gates' since they live and work in public spaces. 'Seek Me, and you will live!' may imply that you should leave a place of evil, for example a city, a country, or an unjust social environment, going through that gate as Amos did. He saved his life before the destruction of the northern kingdom and the following enslavement and deportation of its survivors.

---

3. Jeremiah too was accused of being a traitor because he had prophesized surrender to the Babylonian army besieging Jerusalem (Reading 26).

4. The practice of sealing of contracts and business 'in the gates' is very ancient and recorded in Genesis 23:17-18: 'So Ephron's land in Machpelah near Mamre—the field with its cave and all the trees anywhere within the confines of that field—passed to Abraham as his possession, in the presence of the Hittites, of all who entered the gate of his town.' Abraham bought this piece of land to bury his wife Sarah in the cave of the field of Machpelah now Hebron.

Obadiah

Reading 31 *Humanitarian action prevents transgressions.*

Obadiah 1:10-15
10. For the violence to your brother Jacob,
shame shall be on you,
and you shall be cut off forever.
11. On that day when you stood aloof,
when strangers carried away his goods,
when foreigners entered his gates
and cast lots upon Jerusalem,
you were as one of them.
12. You should not have gazed with glee
on your brother that day,
on his day of disaster!
How could you rejoice
over the people of Judah
on that day of destruction!
How could you loudly jeer
on a day of great distress!
13. You should not have entered the gate of My people
on its day of calamity,
gaze in glee with the others on their misery
on its day of disaster,
And you should not have laid hands on their sustenance
on its day of disaster!
14. You should not have stood at the passes
to cut down those who fled!

How could you betray those refugees
on that day of anguish!
15. As you did, so shall it be done to you;
your conduct shall be reciprocated.

THE BOOK OF OBADIAH is the shortest book of the Old Testament with only 21 verses and without information on the prophet in it or any other document. Because of similar verses in the Book of Jeremiah, Obadiah is considered as a contemporary of Jeremiah and probably witnessed the destruction of Jerusalem and the subsequent waves of deportations to Babylonia. Obadiah has a special place in the Bible because of the message he addressed to the world of his time and even to the world today. Already in Verse 1 Obadiah announces that he is sent out as a messenger among the nations, underlining his universal mission. As a matter of fact, Obadiah's prophecy is a judgment against Edom which is at the same time a warning for all nations. The Edomites were the descendants of Esau who had harbored a grudge against Jacob because of the blessing which his father Isaac had given him. Esau said to himself 'Let but the mourning period of my father come, and I will kill my brother Jacob' (Genesis 27:41). Thus, the Edomites were related to the Jewish people. They lived in a hilly region south of Jerusalem stretching down to Eilat and during their entire history they had fought with Judah. When Judah was destroyed by the Babylonians the Edomites had gloated in the misfortune of Judah. Instead of helping their brothers of Judah, they started to loot the ruined city of Jerusalem and attacked the few survivors.

Obadiah makes a call to all the nations of the world for their aggression and mischievous conduct towards Israel and Judah. Here Israel and Judah symbolize humanity while Edom serves as the example and the warning what would happen to the nations if they mistreated the Israelites or humanity. Unusually, the Book of Obadiah is about regret and change, not addressed to the Israelites but to all other nations. Obadiah delivered the judgment of the LORD against Edom with Verse 10 predicting the end of Edom's existence forever: 'For the violence to your brother Jacob, disgrace shall cover you, and you shall perish forever.' Obadiah makes it clear that the Edomites should have shown humanitarian care for their unfortunate brothers, notwithstanding their enmity for so long. Instead, the Edomites were complicit in the catastrophe caused to Jerusalem and Judah and deserved to disappear from history. In the same vein, Psalm 137:7 mentions 'Remember, O LORD, against the Edomites the day of Jerusalem's fall; how they cried, "Strip her, strip her to her very foundations!"' Obadiah's prophecy is a warning to all nations to respect Israel and Judah, or else disappear from the face of the earth. The Book of Obadiah ends with God's promise that He will restore the good fortunes of Judah, although only a loyal remnant shall survive on mount Zion.

Obadiah is an important book that emphasizes the universal value of the teachings of the Old Testament. Its central theme is the humanitarian message of Verse 15: 'As you did, so shall it be done to you; your conduct shall be reciprocated.' A universal humanitarian standard is now put forward through Obadiah's message: spare life and property as much as possible, do not turn against those civilians who are not fighting, take care of the sick and wounded, show respect for the afflicted people, and show compassion. Even neutrality or merely looking at the victims is already an indictment against the onlookers. We must act with the means we have to stop a humanitarian tragedy. God's punishment of Edom and the other nations is based on serious violations of humanitarian prescriptions.

Jonah

Reading 32 Nineveh is saved by regret.

Jonah 3:1-10
1. The word of the LORD came to Jonah a second time.
2. "Arise, go to Nineveh, that great city, and proclaim to it what I tell you."
3. So Jonah arose and went to Nineveh according to the LORD's command. Nineveh was an exceedingly large city a three days' journey across.
4. Jonah began to enter in the city the distance of one day's journey, and proclaimed: "Within forty days, and Nineveh shall be overthrown!"
5. The people of Nineveh believed God. They proclaimed a fast, and wealthy and poor alike put on sackcloth.
6. When the news reached the king of Nineveh, he arose from his throne, laid down his robe, put on sackcloth, and sat in ashes.
7. And he ordered to announce throughout Nineveh: "By decree of the king and his nobles: No man or beast—of flock or herd—shall taste anything! They shall not feed, and they shall not drink water!
8. They shall be covered with sackcloth—man and beast—and shall cry mightily to God. Let everyone turn back from his evil ways and from the wrongdoing of which he is guilty.
9. Who knows whether God may turn and change His mind? He may turn back from His anger, so that we do not perish."
10. And God saw what they did, how they were turning away from their evil ways. And God annulled the punishment He had planned to bring on them and did not carry it out.

THE BOOK OF JONAH is one of the oldest of the Minor Prophets. Jonah, son of Amittai, may have been a contemporary of the prophet Joel around 830 BC. The central theme of the book is a return to God and God's forgiveness; for this reason, it is read in the afternoon service of Yom Kippur. Jonah is another example of a reluctant man to deliver a divine warning. God called him to go to Nineveh and proclaim His judgment on the city for its wickedness, but he fled from God by sailing away from Israel. In a violent storm the sailors blamed Jonah for his confessed flight from God which would have caused the dangerous storm. He was thrown overboard and landed in the belly of a giant fish. In his trouble, he called to the LORD and realized that He had spared his life notwithstanding his flight from God. Chapter 2 is a poem praising God's forgiveness when Jonah realized that God wanted him to stay alive and carry out his mission. One of the notable verses of Chapter 2 is Verse 7: 'I went down to the bottom of the mountains; the earth with her bars closed upon me forever; yet You have brought my life up from the pit, O LORD my God!' Then the giant fish spewed Jonah out on the beach. It is followed by a second call from God to go to Nineveh and deliver His judgment. In the middle of the city of Nineveh Jonah delivered his only prophecy 'Within forty days, and Nineveh shall be overthrown' (Jonah 3:4). The word 'overthrown' was then understood as complete destruction.

Surprisingly, although Jonah was from Israel and a citizen of a foreign hostile nation, the citizens of Nineveh believed his divine prophecy and spontaneously started to repent with all the external expressions of sorrow and regret in that time such as fastening, putting on sackcloth and sitting in ashes. Even the king of Nineveh ordered a general repentance and gave the example by taking off his royal robes and putting on sackcloth. The royal proclamation called on the citizens of Nineveh to turn back from evil ways and from the injustices of which they were guilty. It was the hope of the citizens that God would reconsider his judgment and relent. And indeed, God renounced the punishment He had planned to bring on Nineveh and did not carry it out. It is an irony that Jonah, who had first refused to make a call to repentance to a foreign city, is the only prophet who was successful in changing the behavior of a foreign people and changing God's decision. The Book of Jonah makes it clear that God not only cares about the Israelites but also about other peoples who are willing to repent and thereby changing the course of their future. It underlines the universal value of the Bible as preached in Obadiah—Reading 31.

Another surprise shows up in the final Chapter 4 which tells that Jonah was displeased because the city of Nineveh was spared by God. One may expect that Jonah would have rejoiced that his warning had been heeded and the people of Nineveh had repented. Instead, Jonah had regret that the city of Nineveh, a long-time enemy to the Israelites, was not destroyed. Then comes the remarkable explanation why he fled from God and Israel: 'For I know that You are a compassionate and gracious God, slow to anger, abounding in kindness, renouncing punishment.' (Jonah 4:2)[1] The negative mental attitude of Jonah and God's rebuke teaches us that God is not only the Father of the Israelites but of all mankind. He shows compassion and forgiveness to anyone who is truly regretful and open-minded to His call. Jonah is punished again for his negative mindset when he is laying in a deprived condition in the streets of Nineveh, begging to die. God tells Jonah that He cares about the remorseful city of Nineveh. However, sometime later Nineveh will relapse in evil attitudes, and this time the prophet Nahum will prophesy the destruction of the city-state (Reading 34).

---

1. The characteristics of God's attitude towards men were already announced by God when Moses went up on Mount Sinai and carved the covenant in the two tablets of stone (Exodus 34:6-7)—see Reading 4.

Micah

Reading 33   God forgives the remnant of His people.

Micah 6:8-9
8. He has told you, O man, what is good,
and what the LORD requires of you:
only to do justice
and to love goodness,
and to walk modestly with your God.
9. Fear the LORD if you are wise!
…

Micah 7:18-20
18. Who is a God like You,
forgiving iniquity
and overlooking transgression;
Who has not maintained His anger forever
against the remnant of His own people,
because He delights in mercy!
19. He will take us back in love;
He will cover up our iniquities,
You will cast all our sins
into the depths of the sea.
20. You will keep faith with Jacob,
loyalty to Abraham,
as You promised on oath to our forefathers
from the days of old.

MICAH

Micah, a contemporary of Hosea and Isaiah, was a Morashite who prophesized in the northern and southern kingdoms.[1] Right from the start, verse 2 is a clear warning for all transgressors in the world: 'Listen, all you peoples, listen carefully, O earth, and all it holds; and let my LORD GOD be your accuser—my LORD from His holy abode.' The prophecy of Micah accuses the political and religious leadership of both the Northern Kingdom of Israel and the Southern Kingdom of Judah for being degraded, oppressing the people and denying God's commands. His accusations are formulated as follows.

> 1. I said:
> Listen, you leaders of Jacob,
> you rulers of the House of Israel!
> for you should know what is just,
> 2. but you hate good and love evil.
> You have fed on My people's flesh;
> Micah 3:1-2

> 9. Hear this, you leaders of the House of Jacob,
> you rulers of the House of Israel,
> who abhor justice
> and pervert all equity,
> 10. who build Zion with crime,
> Jerusalem with iniquity!
> 11. Her leaders judge for rewards,
> her priests teach for a fee,
> and her prophets divine for money ...
> Micah 3:9-11

The heavy emphasis on the failures of the leadership conveys the prophetic message that a country can lapse into decay and undergo divine punishment because of bad leadership alone (Reading 55). Perhaps the people should have revolted against unjust leaders but, by failing to do so, became complicit in the transgressions and crimes of the political and religious regime. Like the Book of Hosea (Reading 28), the Book of Micah makes use of legal terminology when it says that the LORD '... has a case against His people, He has a suit against Israel' (Micah 6:2). The Book of Micah does not contain an explicit call to regret and change for in the mind of the prophet the fate of Israel and Judah is already sealed, a divine judgment will be delivered. The underlying thought seems to be that the people were already warned by several prophets, but these warnings were in vain. Micah

---
1. Morasheth-Gad is a village 25 kilometers south-west of Jerusalem on the plains of Judah.

predicts the destruction of both kingdoms and the dispersal of the population among many nations. He prophesizes that '... Zion shall be plowed as a field, and Jerusalem shall become heaps of ruins, and the Temple Mount an open place in the woods.' (Micah 3:12). Micah is the first prophet to predict the fall of Jerusalem.

The Book of Micah closes with the promise of God's forgiveness. The announced exile of the Jewish people is seen as an act of cleansing all transgressions and a reawakening of the covenantal bond between God and His people. Chapter 7 portrays God as the good shepherd: 'Oh, shepherd Your people with Your staff, Your very own flock.' (Micah 7:14). Micah calls for patience knowing that, one day, God will rescue the regretful and purified remnant of Jacob.

> 7. Yet I will look to the LORD,
> I will wait for the God who saves me,
> my God will hear me.
> 8. Do not rejoice over me,
> O my enemy!
> Though I have fallen, I shall rise again.
> Though I sit in darkness, the LORD is my light.
> 9. I will bear the anger of the LORD,
> since I have sinned against Him,
> until He pleads my cause
> and pronounces a favorable judgment over me.
> Micah 7:7-9

Like a teacher, Micah summarizes the essentials of the Old Testament: to do justice, to love goodness, and to walk modestly with your God. The last recommendation '... to walk modestly with your God' is a warning not to boast authority or prestige by referring to God as if a person can be assured that his opinion would be the same as the considerations of God. Instead, modesty is humility and a combination of fear and love regarding God whose thoughts can never be fully understood by humans. Also Proverbs 3:5 warns for replacing God's understanding by one's own understanding: 'Trust in the LORD with all your heart, and do not rely on your own understanding.' It requires a constant attention to the divine spirit so that we may walk in His paths: 'That He may instruct us in His ways, and that we may walk in His paths.' (Micah 4:2). The mindset of walking modestly with God means that God will show us the way if we listen carefully and without arrogance. Psalm 16:11 declares 'You will teach me the path of life. In Your presence is perfect joy; delights are ever in Your right hand.'

Nahum

Reading 34 *God is slow to anger but does not remit all punishment.*

Nahum 1:1-3
1. This pronouncement on Nineveh. The Book of Nahum the Elkoshite.
2. The LORD is a jealous, avenging God;
the LORD is vengeful and full of wrath.
The LORD takes vengeance on His enemies,
He became enraged against His foes.
3. The LORD is slow to anger and mighty,
but the LORD does not annul all punishment.
…

Nahum 3:18-19
18. Your shepherds are reposing, O king of Assyria;
your sheepmasters are lying inert;
your worthiest are scattered over the hills,
and there is none to assemble them.
19. There is no healing for your grievances,
your wound is grievous.
All who hear the news about you
clap their hands over you.
For who has not suffered
from your never-ending evildoings?

NAHUM PROPHESIZED IN THE time of Jeremiah and Zephaniah. More than one hundred years earlier the Northern Kingdom of Israel had been destroyed by the Assyrians (Nineveh) and its population deported, one of the most catastrophic events in Jewish history. While conquering the land, the Assyrians had committed wide-spread atrocities, such as impaling their captives or skinning them alive.[1] Not surprisingly the neighboring peoples hated Assyria for its extreme violence and injustices. The prophet Jonah had warned Nineveh of God's anger and judgment, but the Ninevites then repented, and God relented. This was to the dismay of the prophet Jonah who had hoped for Nineveh's destruction (Reading 32). The Book of Nahum takes up the same complaints about Assyria but this time the outcome is very different. Like the Book of Jonah, the Book of Nahum teaches us that the LORD is slow to anger but, unlike the Book of Jonah, it adds that the LORD does not remit all punishment. Notwithstanding its earlier repentance, Nineveh continued its cruel, inhumane, and immoral practices. The indictment is delivered in Nahum 3:1 'Ah city of crime! Utterly treacherous, full of violence, where killing never stops!' God is slow to anger and gives time to repent, but He is also righteous by punishing incorrigible transgressors.

Nahum does not make a call to regret and change since Nineveh had been given enough time to do so. His prophecy on the destruction of Nineveh is rather directed at Judah, the surviving kingdom, as an assurance of God's justice. Furthermore, the destruction of Nineveh would take away a constant danger for Judah's existence and freedom. Considering that the destruction of the Northern Kingdom of Israel had been very traumatic for the Jewish world, Nahum tells the people of Judah that Nineveh's imminent destruction also serves to restore '. . . the Pride of Jacob as well as the Pride of Israel' (Nahum 2:3). Finally, the destruction of Nineveh is proof to all nations that justice will be done according to God's considerations of divine justice and His timing. Nahum's prediction came true when a coalition force of Babylonians, rebelling Assyrians, Persians, and Medes conquered and destroyed Nineveh in July 612 BC, around twenty years after Nahum's prophecy. The city became depopulated and was laid in ruins, a symbol of the fall of a mighty empire.[2] The ruins of ancient Nineveh are in present-day Mosul's city center in Northern Iraq.

1. Archeological evidence supports the reputation that amputation, mutilations, decapitations, and skinning were carried out by the Assyrians—see Haim Cohen et al., Assyrian Attitude Towards Captive Enemies: A 2700-year-old Paleo-forensic Study, in: International Journal of Osteoarcheology, November 2012, pp. 265–80.

2. The Babylonian Chronicle, known as ABC3 and written on a clay tablet, describes the fall of Nineveh with these sentences: 'The king of Akkad mustered his army and marched to Assyria. The king of the Medes marched towards the king of Akkad, and they met one another at …u. The king of Akkad and his army crossed the Tigris; Cyaxares had to cross the Radanu, and they marched along the bank of the Tigris. In the month Simanu, the Nth day, they encamped against Nineveh. From the month

Habakkuk

Reading 35 *Though angry, may You remember compassion.*

Habakkuk 1:1-4
1. The troublesome vision of the prophet Habakkuk.
2. How long, O LORD, shall I cry out
and You not listen,
shall I shout to You, "Violence!"
and You not save?
3. Why do You show me iniquity?
Why do You stare at the wrong?
Why are raiding and violence before me?
Strife goes on and contention arises.
4. That is why the law fails
and justice is never done;
for the wicked deceives the just man –
Therefore justice is perverted.
...

Habakkuk 3:1-2
1. A prayer of the prophet Habakkuk. In the mode of Shigionoth.
2. O LORD! I have learned about Your character;
and I am afraid, O LORD, by Your deeds.
Renew Your deeds in these years,

Simanu until the month …bu, for three months, they subjected the city to a heavy siege. On the Nth day of the month … but they inflicted a major defeat upon a great people. At that time Sin-sar-iskun, king of Assyria, died. They carried off the vast booty of the city and the temple and turned the city into a ruin heap.'—www.livius.org/ne-nn/nineveh/nineveh02.html.

oh, make them known in these years!
Though angry, may You remember compassion.

THE BOOK OF HABAKKUK is a short book with three chapters and 56 verses. We know nothing about the life of Habakkuk who is most probably a contemporary of Jeremiah and Obadiah. It is likely that he died shortly before the fall of Jerusalem in 587 BC because he did not mention this momentous event.[1] Habakkuk is desperate to see much wickedness around him. Because there is no remorse or regret it creates more and more injustices. He cries to the LORD with the question why He does not intervene and establish divine justice. The prophet's painstaking cry whether God is listening is echoed in Psalms 4, 10, 13 and 22. Here is one of King David's desperate cries to God questioning whether He is listening.

> 'My God,
> I cry by day—You answer not;
> by night, and have no respite.'
> Psalm 22:3

God replies in Habakkuk 1:6 that He will raise up the Chaldeans (Babylon) against Judah: 'For lo, I am raising up the Chaldeans, that fierce, furious people, who roam the earth to seize houses not their own.' Although the Chaldeans are the instrument of punishment by God, they are even worse than Judah. Therefore, God makes the second announcement in verse 2:8 that He will deal harshly with the Chaldeans afterwards because they plundered many nations. The time has come that all surviving peoples shall plunder the Chaldeans. The two divine announcements recognize the validity of Habakkuk's complaint that justice had disappeared. For this reason, the nations involved in the injustices will be dealt with. God further clarifies that He has set the time for the punishments; it is not the task of the prophet Habakkuk to determine when the punishments will be carried out. Thus, in verse 2:3 God answers that his prophecy will be carried out in the future, one has just to wait for it.

Although God's punishments are punishments of the people, it does not exclude the vindication of the righteous man. In verse 2:4 God promises that the righteous man will be rewarded with life for his fidelity. This verse is often quoted as the fountainhead of Judaism, namely faith ('emunah') in God promises life. God's answer reveals that a wicked man does not really live, he is already mentally dead, but the righteous man fully lives his life.

---

1. According to Jewish tradition, the tomb of Habakkuk is on a hillside in the Upper Galilee, 10 kilometres southwest of Safed.

God also confirms that the treacherous, arrogant man will be punished, it is only a matter of time (Habakkuk 2:5).

Habakkuk's prayer in Chapter 3 remembers the great deeds of God for His people in the past. The prophet asks God to intervene again and renew His great deeds today. 'Oh, make them known in these years!' is a plea of the prophet to reconnect with God in an intimate relationship that nurtures love, security, and justice. We see the prophet speaking on behalf of the people although the people itself are estranged from God and forget to make this plea. Habakkuk realizes that the people are guilty of not asking a reconnection to God and understands that God is angry because of this. Finally, Habakkuk brings forward his last argument in favor of the wrongdoing and hardheaded people: God, show Your compassion! Habakkuk evokes the fact that men are suffering because of their bad behavior and estrangement from God, a never-ending circle of suffering. Habakkuk proceeds with an appeal to one of the main characteristics of God throughout all times: His ability and willingness to show compassion (Readings 4, 26 and 29). In the closing verses of the Book of Habakkuk, realizing the fast-approaching day of punishment by the hand of the Chaldeans, the prophet regains self-confidence because he believes in the eternal nurturing love and protection of the LORD. As a matter of fact, the prophet becomes aware that God will ensure justice although in a way the prophet could not imagine when he began his mission and even doubted God's never-ending interest in humanity.

> 18. Yet I will rejoice in the LORD,
> exult in the God who sets me free.
> 19. My Lord GOD is my strength:
> He makes my feet like the hind's
> and lets me walk upon the heights.
> Habakkuk 3:18-19

Zephaniah

Reading 36 *Seek the Lord before the day of the Lord's anger.*

Zephaniah 2:1-3
1. Gather yourselves together, gather together,
O shameless nation,
2. Before the day the decree is proclaimed—
the day flies by as the chaff –
before the fierce anger
of the LORD comes down on you,
before the day of anger
of the LORD comes down on you.
3. Seek the LORD,
all you humble of the earth
who have followed His commandments;
seek righteousness,
seek humility.
Perhaps you will find refuge
on the day of the LORD's anger.

THE BOOK OF ZEPHANIAH opens with the statement that Zephaniah was '... the son of Cusi, son of Gedaliah, son of Amariah, son of Hezekiah during the reign of King Josiah, son of Amon of Judah.' He is regarded as a contemporary of the prophets Nahum and Jeremiah and prophesized in Judah shortly before the fall of Jerusalem. In his age the Assyrian power began to decline, and Babylonia was in the ascent culminating in the defining year 605 BC when the allied troops of Egypt and Assyria were defeated by

Babylon at the Battle of Carchemish.[1] Judaism was still the official religion in Judah although other gods like Baal were also worshipped (Zephaniah 1:4-6).

A great theme of Zephaniah is the quick approach of the 'Day of the LORD'. On that day, God will punish the officials and the royal family of Judah (verse 1:8). Zephaniah prophesized that on that great day of the LORD, God will '. . . search Jerusalem with lamps' and punish those who say, "The LORD will neither do anything good, nor will He do bad." (Verse 1:12). Such a thought was in fact a denial of the existence of God. Yet the prophet makes a final call to a change of heart and mind in Chapter 2. The nation Judah is urged to repent before it is too late, and the decree has been proclaimed by God. Zephaniah's call is made with a feeling of immediacy and the prophet seems to address himself in the first place to the common people because he viewed the rich and powerful of Judah as beyond salvation. He even declares with strong words that their fat will be spilled like dung and their silver and gold will not save them (verses 1:17-18). Zephaniah's hope rests on the 'humble of the land' who follow God's commands and law. For one moment he doubts whether even this will be satisfactory for God to spare but a few righteous people, saying 'Perhaps you will find shelter' although his hesitation about the survival of ta remnant of the people of Judah is removed in Chapter 3. Zephaniah was a nationalist prophet who believed in the salvation of 'the remnant of Israel' which he described as 'poor, humble, purified by the future calamities' (verses 3:12-13).

Zephaniah's final words address future generations when he prophesized in 3:15

> 15. The LORD has annulled the judgment against you,
> He has swept away your enemies.
> Israel's Sovereign the LORD is within you;
> you shall fear calamities no more.
> Zephaniah 3:15

After self-examination, the regretful one's heart and mind are reconciled with God, and he regains strength by God's healing power. He is reborn and free of anxiety or depression. There is no more reason for shame. Moreover, shame is replaced by praise by those who ashamed you! Verse 3:20 is the closing verse of the book: 'For I will make you renowned and famous among all the peoples on earth, when I restore your fortunes before their very eyes.'

---

1. Carchemish, on the Euphrates River, was then the temporary capital of the Assyrians after they had lost their capital Nineveh in 612 BC and the first relocated capital Harran, lost in 609 BC.

Haggai

Reading 37   *The returned exiles repent and rebuild the House of the Lord.*

Haggai 1:7-15
7. This said the LORD of Hosts: Consider your ways:
8. Go up the hills and search for timber and rebuild the House; then I will take pleasure in it and I will be glorified, said the LORD.
9. You have been expecting a lot but got little; and when you brought it home, I would blow on it! Why? asked the LORD of Hosts. Because of My House which lies waste, while you take only care of your own houses!
10. That is why the skies above you have withheld their dew and the earth has withheld its crops,
11. and I have called for a drought upon the land—upon the hills, upon the corn and wine and oil, and the earth withheld its produces, upon man and cattle, and upon all the labor of your hands.
12. Zerubbabel son of Shealtiel and the high priest Joshua son of Jehozadak and all the remnant of the people listened carefully to the summons of the LORD their God and to the words of the prophet Haggai, when the LORD their God sent him; the people feared the LORD.
13. Then spoke Haggai, the LORD's messenger, fulfilling the LORD's mission, to the people, "I am with you—declares the LORD."

THE BOOK OF HAGGAI is another very short book of the Old Testament, consisting of only two chapters and 38 verses. A decree of the Persian King Cyrus the Great in 539 BC had allowed the Jewish exiles of Babylonia and Assyria to return to their home country which is recorded in the Book of Ezra. King Cyrus ordered the exiles, who wanted to return, to rebuild the

Temple of Jerusalem while the exiles, who chose to remain in Babylonian exile, were asked by the Persian king to support the rebuilding of the temple with donations. The Persian king himself released the vessels of the Temple of Jerusalem which the Babylonian King Nebuchadnezzar had taken away from Jerusalem after the fall of the city (Ezra 1:2-8). The Book of Haggai begins in the second year of King Darius (550-486 BC), a successor of King Cyrus and the third king of the Persian Achaemenid Empire.[1]

Nothing is known about the prophet Haggai, except for what is written in the Book of Haggai. All his prophecies were done in the last four months of 520 BC according to the Book of Haggai. The LORD first spoke to Haggai by expressing His displeasure that the returned exiles were building nice houses for themselves while His House was still in ruins. He then referred to the failed harvests of Judah which were caused by Him as a warning. The leaders and the people, when hearing the message of Haggai, immediately felt remorse and feared the LORD. The response of immediate regret is in marked contrast to the fruitless efforts of the prophets Jeremiah and Amos. However, this time the Babylonian captivity and the downfall of Jerusalem served as a vivid reminder in the post-exilic period that God was just and would punish those who neglected His calls through the prophets. Now the people were responsive and listened to God.

The message of Haggai is a warning that material wealth and regained freedom are not enough to expect a secure and prosperous future. Without a place for God in their hearts, the country risked curses instead of blessings. Only when the people recognized God in their midst, the LORD would give His blessings: 'The glory of this latter House shall be greater than that of the former one, said the LORD of Hosts; and in this place I will grant peace—declares the LORD of Hosts.' (Haggai 2:9). After the people had repented, the LORD roused the spirit of the leaders and the people. They came together and speeded up their work on the House of the LORD. This serves as another lesson for all future generations. Those who seek the LORD will feel their spirit lifted, and they know that the spirit of the LORD is in their midst. They will not fear (Haggai 2:5). A spirit of defeat is a sign on the wall that we are disconnecting from God. Finally, the LORD makes His greatest promise after we have reconnected with Him: 'I am with you!' (Haggai 1:13).

---

1. King Darius tried to subjugate Greece but was ultimately stopped by the Battle of Marathon in 490 BC. This landmark battle is the start of the demise of Persia which ended with the decisive victories of Alexander the Great.

Zechariah

Reading 38   *Humanity is not inherently evil and can cleanse itself from its mistakes.*

Zechariah 3:1-5
1. He further showed me Joshua, the high priest, standing before the angel of the LORD, and the Accuser standing at his right to accuse him.
2. But the angel of the LORD said to the Accuser, "The LORD rebuke you, O Accuser, may the LORD who has chosen Jerusalem rebuke you! For this is a brand plucked from the fire."
3. Now Joshua was clothed in filthy garments when he stood before the angel.
4. The latter spoke up and said to his attendants, "Take the filthy garments off him!" And he said to him, "See, I have removed your guilt from you, and you shall be clothed in priestly robes."
5. Then he gave the order, "Let a pure diadem be placed on his head." And they placed the pure diadem on his head and clothed him in priestly garments, as the angel of the LORD stood by.

ZECHARIAH IS A CONTEMPORARY of Haggai (Reading 37) and both prophets encouraged the rebuilding of the Temple of Jerusalem, the resettlement of Babylonian exiles in Judah and an embrace of a new nationalistic spirit with visions of a bright future for the Jewish people. The first verse of the first chapter makes an exact dating of the Book of Zechariah possible, namely in 520 BC. Two decades earlier the first group of Babylonian returnees had arrived in Judah and started rebuilding their lives there. Before embarking on the explanation of the major elements of national reconstruction, the prophet Zechariah starts with a call to reconcile with God. The calamities of the northern and southern kingdoms and the destruction of the Temple of Jerusalem were seen as the inevitable outcome of ungodly behavior by the forefathers. They had not really embraced God in their lives while their religious practices were at best ritualistic and conformist. In verse 3 above, Zechariah portrays God as waiting for the people to return to Him. It only requires an answer by the people to return to God.

The Book of Zechariah contains eight visions which the prophet received for one night. In the fourth vision Zechariah saw Joshua, the high priest, standing with filthy clothes before the angel of the LORD, and the Accuser standing at his right to accuse Joshua. A judicial proceeding before God as the Judge is suggested. The filthy clothes symbolize the defilement of Joshua because of transgressions in his life. The Accuser, as the personification of evil and called Satan, uses every rational argument with the mischievous purpose of misrepresenting and debasing the person who is accused. Otherwise said, the Accuser brings forward false accusations by distorting the portrayal of the actual situation. In some Bible translations, the Accuser in Zechariah 3:1 is translated as Satan. The misrepresentation by the Accuser rests on the premise that no man is without sin or fault and thus unworthy to stand before God. The fact that the high priest, who is the religious leader of the people in that time, is accused of sins necessarily implies an accusation against humanity. Very surprisingly, the high priest doesn't plead in his favor but stands silently. But the angel of the LORD comes to his defense and says to the Accuser: 'The LORD, Who has chosen Jerusalem, rebuke you, O Accuser; The angel said to his attendants, 'Take the filthy garments off him!' and said to Joshua, 'See, I have taken away your guilt from you, and you shall be clothed in priestly garments.' Since the angel acts on the commandment of the LORD, the new garments symbolize God's will to take away the guilt of Joshua and of humanity. However, the angel of the LORD gave the following instruction to Joshua: 'Thus said the LORD of Hosts: If you walk in My ways and keep My charge, and rule My house and keep My courts, then I will allow you to move among these attendants. Hear now, O High Priest Joshua, you and your fellow priests sitting before you!' Zechariah's vision is a warning against any grave misrepresentation of humanity as inherently corrupt and evil and thus not worthy to exist. Notwithstanding the mistakes and failures, humanity will be save if it regrets and corrects itself with a reconnection to God, the eternal source of perfection. Moreover, Zechariah also teaches that misrepresentations and false accusations against a person are character assassinations and therefore satanic acts of evil like the Accuser did regarding humanity. King David repeatedly suffered under the injustice of false accusations and wrote in Psalm 109:1-5 about this painful experience.

1. O God of my praise,
do not remain silent,
2. for the wicked and the deceitful
Have opened their mouth against me;
they have spoken against me with lying tongues.
3. With words of hate they surround me;
they attack me without cause.
4. They meet my love with accusation
and I must stand judgment.
5. They repay me with evil for good,
with hatred for my friendship.
Psalm 109:1-5

Finally, the Book of Zechariah contains repeated warnings not to behave like the fathers or else to make the same mistakes which would only lead to further calamities.[1] Usually, the fathers are portrayed as an example to follow by the children and grandchildren. This is not the case in Zechariah's prophecy. The present generation should look to God, forget the past and the transgressive practices of their forefathers, and rebuild their lives and the Temple of Jerusalem as the House of the LORD. In a way, Zechariah tells the people and the leadership that they are in the year zero in which everything must be reconsidered. Only a new start with God could erase the traumatic experiences of the past.

---

[1]. The same exceptional warning not to follow the example of the forefathers is given in Psalm 78:8. '... and not be like their fathers, a wayward and defiant generation, a generation whose heart was inconstant, whose spirit was not true to God.' And in Jeremiah 44:9 'Have you forgotten the wicked acts of your forefathers...'

Malachi

Reading 39 *All the nations shall account you happy because you returned to Me.*

Malachi 3:6-12

6. I have not changed for I am the LORD; and you are the children of Jacob, you have always been.

7. From the days of your forefathers you have turned away from My commandments and have not kept them. Return to Me, and I will return to you, said the LORD of Hosts. But you ask, "How shall we turn back?"

8. Shall a man rob God? Yet you rob Me. And you ask, "How have we been robbing You?" In tithe and offerings.

9. You are cursed with the curse, yet you go on robbing Me, even the whole nation.

10. Bring the full tithe into the storehouse so that there is food in My House, and thus put Me now to the test, said the LORD of Hosts. I will surely open the clouds of the sky for you and pour out blessings on you;

11. and I will devour the insects from you, so that they will not destroy the fruits of your soil; and your vines in the field shall no longer dwindle away before their time, said the LORD of Hosts.

12. And all the nations shall call you happy, for you shall be the most delightful land, said the LORD of Hosts.

THE BOOK OF MALACHI is the last book of the twelve Minor Prophets and the last book of the prophets, the Nevi'im. It was written around 450 BC when the walls of Jerusalem and the Temple were already rebuilt. The book marks the time of the closing of the Sacred Scriptures (the canonization) and the start of the long process of their canonization. It coincides with the end of the Persian period and the beginning of the Hellenistic period with the sweeping conquests of Alexander the Great (356 to 323 BC). The prophet Malachi criticized the priests for not faithfully serving the LORD in the Temple and the people for their immoral conduct.

The people complained how God had shown His love for them in the past and asked where the God of justice is in their days. This questioning amounted to a rebellion and the rejection of the notion of a just and loving God. In the Book of Malachi, the people even accused God that those who did evil were rewarded by God: 'All who do evil are good in the sight of the LORD.' (Malachi 2:17). God replied to the skeptical remarks of the people by raising the question in Malachi 2:10 'Have we not all one Father? Did not one God create us?' In the citation above, God confirms that He still loves the people. In verse 3:7 God acknowledges that, from the beginning of the covenantal relationship, there has been a recurrent tendency to turn away from Him although He steadfastly repeated that there is always a possibility to return to Him. God's answer is straight and easy: if we turn back to Him, He promises to turn back to us (verse 3:7). We may say that the process of reconciliation is initiated with our step back to God who will favorably respond to us.

When the people asked how they could return to Him, He answered that the people should honor Him by giving 'the full tithe'. In the time of Malachi, the full tithe were the sacrificial offerings in the Temple, usually in the form of agricultural products or animals. Today these offerings represent the time and attention we give to God during our life. If we do this, God promises to open the floodgates of the sky and to pour down blessings on us (verse 10), meaning that God promises to give more to us than we can ever give to Him. How does God give His blessings? The blessings can be material wealth and prosperity, as the Israelites hoped for, but they always work towards spiritual and personal enhancement. The true nature of the blessings is the daily awareness that we have an intimate relationship with God who will care about us. Even in a time of greatest need and distress, we can trust in Him, our Father. Psalm 62:8-9 testifies to the promise of this blessing.

> 8. I count on God, my deliverer and glory,
> my rock of strength;
> in God is my refuge.

9. Trust in Him at all times, O people;
pour out your hearts before Him;
God is our refuge.
Psalm 62:8-9

Part III

THE WRITINGS

Psalms

Reading 40   *A plea for forgiveness and protection from enemies*

Psalm 6:1-11

1. For the leader; with instrumental music on the *sheminith*. A psalm of David.

2. O Lord, do not punish me in Your anger,
do not chastise me in Your wrath.
3. Have mercy on me, O Lord, for I languish;
heal me, O Lord, for my bones shake with terror.
4. My soul is stricken with anxiety,
while You, Lord—O, how long?
5. Return, O Lord, return! Save me!
Rescue me as befits Your faithfulness.
6. For the dead cannot praise You
in Sheol, who can laud You?

7. I am weary with my groaning;
every night I soak my bed in sweat,
I melt away my couch with tears.
8. My eyes are weakened because of vexation,
worn out because of all my adversaries.
9. Leave me, all you evildoers,
for the Lord listened to the sound of my weeping.
10. The Lord has heard my plea,

the LORD accepts my prayer.
11. All my enemies will be ashamed and stricken with terror;
they will suddenly turn back, frustrated.

KING DAVID IS ONE of the most inspiring persons of the Old Testament. We know much about his life and character thanks to the two books of Samuel, the books of 1 Kings and 1 Chronicles as well as 73 Psalms that are attributed to him. For many good reasons, the 150 Psalms or songs of praise are widely used ever since Temple times when they were sung as a hymn or a poem song to the accompaniment of a stringed instrument.[1] The beauty and strength of the Psalms shine in their thoughts and emotions rather than stanza or rhyme, giving them a direct touch. They are addressed to God, not to men, creating an intimate sphere of communion with God. Moreover, the spontaneous flows of thoughts and emotions are written in concise verses in which every word has a special purpose; not a single unnecessary word is used. The open format of the Psalms gives the Psalms a suppleness and simplicity which make them easily accessible to very different audiences throughout time. And because the Psalms express thoughts and emotions rather than form, little is lost in translation. The Psalms are the best examples of how to pray, confirming trust in God as the ultimate source of protection, expressing regret for mistakes and seeking forgiveness.

In the Psalms we see David as a man who was aware of God's presence in every aspect of his life, anytime. He was anxious not to lose the divine presence and prayed regularly for confirmation of God's presence and favor. Although he was a king, he remained humble and saw himself in the first place as a servant of the LORD; he used very frequently the words 'Your servant'. The Psalms speak vividly to us today because we can easily empathize with David who is not portrayed as a superhuman or distant ruler. He suffered, he had desires, he transgressed, he was persecuted but was able to re-examine himself sincerely and with a contrite heart. He hoped to save his disorderly family through the many tribulations, even a rebellion by Absalom, one of his many sons.[2] David became a refugee several times in his life, even when he was the king, yet he persevered and never doubted that God would come to his rescue. This firm belief kept him alive through all turbulent times until he died at an old age. Another great quality

---

1. The Greek translation of 'Mizmor' or מִזְמוֹר (song of praise) is ψαλμός (psalmos) from which the English name Psalm is derived. Sometimes the collection of psalms is called the Psalter.

2. Absalom was his son with Maacah daughter of King Talmai of Geshur; for the list of David's sons, see 1 Chronicles 3:1-9.

of David was his integrity, deeply honest in his actions and straightforward. He was aware that you cannot fool the LORD for he knew that the LORD investigates the heart and soul of men; nothing can be hidden. God is not impressed by outward appearances.[3] The importance of personal integrity is articulated in Psalm 37:37 'Mark the blameless, note the upright, for there is a future for the man of integrity.'

Psalm 6 is often called a 'Psalm for healing' because in Verse 3 David calls to God 'Heal me, O LORD, for my bones shake with terror.' Although we do not know whether he was physically ill, it is without doubt that he had a troubled mind for two opposing reasons. On the one hand he was afraid that he had erred and made transgressions which were displeasing the LORD. The rebuke by the prophet Nathan was still fresh in his mind (Reading 21). On the other hand, he felt threatened by his enemies who still opposed his kingship after he had succeeded King Saul.[4] The essence of Psalm 6 deals with these opposing feelings and possible ramifications. He is caught between two life-threatening conditions, namely the possible severe chastisement by God and the real danger of an ongoing rebel campaign against him. David shows how an integer man should act in such a desperate situation. The first verses are addressed to God with an appeal not to punish him severely for his transgressions. He was aware that the LORD might even use his enemies as an instrument to punish him.[5] His plea not to chastise him in fury is a plea for a moderate chastisement like a father would discipline his children with the intent not to destroy them but to improve them. In a later time, Jeremiah will make the same plea when he asks, 'Chastise me, O LORD, but in measure; not in Your wrath, or You reduce me to nothing.' (Jeremiah 10:24). David then entreated God with the acknowledgment that his energy was ebbing away like a sick man who is exhausted. He proceeded with the cry that he already waited a long time for God's rescue ('O LORD, turn! Rescue me!').

David was waiting for God with sincere regret for his mistakes and asked God to turn to him. This movement captures the mind of regret, namely a return to God and the expectation that God will answer by turning to the repentant. When God will turn to the repentant is a matter of God's choice alone although for David God's turn could not be fast enough '... while You, LORD—O, how long!'.

3. See 1 Samuel 16:7.

4. 2 Samuel 3:1 mentions that the war between the House of Saul and the House of David was long-drawn.

5. From time-to-time God used enemies of the Israelites to punish them for their transgressions. For example, during David's life King Saul was defeated and killed on the battlefield by the Philistines, the enemies of Israel (1 Samuel 31).

One final argument was put forward: please let me not perish but let me continue to be Your servant, since a dead servant can no longer serve God (verse 6). Once David had shown his faithfulness and admission of guilt to God, he confronted the second danger of his many enemies. In verses 7 and 8 he complained to God that his enemies caused sleepless nights, drenching his couch in tears, and making his eyes wasted by vexation. Such mental suffering paralyzed his dynamic and held him in bed as a sick and depressive man. Though, after letting known his bad condition, David regained trust in God and His rescue which is most visible in verse 9. It restored his self-confidence, and he is now convinced that the LORD will heed his plea and accept his prayer.

Psalm 6 concludes with the hope that his enemies will be frustrated and will finally give up their malice practices. After having read and understood Psalm 6 we may say that there was no moral equivalence between the transgressions of David and the unrelenting hate campaign of his enemies. At least David returned to God, was patient and trusted God's mercy. The same cannot be said about his pursuers and slanderers who continued to conspire against him without any justification except their hunger for power.

Psalm 6 also shows that a person's change of heart and mind becomes much harder to do if he is persecuted by his enemies at the same time. Yes, we are all transgressors, but we should be careful to distinguish between our own mistakes and the mistakes of our enemies against us. When we face this dilemma with integrity in the way David did, we may hope to be healed by God who will take away the troubles of our mind. The integer approach by David excludes any moral equivalence with his enemies who were far more wicked and unrelenting in their destructive actions.

Reading 41 *The decision to acknowledge transgression.*

Psalm 32:1-7

Of David. *A maskil.*

1. Happy is he whose transgression is forgiven,
whose sin is removed.
2. Happy the man whom the LORD does not hold guilty,
and in whose spirit there is no deceit.
3. While I kept silent,
my bones wasted away
from my anxious roaring all day long.
4. For day and night
Your hand was heavily on me;
my strength waned
as in the drought of the summer *Selah.*
5. I acknowledged my sin to You;
I did not hide my guilt;
I said, "I will confess my transgressions to
the LORD,"
and You, You forgave the guilt of my sin. *Selah.*
6. Therefore let every faithful man pray to You
At a time when You are present,
that the rushing turbulent waters
do not engulf him.
7. You are my shelter;
You preserve me from adversity;
You cover me with the joyful sounds of
deliverance. *Selah.*

PSALM 32 IS WRITTEN in a reverse mode. Verses 3 to 5 are the core message of the psalm and represent the first step of regret. They say that the first step in the process of 'teshuvah' is also the most difficult one. Verse 3 evokes the mental pain and vexations when a person keeps his transgression hidden or denies it. Some find it convenient not to think about what they did wrong and go on as if nothing had happened. As a side thought, many transgressions are not even punishable by the laws of a country or can remain unnoticed and unsanctioned. Likewise, a thief always hopes that he will not be caught. All too often pride dictates that we should not acknowledge guilt to ourselves. Finally, humans are creative in devising all kinds of reasons not to acknowledge the reality of a transgression although a not acknowledged transgression is self-deception and it worsens the corruptive effect on a person's integrity. To make things more troublesome, Verse 4 adds another layer to the burden of denial by our awareness that God knows what we do, feel, or think. In David's experience it is as heavy as the hand of God: 'For night and day Your hand was heavily on me'. He went even further by saying that his physical condition was weakened because of the mental burden of his denial. His limbs wasted away, and his vigor waned.

Over some time, David gained the mental strength to confess his transgressions to the LORD and was immediately overwhelmed by the emotion that God had forgiven him that same moment. 'I did not hide my guilt' is in contrast with the exclamation of joy and happiness in the opening verse 1 where it is stated that his sin is removed by God's forgiveness. The forgiveness by God does not take away the factual element of the transgression, but it takes away the negative effects on the transgressor's future, including his mental state. What is irrevocably part of the past cannot be erased but it can be put aside so that the person no longer suffers from his transgressions. Verse 6 depicts the moment of decision to acknowledge guilt as the moment of discovery of sin. Here again, to discover is to reveal although in God's mercy the revelation of the transgression is immediately covered by God's forgiveness.

The joy of verse 1 because of God's forgiveness is dependent on two considerations. First, the forgiven transgressor enjoys God's acquittal like in a divine judgment although God's laws of justice are not comparable to human notions of justice. The LORD also has mercy for us. Secondly, God's forgiveness will only be granted to a man '. . . in whose spirit there is no deceit.' Thus, the transgressor is granted divine forgiveness because he sincerely regretted his wrong action and firmly decided not to repeat such mistake. The joy of verse 1 is repeated in verse 7 by proclaiming that God is my shelter. He will preserve me from further distress caused by my confessed transgressions. The experience of David is again a physical reality when he heard 'joyful sounds of deliverance' around him. We may say that the harpist David was aroused by a musical impulse when he felt relieved from the sickening burden of transgression.

Reading 42   *But I wait for You, O Lord.*

Psalm 38:1-23
A psalm of David. *Lehazkir.*

2. O LORD, do not punish me in fury;
do not chastise me in wrath.
3. For Your arrows have struck me;
Your hand has come down on me.
4. There is no soundness in my flesh because of
Your outrage,
no health in my bones because of my sin.
5. For my wrongdoings have overrun me;
they are like a heavy burden, too heavy for me.
6. My wounds stink and fester
because of my foolishness.
7. I am all bent and bowed;
I walk mourning all day long.
8. For my loins are filled with fever;
there is no soundness in my flesh.
9. I am benumbed and crushed;
I groan because of the vexation of my mind.
10. O LORD, You are aware of all my desires;
my groaning is not hidden from You.
11. My mind reels;
my strength fails me;
the light in my eyes has gone.
12. My friends and companions keep a distance from my
affliction; my kinsmen stand far off.
13. Those who seek my life lay in ambush;
those who wish me harm speak with hate;

they utter deceit all the time.
14. But I became a man who cannot speak, I do hear not
and I am as a dumb man who cannot find words;
15. I am like one who does not hear,
who has nothing to say.
16. But I wait for You, O LORD,
until You will answer, O LORD, my God.
17. Without You I fear they will rejoice over me;
when my foot gives way they will boast
against me.
18. For I am on the verge of collapse;
and I am always in pain.
19. I acknowledge my transgressions;
I am fearful over my guilt;
20. for my enemies are forceful;
my treacherous foes are many.
21. Those who repay evil for good
are my adversaries for acting justly.

22. Do not abandon me, O LORD;
my God, be not far from me;
23. hasten to my aid,
O LORD, my deliverer.

THE OPENING VERSE 2 of this psalm is almost identical to the opening verse of Psalm 6 (Reading 40). Both psalms begin with an expression of fear for God's punishment and end with a plea for protection from enemies. Even more than in Psalm 32, Psalm 38 deals in stark images of sickness and sums up David's medical condition by a list of symptoms: a low level of energy, stinking and festering wounds, walking in a depressive mood, inflamed ligaments, turmoil in the mind, weakened eyes, deafness, dumbness, and pain. David attributes his illnesses to his transgressions of the past for which he is now chastised by God. He confesses twice his transgressions to God: '…my wrongdoings have overrun me' (verse 5), and '. . . I acknowledge my transgressions; I am fearful over my guilt' (verse 19). He feels the bodily pain of this punishment as a wounded soldier: 'For Your arrows have struck me; Your hand has come down on me' (verse 3). His wounds fester and stink because of the folly of his transgressions (verse 6). Since the psalm does not mention the transgressions acknowledged by David, they will always remain a secret between David and God. Other psalms, for example Psalm

51 and 2 Samuel contain a similarly unreserved acknowledgment of transgression by David.

The openness and directness in the acknowledgment of transgression is very uncommon for a king in the ancient world and they prove David's moral integrity and deep faith. His troubled mind causes physical illnesses to such a degree that he complains there is no soundness in his flesh, that he feels benumbed and crushed (Verses 8 and 9). This lowest condition is in contrast with David's youth when he was a hero warrior who defeated Goliath in a personal combat after nobody else dared to take on this giant enemy.

In Psalm 38 David is also afflicted by social isolation. His friends and companions now shun his company and offer no solace. Even his kinsmen have abandoned him. How often does it not happen that a valiant man is abandoned in a time of great distress or adversity? Especially when he is attacked by enemies, friends and kinsmen may avoid taking sides and flee. However, the story of a man's affliction is always a test of the social soundness and cohesion around him. If friends and relatives lack moral courage to come to the aid, the moral fabric of society unravels, and even more troubles will show up for all those involved. In this kind of social isolation David further complains that his enemies continue to defame him with false accusations and can do this with impunity because he cannot even defend himself against such unrelenting hate (Verse 13). Contrary to David's attitude, his enemies are remorseless and unrelenting. Again, he uses physical images to describe his defenseless position: he is like a deaf man, like one who cannot speak, who has no retort on his lips (Verses 14 and 15).

Abandoned by friends and his own family, under attack by his enemies, David returns to his inner self—which is the image of God created in us—and addresses himself to God with the words 'But I wait for You, O LORD; until You will answer, O LORD, my God.' (Verse 16). David has a long-time personal relationship with God—he repeatedly says 'my God'—and he knows that God will answer according to His timing. When God will answer is not known but David has patience. Nobody, in whatever circumstance, can demand that God must answer immediately. It proves David's deep understanding that God always acts according to His will and plan, so David shows patience as he did on many other occasions. Arguably, Verse 16 is the most critical verse of the entire psalm by the firm belief that God will answer if we are patient. Waiting for God can be a hard experience for many people, but not so for David. Perhaps for this reason David was very much liked by God who showed him favor and protection during his long life.

Reading 43   *Teach me wisdom about secret things so that I do not stumble.*

Psalm 51:1-16

For the leader. A psalm of David,
2. when Nathan the prophet came to him after he had come to Bathsheba.

3. Have mercy on me, O God,
according to Your mercy;
according to Your abundant compassion,
blot out my transgressions.
4. Wash me thoroughly of my iniquity,
and cleanse me from my sin;
for I recognize my transgressions,
and my sin is ever before me.
6. Against You alone I have sinned,
and done what is evil in Your sight;
so You are just in Your sentence,
and right in Your judgment.
7. Truly I was born in iniquity;
in sin my mother conceived me.
8. Indeed You desire truth about the inward parts;
teach me wisdom about the intimate things of the heart.

9. Purge me with hyssop till I am clean;
wash me and I shall be whiter than snow.
10. Let me hear joy and gladness;
let the bones You have crushed rejoice.
11. Hide Your face from my sins;

and blot out all my iniquities.
12. Create me a clean heart, O God;
and renew a steadfast spirit within me.
13. Do not cast me out of Your presence,
or take Your holy spirit away from me.
14. Let me again rejoice in Your rescue;
and let a vigorous spirit uphold me.
15. Then I will teach transgressors Your ways,
and sinners shall return to You.

16. Deliver me from bloodguilt,
O God, God, my deliverer,
that I may sing aloud Your righteousness.

PSALM 5, A SONG accompanied by instruments, is regarded as the penitential psalm *par excellence* because of the many striking metaphors connected to the feeling of guilt and remorse. The opening words in Greek are 'Kyrie eleison' ('Κύριε, ἐλέησον') and in Latin 'Miserere mei, Deus'. Psalm 51 has been used in the history of music, e.g. Orlande de Lassus's 'Psalmi Davidis poenitentiales' of 1584 (the fourth psalm), Gregorio Allegri's 'Miserere mei, Deus' (1638), Heinrich Schütz's 'Erbarm dich mein, O Herre Gott' of 1628 and revised in 1661 (SWV 148), or Johann Sebastian Bach's 'Tilge, Höchster, meine Sünden' of 1743 (BWV 1083). It proves the everlasting appeal and recognition of the emotional depth of Psalm 51. Even after several thousands of years, Psalm 51 comes in a fresh, straight way to the reader or listener, without restraint or shyness. It is the more remarkable since here spoke a king, not a commoner, who confessed his transgressions openly by means of the psalm ('mizmor').

Behind the psalm is the story of David's greatest transgression, namely his adultery with Bathsheba in combination with the concealed plan for the murder of Bathsheba's husband Uriah (Reading 21). The prophet Nathan is sent by God to rebuke David for his bloodguilt and felony, not the adultery itself. The punishment for intentional homicide was the death penalty in his time[1] (see Genesis 9:5-6). David does not deny his crime but confesses

---

1. There is no bloodguilt incurred in the exercise of the right to self-defense (Exodus 22:1), in an execution implementing a death sentence warranted by a competent tribunal (Leviticus 20:9-16) or in war operations (1 Kings 2:5-6). However, God announced that He did not want David to build the Temple because he had fought too many battles and shed too much blood—see 1 Chronicles 22:7-8—'David said to Solomon, "My son, I wanted to build a House for the name of the LORD my God. But the word of the LORD came to me, saying, "You have shed much blood and fought great

and asks for forgiveness. After his immediate confession Nathan told David that the LORD has forgiven his sin and that he shall not die (2 Samuel 12:13). However, there is a punishment looming over his family by means of a calamity against David from within his own house and the death of the first son born to him and Bathsheba. Although Psalm 51 is the prototype of a penitential psalm, it ends with joy by the knowledge that his transgression is forgiven and that he will not die. David realizes that God wants him to live by sending the prophet Nathan who shows him the way to change.

Psalm 51 opens with a cry for mercy, an attribute of God for mitigating the harsh punishment that is reasonably expected for such a crime. God is also a compassionate God Who knows that man is prone to corruption due to man's evil inclination. David is not spared from the faulty human nature, but he seeks pardon for his uncontrolled passion and sexual desire that made him stumble. Although he acknowledges to deserve a severe punishment, David calls on God's compassion and mercy. He asks a special favor and admits that his judgment was impaired by his unguided desires. He wishes that he had never committed such transgression and now pleads that any trail of it would be wiped off, '. . . blot out my transgressions'. Cleansing away impurities is deeply rooted in Jewish religious thought (Readings 5 and 6 related to 'kipper'). The metaphor used here is washing thoroughly of his iniquities (verse 4), an expression normally used for the laundry of clothes. However, there is more in this verse than just washing of clothes.[2] He prays that his soul might be washed and cleansed of any stain. To purify him from transgression is to remove it out of his life because if sin is attached to a person there is an increased risk of transgressing again. Once a thief has committed a theft it becomes easier for him to commit the same crime again in the future. Sin transgresses a line that should not be crossed, and without regret and the blotting out of the sinful root there will always be a risk of repeating the same mistake.

The purification ('kipper') is repeated in Verse 9: 'Purge me with hyssop till I am pure; wash me till I am whiter than snow.' Psalm 51 adds an element of realism in David's request by admitting that he is and always will be conscious of his transgressions (Verse 4). In the eyes of God, he can be thoroughly washed and become pure again, but he will never be able to forget his wrongdoings which serve as a kind of living warning. From now on David will take any necessary precaution neither to transgress again nor let him bring in a situation that his evil inclination sees an opportunity

---

battles; you shall not build a House for My name for you have shed much blood on the earth in My sight."

2. After the death of his first-born child with Bathsheba David bathed and anointed himself, and he changed his clothes (2 Samuel 12:20).

to seduce him again in wrongful conduct. He further accepts that he had sinned against God alone because he was God's anointed king with the responsibility to give the upright example to his co-citizens. In the following move, the psalm recognizes God as the Supreme Judge whose judgments are always right and undisputable (Verse 6).

In the development of Jewish thought, the idea of God as the Supreme Judge is further highlighted in the theme of the 'Day of the LORD' when God will judge every person, dead or alive—see above Joel (Reading 29) and Zephaniah (Reading 36) and righteousness is one of the attributes of God in His self-revelation (Reading 4). David pleads that further chastising him is not necessary to open his eyes for his transgressions because he is now fully aware of his shortcomings. Then David returns to the subject of his uncontrolled passion and sexual desires, the reason for his misconduct, and remarks that he was conceived by his mother in the heat of passion inherent in the sexual act. This kind of arousal and heat of passion will always be part of a person's life and an everlasting challenge. In his way David argues that the sexual drive is more understandable than other crimes such as murder, arson, theft, or assault. Taking this into consideration, he is aware that his crime of passion had very damaging results for the persons around him, in the first place Bathsheba, Uriah and his first-born son with Bathsheba. Moreover, as a king he discredited the position of his kingship and disappointed his citizens who expect their leader to give the example of a righteous life. Conscious about the many ramifications of his inability to effectively control his passions, David then asks for help of the LORD. In Verse 12 David pleads for replacing his passion of the heart by a pure heart and a steadfast spirit.

In Verse 8 he acknowledges that God seeks truth about the passions inside a man ('that which is hidden')—including his sexual conduct—and he asks the LORD '. . . to teach wisdom about secret things.'[3] In a general sense this is a question for help to maintain his personal integrity, even related to things that are part of his private life. The answer of God comes with the words of the prophet Nathan: 'You acted in secret, but I will make this happen in the sight of all Israel and in broad daylight.' God's warning here is that even private wrongdoings will see the daylight and be revealed in one way or another. Thus, righteousness must prevail so that there is no deceit. The beautiful metaphors continue with Verse 9 where David asks

---

3. Rashi commented as follows on the expression 'that which is hidden' of verse 8: 'The hidden places are the reins, which are smooth. Menachem (page 97), however, associated it with "as it were a bowshot" (Genesis 21:16); and so Job 38:36: "Who placed wisdom in the inward parts". And their interpretation is an expression of drawing, for just as a bow is drawn, so is their yearning for knowledge.'

God 'Purge me with hyssop till I am clean; wash and I shall be whiter than snow.' According to Rashi the purification with hyssop refers to the purification of a deceased person and the one who became unclean through contact with a corpse. David's call for purification is followed by another call to gain strength to maintain the standards of a righteous man.

The psalm then proceeds with expressing the lifelong desire of David: 'Do not cast me out of Your presence or take Your holy spirit away from me.' (Verse 13). The greatest fear of David has always been the loss of God's company, the estrangement from God. He realized that he could not live without feeling the divine presence close to him in a personal bond. It is echoed in a more expressive way in Psalm 23:6 'Only goodness and steadfast love shall pursue me all the days of my life, and I shall dwell in the house of the LORD forever.' Psalm 51 continues with the thankfulness of David who promises to become a teacher for others based on his experience of transgression and God's forgiveness so that transgressors can be saved: 'I will teach transgressors Your ways, that sinners may return to You.'

Reading 44   Out of the depths

Psalm 130

A song of ascents.

Out of the depths I call You, O LORD
2. O LORD, hear my cry;
let Your ears be attentive
to my plea for compassion.
3. If You keep a record of sins, O LORD,
Lord, who could stand?
4. You have the power to forgive
so that You may be held in fear.

5. I wait for the LORD;
My soul waits;
and I hope to hear His word.
6. I am more impatient for the LORD
than watchmen for the morning,
yea, more than the watchmen for the morning.

7. O Israel, hope for the LORD;
for with the LORD there is compassion
and with Him is plentiful redemption.
8. And He will redeem Israel from all its
iniquities.

PSALMS 120 TO 134 are songs of ascent, sometimes called songs of steps, songs of degrees or pilgrim songs. According to tradition, the translation 'Songs of Steps' would refer to the fifteen steps that led to the inner section of the Temple courtyard. The Levites would sing these songs when they ascended to this courtyard. The translation 'Pilgrim Songs' would refer to the fact that they were sung by pilgrims on their way to Jerusalem at the Feasts of Tabernacle, Passover, and the Feast of Weeks. However, no historical evidence supports any of these explanations. However, the composition of the fifteen songs makes them well suited to be sung. Psalm 130, 'Out of the dephts' and translated in Latin as 'De profundis', is a penitential psalm that has been used in musical compositions such as Josquin des Prez's 'De Profundis clamavi'(a motet) of 1521, Orlando di Lasso's Psalmi Davidis poenitentiales, part six, of 1584, Johann Sebastian Bach's 'Aus der Tiefen rufe ich zu dir' of 1708 (BWV 131) and 'Aus tiefer Not schrei ich zu dir' of 1724 (BWV 38), Heinrich Schütz's 'Aus der Tiefe' of 1619 (SWV 025) and 'Aus tiefer Not Schrei ich zu dir' (SWV 235), and John Rutters' second movement of his Requiem of 1985. The psalm is also used as a funeral song in general.

Psalm 130 is anonymous and thus not ascribed to David or Solomon. Its indication of 'ascent' is well chosen because the psalm starts with a lamentation on the dire and sinful condition of an individual Israelite and ends with the promise of redemption for the people of Israel. In one sweeping move, the psalm moves in a straightforward way from a very low point to an exaltation and at the same time it expands from one person to the whole people. Psalm 130 is short and deals most poignantly with regret and God's forgiveness. It starts with a feeling of despair and a direct call to the LORD for help. The reason for the despair is an awareness of guilt. Verse 3 makes it clear that no specific transgression is the reason of the despair but the evil inclination of man itself which causes every man and woman to err in life. The psalmist realizes that nobody is blameless and, if a blameless life would be the yardstick of the LORD, nobody would survive. The only option to gain God's help is a call for His mercy and forgiveness and to wait for His answer. Emphasis is now put on the certainty that God will answer if we are waiting for it. The metaphor that the psalmist is more patient than watchmen, combines in one sentence the tension between eagerly waiting for an answer and having the discipline to wait until the night is over. Yet, there is always the certainty that the night will end. 'Looking for the LORD confirms the presence of God in the world, but how and when we will experience His Holy Spirit (Shekhinah in Hebrew) remains unknown and unpredictable. The psalm ends with a call to the people of Israel to look for the LORD with the promise that redemption and steadfast love is the reward. In summary, the psalm begins with darkness and, after a few verses, ends with brightness and light.

Proverbs

Reading 45 *Rely on the wisdom of the Lord.*

Proverbs 3:5-12

5. Trust in the LORD with all your heart,
and do not count on your own understanding.
6. In all your ways acknowledge Him,
and He will show your paths.
7. Do not be wise in your own eyes;
fear the LORD and avoid evil.
8. It will be a cure for your body,
and marrow for your bones.
9. Honor the LORD with your means,
with all your income,
10. And your barns will be filled,
your vats will burst with new wine.
11. My son, do not reject the discipline of the LORD,
do not despise His correction.
12. For whom the LORD loves, He disciplines,
as a father the son in whom he delights.

PROVERBS, JOB, AND ECCLESIASTES are the three books of the Old Testament considered as wisdom writings, a genre that was widespread in the ancient Near East, Mesopotamia, and Egypt.[1] Traditionally wisdom writ-

---

1. Proverbs has striking similarities with the Egyptian 'Instructions of Amenemope' considered to be written between 1300 and 1075 BC. The scribe Amenemope wrote 30 sections of advice for a happy life as instructions for his son.

ings addressed issues of moral conduct, a righteous life, and the meaning of life. Various sections of Proverbs mention multiple authors for this book although King Solomon is the most prominent author who is mentioned in the first 29 sections of the book.[2] 1 Kings 3:5-9 recounts that God appeared to Solomon in a dream at night and asked what to grant him. Solomon answered, 'Grant then Your servant an understanding mind to judge Your people, to distinguish between good and bad.' In legend and tradition Solomon has always been portrayed as a wise king. He was the son and successor of King David and supervised the construction of the First Temple of Jerusalem.

The central theme of Proverbs is mentioned right from the beginning in Verse 1:7: 'The fear of the LORD is the beginning of knowledge; fools despise wisdom and discipline.'[3] Fear of the LORD is understood as reverence for God as the Creator of the universe, to guide our lives according to His revealed words, and to humbly accept and rely on His wisdom and plans. The emphasis on the Creator is repeated in Verse 3:19 'The LORD founded the earth by wisdom; He established the heavens by understanding.' If we understand this invisible truth, we will discover wisdom on how to become or remain a righteous man or woman. A regular reading of the Bible is generally accepted as a necessity to maintain the right mental state. Living according to the sacred book starts with reading it supplemented with clarification and interpretation via other sources, for example contemporary publications about religion and spirituality, older texts, or religious gatherings.

The style of Proverbs is characterized by contrasting the wise man with the fool, leaving not much room for personal change when he regrets. The Sages of the Talmud also had their doubts and considered to exclude Proverbs and Ecclesiastes from the Old Testament because some of their maxims were self-contradictory. In the end they accepted both works as part of the Written Law because of the religious teachings in the books (Talmud, Shabbat 30B). Special attention is thus needed to connect the wisdom sayings in the two books with the words of the entire Bible. An evident connection is found in Jeremiah 9:22 where it is said 'Let not the wise man glory in his wisdom'. Jeremiah clarified this point by underlining the necessity to always return to God and trust Him instead of relying only on one's own talents and knowledge (Reading 26). Another warning against self-perceived wisdom

---

2. Proverbs contains 31 sections. Agur son of Jakeh, man of Massa is named as the author of Section 30 while section 31 is ascribed to Lemuel, king of Massa.

3. Verse 1:7 is repeated in 9:10 'The beginning of wisdom is fear of the LORD, and knowledge of the Holy One is understanding.'

comes from Isaiah 5:21 'Ah, those who are so wise in their own eyes; so complacent in their own judgment!'

Proverbs 3:5 is a call to trust the LORD and not rely on your own understanding alone. In a knowledge-based society, as our society today, strong emphasis is put on understanding through knowledge, education and information gathering. We are used to make our own judgments daily. Indeed, everybody must make up his mind and act according to his knowledge and good judgment. Personal judgment is an inherent human capacity that was given to us by God. Notwithstanding the human capacity for judgment, Proverbs 3:5 warns us not to rely solely on our understanding since the human mind cannot comprehend everything because there is a limitation on human knowledge and capacity to understand. True wisdom is the humility to accept God's wisdom and unrevealed plans with humanity. In this sense Proverbs 3:5 can be seen as a warning not to rely only on our understanding or even the wisdom writings of Proverbs itself. No matter how learned a man may be, he can act as a wise man or a fool, or one day he can be wise while on another day he errs in his judgment. If we are fully aware of the transitory character of life itself, we can only turn to God and seek His advice to guide us through the many phases of life. Self-examination and control over the evil inclination is the real wisdom in this world. Proverbs 3:11 asks us to view the difficult and painful moments in our life as a call of God to return to Him. If He chastises us, He does so because He is like a loving father who rebukes his children so that they develop and live well.

Job

Reading 46 *The self-righteous Job examines himself.*

Job 42:1-6

Job answered the LORD:

2. I know that You can do everything,
that nothing is impossible for You.
3. What obscures counsel without knowledge?
Indeed, I uttered words without understanding
of the things beyond my comprehension, which I did not know.
4. Hear now, and I will speak;
I will ask, and You will teach me.
5. I had heard You with my ears,
but now I see You with my eyes;
6. Therefore, I regret my words and repent,
seeing I am but dust and ashes.

THE BOOK OF JOB is very different from the other books of the Old Testament which assert God's justice as a retributive justice according to which transgressors are punished and righteous ones rewarded. In the Book of Job God's justice is clouded in mystery, even put in doubt. Above all, it raises the question why a righteous person should suffer. There seems to be an apparent lack of justice in human history, and we can often observe that the righteous suffer while the wicked prosper. Many of us know people who were long-time believers but lost their belief in God after they had suffered an enormous personal loss, for example the death of a child. Job could no longer reconcile his belief in a just God after he had suffered a series of serious afflictions. He even concluded that God is not interested in the fate of humans. This view is not far away from the view exposed in many ancient Greek dramas where humans are merely play tools for the gods. Some commentators even contend that the Book of Job represents God as cruel and not interested in the life of humans. Job himself complained about God's apparent lack of justice: 'I cry to You, but You do not answer me; I wait, but You are not involved. You have turned to be cruel to me; with the might of Your hand, You harass me.' (Job 30:20-21).

Job, a very wealthy man with seven sons and three daughters, is put forward as a blameless and upright man who lived in the land of Uz. One day the angels, called 'divine beings', presented themselves before the LORD and the Adversary came along with them. The Adversary is sometimes called the Accuser, another word for Satan (Reading 38). The word 'Adversary' is chosen to underline his intention of debasing humanity and putting it in a bad light. God told the Adversary that there was no one like Job on earth, a blameless and upright man who feared God and shunned evil. The Adversary answered that Job was righteous out of self-interest because he was blessed by God, thereby questioning the real motives of Job's apparent God-loving life. God allowed the Adversary to test Job's disinterested righteousness by taking away all what he had except his life. In a rapid sequence of events Job lost his ten children and all his possessions. Job tore his robe, cut off his hair and threw himself on the ground and worshipped. He said, 'the LORD has given, and the LORD has taken away' (Job 1:21). Then the Adversary inflicted severe inflammations on Job who took a potsherd to scratch himself as he sat in ashes. Yet he did not complain but instead replied to his wife's call to curse God 'Should we accept only good from God and not accept evil?' (Job 2:10).

Next came three adversarial friends of Job, Eliphaz, Bildad and Zophar. They tried to convince him that he must have been punished by God for his transgressions although Job consistently replied that he was blameless. He then asked God 'If I have sinned, what have I done to You, Watcher of men?' and he also asked ,'Why do You not pardon my transgression and forgive my iniquity?' (Job 7:20-21). The three adversarial friends insisted that God did not pervert justice and that Job must have transgressed. Job addressed God again with the question 'If I have sinned, tell me what You charge me with.' (Job 10:2). In a reply to Zophar, Job referred to wicked people who seemed to prosper. 'Robbers live untroubled in their tents, and those who provoke God are secure' (Job 12:6). Job repeated his question to God why he was afflicted to such an unimaginable extent 'How many are my iniquities and sins? Let me know my transgressions and sin. Why do You hide Your face, and treat me like an enemy?' (Job 13:23-24). But Eliphaz said in reply 'Your sinfulness dictates your mouth, so you choose the tongue of the crafty.' (Job 15:5). However, Job persistently denied the arguments of his adversarial friends and called them 'mischievous comforters'. Again, Job said in reply that the wicked live on, prosper and grow wealthy. They did not feel the rod of God. Notwithstanding the many drama's in his life, Job succeeded in maintaining his integrity: 'Until I die I will maintain my integrity. My righteousness is steadfast and will not go away; my heart shall not reproach me as long as I live.' (Job 27:5-6). The three adversarial friends left Job because he thought himself right against God.

Finally, God replied to Job out of a tempest and reminded him that He is the Creator of the universe and omnipotent. He is not under man's judgment, as said with the words 'Would you condemn Me that you may be right?' (Job 40:8). After God's answer Job became fully aware of his unduly held belief of his own righteousness. Compared with God, who is perfect and cannot be fully understood by men, Job considered that he was not more than 'dust and ashes' created into a human being by God—see also Genesis 2:7 ('Then the Lord God formed man from the dust of the ground.') and Genesis 3:19 ('You will turn to dust again.'). A correct awareness of God induces humility and self-examination. Self-righteousness is a transgression for no human is blameless, as David said in Psalm 143:2 'Do not enter into judgment with Your servant, for before You no creature is in the right.' In the end Job regretted that he had questioned God's justice and wisdom and he repented. The LORD restored Job's fortunes when he prayed on behalf of his friends and the LORD gave Job twice what he had before.

The Song of Songs

Reading 47   *Dark but comely*

The Song of Songs 1:1-6

The Song of Songs, by Solomon.

2. Oh, give Him kiss me with the kisses of his mouth,
for your love is better than wine.
3. Your ointments have a sweet fragrance,
Your name is like purest oil –
Therefore do maidens love you.
4. Draw me, let us run!
The king has brought me into his chambers.
Let us enjoy and rejoice in your love,
love is more seducing wine!
They really love you!
5. I am dark, but comely,
O daughters of Jerusalem—
Like the tents of Kedar,
like the curtains of Solomon.
6. Don't glare at me because I am swarthy,
because the sun has tanned me.
My mother's sons were incensed against me,
they made me keeper of the vineyards;
but my own vineyard I did not guard.

THE SONG OF SONGS is a long poem consisting of 117 verses in the form of a dialogue between a young woman and her lover. The title suggests that it is the greatest song of the Bible written by King Solomon according to verse 1:1.[1] The Song of Songs is read entirely on the Sabbath during Passover. The book describes the profound love between a man and a woman who intensely desire the physical pleasures of their intimate relationship. The lover's physical appearance is extolled in many metaphors related to nature and pastoral life. One of the most beautiful verses is Verse 2:3 which illustrates well the sensation of the poem.

> As an apple tree among trees of the wood
> so is my beloved among the sons.
> Under his shadow I delight to sit,
> and his fruit was sweet to my mouth.

The Song of Songs does not contain any explicit reference to God or the covenant between God and His people, so we may wonder why this book was included in the Old Testament. In the first century, Rabbi Akiva said that on the day the Song of Songs was given to the world, the world was not worthy of it. This song was greater than the world itself. He also said 'The entire Old Testament is holy but the Song of Songs is the Holiest of the Holy.' (Mishnah, Yadayim 3:5). Rabbi Akiva saw the Song of Songs as an allegory of God's love for humankind, an interpretation that was immediately adopted by Jewish and Christian traditions.

In the second century, Origen's commentary on the Song of Songs pioneered the interpretation of the Song of Songs allegorically, understanding the Bridegroom as Christ and the Bride as the church or the individual soul. Origen was the best-known theologian of his generation and perhaps the greatest genius of the early church.[2] After him, the Song of Songs was part of an exegetical debate in Carolingian society of the nineth century which was oriented and shaped by the study and interpretation of both the Old Testament and the New Testament. The Carolingian exegetes sought to mold Frankish society according to biblical principles. The early-medieval comments on the Song of Songs brought together the rich imagery of the Song with traditional ideas about the church as mother. Great figures as Bede and Alcuin speculated about the nature of the church and their own position and authority within it.[3] The church and the clergy were depicted

---

[1]. The title has become famous in various languages: שִׁיר הַשִּׁירִים or Šîr Haššîrîm in Hebrew, Ἆισμα Ἀισμάτων (asma asmaton) in Greek, Cantica Canticorum in Latin, Cantique des Cantiques in French, and Hohelied in German.

[2]. John McGuckin, The Westminster Handbook to Origen, Westminster John Knox Press, 2014, p. 25.

[3]. Bede (672-735) was an English monk and one of the greatest teachers and writers during the Early Middle Ages. He is also the father of English history because of

in maternal terms and one of its consequences was the early-medieval articulation of a vocabulary to express clerical authority through the female body, specifically the maternal female body. The comments on the Song of Songs emphasized the beautiful and sensual figure of the Bride as a maternal figure and this imaginary bled over into descriptions of the church and its single class of senior ecclesiastics, the doctors or teachers. It is regarded as a tactic by Carolingian authors to resort to words of 'soft power' to encourage and compel obedience.[4]

However, the most famous catholic comment on the Song of Songs became the 'Sermones in Cantica Canticorum' of Bernard of Clairvaux (1266-1276) consisting of 86 sermons.[5] These are the words written in one of his sermons: "Of what use to me the wordy excessive emotions of the prophets? Rather let him who is the most handsome of the sons of men, let him kiss me with the kiss of his mouth (Song 1:2). Even the very beauty of the angels can only leave me weary. For my Jesus utterly surpasses these in His majesty and splendor. Therefore, I ask Him what I ask of neither man nor angel: that He kiss me with the kiss of His mouth." In our time Stephen Moore raised questions about the Song of Songs from the perspective of the history of sexuality: 'The woman of the Song—and, by extension, woman in general—is symbolically annihilated in the very gesture through which she is idealized. The symbolic world created by these male celibates in their allegorical appropriations of the Song is as free of the polluting presence of real women as the chapterhouse at Clairvaux, an inner sanctum of homosocial sanctity of the literary setting of Bernard's eighty-six sermons on the Song, delivered to an implied audience of women-free men, the minutiae of whose daily lives are so disposed that they are almost never obliged to lay eyes on a flesh-and-blood daughter of Eve.'[6]

Verses 1:5-6 are the allegorical expression of an awareness of past mistakes but with the comforting belief that these mistakes are overcome and forgiven. The young woman, representing the Israelites, confesses that she is blackened because of her mistakes of the past, yet she says that she has become comely after the cleansing of them. Since then, she has been washed

---

his manuscript 'Ecclesiastical History of the English People'. Alcuin (755-804) was a clergyman and teacher from York. He was invited by Charlemagne to lead his newly established Carolingian school at the court. He is considered as the most important intellectual of the Carolingian Renaissance.

4. Hannah Matis, Early-Medieval Exegesis of the Song of Songs and the Maternal Language of Clerical Authority, in: Speculum, 2014, pp. 358-63.

5. Sermones in Cantica Canticorum, Christian Spiritual Growth Books, 2019.

6. Stephen Moore, "The Song of Songs in the History of Sexuality," in Church History, 2000, pp. 339-40.

thoroughly through her regret and change. In their comments on the Song of Songs, the Jewish Sages taught that God said, 'Make an opening for Me like the eye of a needle, and I will open wide for you the gates of heaven.' (Shir Hashirim Rabbah 5:3) The 'daughters of Jerusalem' act like a chorus of like-minded people who are testifying the truthfulness of her words. The 'tents of Kedar' are like the tents of nomadic people in the desert who set up their tents every day, so they became blackened by the weather. Although worn out by wind and sand, the tents are still reliable and protective. This refers to the inner self of humans that is weakened by mistakes, but the soul is capable of protection, restoration, and improvement. The 'tents of Kedar' only need to be cleansed and washed so that they can shine again in the desert sun. It is followed by the expression 'like the pavilions of Solomon' which hold curtains that are richly decorated and always clean. Our soul may be blackened by mistakes but through regret and change we regain our true inner-self and show our purity as the curtains hanging in the building of God. Verse 1:6 is a call, even a negative command, to outsiders not to look at our mistakes of the past which are publicly known ('Don't stare at me because I am swarthy'). We became blackened because of the burning sun. The gazing sun stands for the sun of justice (Malachi 3:20) which uncovers and brings our mistakes in bright light although this is the precondition for the healing process. Only by admitting and exposing our mistakes, we can hope for healing. We reestablish our personal integrity by accepting the sun of justice which is God's power to forgive us and restore our relationship with Him.[7] According to Rashi, the 'mother's sons' are the Egyptians among whom the Israelites grew up. They seduced the Israelites to worshipping false gods such as the Golden Calf at Mount Sinai (Reading 4). Their vineyards I guarded are the false gods or idols of the Egyptians, and the Israelites neglected to keep faith with the LORD, their own vineyard.

---

7. The expression 'sun of justice' gained acceptance in modern European poetry. For example, Odysseas Elytis' 'Το Ἄξιον Εστί' (Axion Esthi, 1959) contains the song with the title 'Της δικαιοσύνης ήλιε νοητέ' (The sun of justice will shine). It has been put on music by Mikis Theodorakis.

Ruth

Reading 48   A change of heart

Ruth 1:11-19

11. But Naomi said, "Turn back, my daughters! Why would you go with me? Have I any more sons in my womb who might be husbands for you?

12. Turn back, my daughters, go your way, for I am too old to have a husband. Even if I thought there was hope for me, even if I had a husband tonight and I also bear sons,

13. should you wait for them till they grow up? Should you shut yourselves off for them and have no husbands? Oh no, my daughters! My lot is far more bitter then yours, for the hand of the LORD has struck out against me."

14. They raised their voice and wept again, and Orpah kissed her mother-in-law farewell. But Ruth cleaved unto her.

15. And she said, "See, your sister-in-law has returned to her people and her gods. Go follow your sister-in-law."

16. But Ruth said, "Do not pressure me to leave you, to turn back and not follow you. Wherever you go, I will go; wherever you lodge, I will lodge; your people shall be my people, and your God my God.

17. Where you die, I will die, and there I will be buried. May the LORD do this, and even more, to me if anything but death parts me from you."

18. When Naomi saw how steadfast she was to go with her, she stopped to argue with her;

19. and the two went on until they came to Bethlehem.

THE BOOK OF RUTH is named after Ruth, the Moabitess who became the great-grandmother of King David.[1] During a famine Elimelech, a citizen of Bethlehem, travelled with his wife Naomi and his two sons, Mahlon and Chilion, to Moab in search for a better life. Elimelech died and Naomi was left with her two sons who married Moabite women, one named Orpah and the other Ruth. Sometime later the two sons also died leaving Naomi without a husband and without her two sons. After the famine and on the road back to Judah, Naomi instructed her two daughters-in-law to return to Moab, their home country. She thought that her daughters-in-law, now widowed, would not be welcomed in Judah because they were foreign women. In that period intermarriage in Judah had become controversial—see Ezra 9:1 (Reading 53) and Nehemiah 13:1 (Reading 54).[2] Orpah heeds the advice and returns to Moab while Ruth disagrees and insists to go with Naomi to Bethlehem in Judah. The story continues with Naomi arranging a Levirate-like marriage between Ruth and Boaz, a close relative of the deceased husband of Naomi who lived in Bethlehem. Out of this marriage a son, Obed, was born. He became the father of Jesse who was in turn the father of David. The women of Bethlehem praised Naomi whose life was renewed by this surprising turn of events. The women also praised Ruth who was regarded as a loving daughter-in-law and better to Naomi than seven sons (Ruth 4:15).

The essence of the Book of Ruth is about a non-Jewish wife (Ruth) who became Jewish by conversion. Ruth remained loyal to her new faith and ideology notwithstanding the discouragement of the contemporary practices and Naomi's instruction to return to her home country Moab and not to convert to the Jewish faith. The conscious turn of Ruth to God was accepted even at the risk of being an outcast in Judah because of her Moabite background. In this context Ruth's change was not the admission of guilt and the expression of remorse but a plea to God for help. It is said that Ruth overcame the Torah laws, as applied in that time, by firmly believing in God's loving kindness that breaks the rigidity of the law. A black letter interpretation of the law cannot break our love for God and His loving kindness. God implicitly but clearly confirmed Ruth's faith by blessing her and her family so much that King David would be born as a descendent of Ruth. The people of Bethlehem approved Ruth's conversion and marriage to Boaz notwithstanding the then ongoing controversy on marriage with someone who was not born Jewish (Ruth 4:11-12)

---

1. The history recorded in the Book of Ruth happened between Joshua and Othniel, the first Judge (Reading 16).

2. For example, Deuteronomy 23:4.

Documenting a dramatic shift in attitude about 'Jewishness', Naomi changed her heart which was to become her 'teshuvah', her regret and change. The story begins with Naomi's bitter complaint about her fate and ends with an exaltation of Naomi's newly found family happiness. The Book of Ruth is a convincing lesson in the power of a change of the heart and the subsequent blessing of God for trusting His loving kindness without regard to our birthplace or origin.

Lamentations

Reading 49   *Take us back, O Lord!*

Lamentations 1:8
8. Jerusalem has grievously sinned,
therefore she is become unclean.
All who honored her despise her,
for they have seen her nakedness;
and she can only sigh
and turn backward.
...

Lamentations 3:31-34

31. For the LORD does not
cast aside forever,
32. Although he first afflicts, then forgives
in His abundant kindness.
33. For He does not afflict without a purpose
or grieve the children of men,
34. Crushing under His feet
all the prisoners of the earth.
...

Lamentations 5:19-22

19. You, O LORD, are enthroned forever,
Your throne is from generation to generation.
20. Why have You forgotten us totally,
and forsaken us for such a long time?

21. Take us back, O LORD, to Yourself,
and let us return;
Renew our days as of old!
22. Indeed, You have totally rejected us,
bitterly outraged against us.

> Take us back, O LORD, to Yourself,
> and let us come back.
> Renew our days as of old!

THE WRITER OF LAMENTATIONS is unknown although tradition ascribes it to Jeremiah. The book is written in the form of a dirge shortly after the destruction of Jerusalem and its First Temple by the Babylonians in 586 BC. It is read entirely during the evening services of the day called 'Tisha b'Av' mourning the destruction of the First and Second Temples in Jewish liturgy. 'Tisha B'Av' falls in July or August according to the Jewish calendar of the year concerned. Lamentations expresses the lowest point in human suffering and catastrophe and for this reason it is appropriate to read it for all catastrophes, for example the Shoah or Holocaust during the Second World War and the expulsion of the Jews from Spain in 1492.

Lamentations pictures the pitiful state of a ruined Jerusalem which is now ruled by her enemies. Her foes rejoiced in her downfall and deported approximately 50,000 men, women, and children or 30 per cent of Judah's population to Babylon. The Judean deportees were the wealthy and professional citizens, the most able of the people. Right from the beginning of the dirge in verse 1:5 Jerusalem's misfortune is explained by her many transgressions, which is repeated in Verse 1:8. God's punishment turned against the city and its citizens for their wicked life, notably idolatry and neglect of the biblical prescriptions. Sadly, Verse 1:9 leaves no doubt that Jerusalem cannot count on compassion or comfort and her immense emotional suffering is brought forward in an outburst of sorrow described in Verse 1:16

> 16. For these things do I weep,
> my eyes flow with tears:
> far from me is any comforter
> who might revive my soul;
> my children are downhearted
> for the foe has prevailed.
> Lamentations 1:16

Despite the catastrophe, the LORD's justice is accepted in Verse 1:18 with the words 'The LORD is in the right, for I have disobeyed Him.' and in Verse 1:20 'My heart is in anguish, I know how wrong I was.' Acceptance of God's justice, in this case a harsh judgment, requires a lot of courage and strength. The writer asks God for equality and divine justice in dealing with the enemies who are even worse than the citizens of Jerusalem; Verse 1:22 pleads that the enemies too would be punished according to the same standard of divine justice: 'Let all their wrongdoing come before You, and deal with them as You have dealt with me.'[1] Lamentations proceeds with the description of the destruction of the city which is seen as God's raging anger against His people. Amidst such utter destruction the Book of Lamentations has confidence in God's grace and kindness to return to His people and restore the good fortunes of the citizens of Jerusalem.

> 21. This do I recall to my mind,
> therefore I have hope:
> 22. The kindness of the LORD has not ended,
> His compassions are not spent.
> 23. They are new every morning -
> Great is Your faithfulness!
> 24. "The LORD is my portion," I say with my soul;
> therefore I will hope in Him.
> Lamentations 3:21-24

Verses 3:31-34 look at the LORD's punishment as a necessary predicament for the future restoration of the people. He afflicts us, then pardons us and finally rebuilds us. Obviously, the Jerusalemites needed a serious warning to change their life. God does not delight in bringing catastrophic events but uses them to cleanse the people from its persistent transgressive behavior. We know that God shows an abundant kindness once we are cleansed and reunited with Him in heart and spirit. Verses 3:31-34 are in the middle of the Book of Lamentations and are the most important message given by the book. God will not crush the prisoners of the earth under His feet for He knows that they are sitting out their punishment and are not condemned to die. Only to make possible a change of heart and spirit was the purpose of their divine punishment. Probably the verse was written to reveal a contrast with the despotic Babylonian King Nebuchadnezzar II who deported Judah and held its people like prisoners in a foreign land when Lamentations was written. Verse 3:40 is an important verse because it urges introspection and self-examination: 'Let us search and examine our ways and turn back to the

---

1. The far greater wickedness of Jerusalem's enemies is again mentioned in verses 3:56-66 with a cry for a deserved divine punishment. As a matter of fact, this happened in 539 BC when Babylon was conquered by the Persian King Cyrus the Great and became a Persian province (satrapy) for one thousand years. Babylon never again regained her independent status and identity.

LORD.' A person who examines his life and deeds will know when to regret, change and return to God. He will protect himself by not making the same transgression again.

'Why have You forgotten us utterly?' of verse 5:20 is a cry out of despair challenging God to make His presence visible by offering help and protection. It is a cry when a man feels abandoned and most vulnerable, when his life is at stake. It is immediately followed by the urgent question of Verse 5:21 'Take us back, O LORD, to Yourself.' The question has been addressed by Eikhah Rabbah 5:21 with these words: "Take us back, O LORD, to Yourself and let us come back" (Lamentations 5:21). The Community of Israel spoke before the Holy One, blessed be He: "Master of the Universe, it depends on You, so 'Take us back to Yourself.'" He said to them: "It depends on you, as it is said (Malachi 3:7) "Turn back to Me, and I will turn back to you" said the LORD of Hosts. The Community of Israel said before Him: "Master of the Universe, it depends on You, as it is said (Psalm 85:5), "Restore us, O God, our helper." Hence it is said: "Turn us to You, O LORD, and we shall be turned." (Eikhah Rabbah 5:21).[2] The rabbis wanted to explain that God and man act together in the process of restoring their relationship. Although God reaches out to mankind, He cannot be sure that man will reach out to Him. Yet, a man, reaching out to God, can be sure of God's indisputably positive response. Man must call to God first before God can help man. Thus, the restoration of the relationship between God and man can only become true if God helps man to turn back to Him. It is the restoration process as vigorously expressed by Lamentations 5:21.

---

2. Lamentations Rabbah is the Midrash on Lamentations and one of the oldest works of the Midrash.

Ecclesiastes

Reading 50 — God will call everyone to account.

Ecclesiastes 1:1-3

The words of Koheleth son of David, king in Jerusalem.

2. Utter futility! said Koheleth
Utter futility! All is futile!
3. What real value is there for a man
for all the work he has done beneath the sun?
...

Ecclesiastes 2:15-16

15. Then I said in my heart:
"The fate of the fool will also be my fate; for which reasons, then, have I been wise?" And I concluded that that too was futile,
16. because the wise man, just like the fool, is not remembered forever; for, as time passes by, both are forgotten. Alas, the wise man dies, just like the fool!
...

Ecclesiastes 12:13-14

13. To summarize: when all is said and done: Love God and observe His commandments! For this applies to all humanity:

14. that God will call every deed to account for everything hidden, whether it be good or bad.

To summarize when all is said and done: Love God and observe His commandments! For this applies to all humanity.

THE TITLE 'KOHELETH' MEANS somebody who convenes an assembly to make an address. Tradition holds that the writer of the book is King Solomon in his old age when he had sorrow after considering his transgressions during his sumptuous life at the royal court. Another example tells that the LORD was angry with Solomon because '... his heart had turned away from the LORD. God decreed the punishment that the kingdom would be split apart after his death (1 Kings 11:9-13). In Chapter 2 of the Book of Ecclesiastes, Solomon sums up the wealth he has amassed during his life and concludes that it is futile. The book even starts with the reflection that all we do or aspire to become is futile. The Book of Job too doubts God's justice (Reading 46) and the Book of Ecclesiastes seems to doubt divine judgment on earth by saying that all men, the righteous and the wicked ones, have the same sad fate:

> That is the sad thing about all that goes on under the sun:
> that the same fate is in store for all.
> Not only that, but men's hearts are full of sadness,
> and their minds of madness,
> while they live; and then ... to the dead!
> Ecclesiastes 9:3

At this point the book comes close to a nihilistic worldview without a place for God's intervention and grace. Although the Book of Ecclesiastes, together with Proverbs and Job, is one of the three wisdom books of the Old Testament, it surprises with the saying in 3:15-16 that wisdom too is futile and that death levels all humans without distinction. It is an irony that King Solomon asked God for the gift of wisdom and was considered the wisest of all men in his time (1 Kings 3:9-10 and 5:9-11), while the same king in the Book of Ecclesiastes would deny the value of wisdom in some of its verses. By repeatedly referring to death as the destruction of all men into nothing, Ecclesiastes borders again along a nihilistic penchant. The subject of regret and change is touched upon in an indirect way throughout Ecclesiastes. Echoing the concluding message from the Book of Job, Ecclesiastes states that there is not one good man on earth who does what is best and doesn't err (Ecclesiastes 7:20). From this follows that man should pay daily attention to his words and deeds and have the courage to change when he becomes aware that he erred. The book goes further by saying that one transgression may obscure much good: 'Wisdom is more valuable than weapons of war, but a single error destroys much of value.' (Ecclesiastes 9:18).

In the end, the Book of Ecclesiastes might surprise us again. The writer calls to revere God and follow His commandments. His addition that it is true for all mankind invites everybody to allow God in daily life, regardless of social origin or ethnicity or any difference. After having doubted the distributive justice of God on earth, Koheleth ends with the statement that God will call every person to account for everything unknown, be it good or bad. Again, the universal call to follow the path of God is underlined, without distinction who is a Jew or not. The Book of Koheleth concludes that God will be the Judge for every person and that a life without God is utterly futile and unfulfilling. Ultimately and after many doubts, the writer believes in divine justice in the World to Come, when the Day of the LORD will arrive (see Book of Joel in Reading 29). In this view divine justice is not necessarily done in earthly life. Perhaps the hidden wisdom of Ecclesiastes is the biblical promise of an eternal life with God after death for those who are written in the Book of Life according to the Jewish belief. It reminds the beautiful Psalm 23 which ends with these verses.

> Only goodness and steadfast love shall pursue me
> all the days of my life,
> and I shall dwell in the house of the LORD
> for ever and ever.
> Psalm 23:6

The promise of eternal life is part of the Christian liturgies with the expression 'unto the ages of ages' which is translated in the Septuagint as "εἰς τοὺς αἰῶνας τῶν αἰώνων" and in the Vulgate as "in saecula saeculorum, Amen".

Esther

Reading 51 — We should not hide who we are.

Esther 4:15-17

15. Then Esther sent back this answer to Mordecai:

16. "Go, gather all the Jews who live in Shushan, and fast in my behalf; do not eat or drink for three days, night or day. I and my maidens will observe the same fast. Then I shall go to the king, although it is contrary to the law; and if I am to perish, I shall perish!"

17. So Mordecai went to the city and did just as Esther had asked him.

…

Esther 9:20-23

20. Mordecai wrote these things, and sent letters to all the Jews across the provinces of King Ahasuerus, near and far,

21. instructing them to observe the fourteenth and fifteenth days of Adar, every year

22. the same day on which the Jews rested from their enemies and the same month which had been turned for them from one of grief and mourning to one of great joy. They were to observe them as days of feasting and merrymaking, and as an occasion for sending gifts to one another and to the poor.

23. Accordingly the Jews assumed as an obligation that which they had begun to practice and which Mordecai had written to them.

THE BOOK OF ESTHER is a book on the astounding rescue of the Israelites in exile from an attempt of extermination. The story is in the reign of the Persian King Ahasuerus, traditionally thought to be Xerxes I (519 to 465 BC).[1] King Ahasuerus divorced from Queen Vashti and asked his courtiers to travel throughout the country in search of a suitable young wife. After many beautiful maidens were brought to court, King Ahasuerus chose Esther. Although Esther was her Persian name, her hidden Jewish name was Hadassah (myrtle). She was told by her foster father Mordecai not to reveal her religion, apparently a minority religion and it is likely that there was animosity in Persia against the Jews. One day, Haman, the recently appointed grand vizier, ordered Mordecai to prostrate before him but Mordecai refused to do so '... for he had explained to them that he was a Jew.' (Esther 3:4). The most credible explanation for Mordecai's refusal is that he knew that Haman held anti-Semitic feelings and he did not want to pay public homage to an anti-Semite.[2] After this incident Haman plotted to take on the Jews. He obtained permission from the king to destroy, massacre and exterminate all the Jews in the country on a specific date. Dispatches were sent to the governors to act accordingly on that day. However, Mordecai heard about this plan, informed Esther, and asked her to put up resistance from within the palace.

Esther's answer is in the quotation of Esther 4:15-17. Before addressing her king-husband, Esther ordered three days of fasting. Her encounter with the king was a momentous event to come, and the decision of Esther was to pray to God first, repenting for things that had gone wrong by mistakes, and pleading for God's intervention for the rescue and the survival of the

---

1. Xerxes I invaded Greece in August 480 BC after he had bridged the Hellespont with pontoons. The first encounter with the Greek army came at the Battle of Thermopylae where a small Greek force under the command of the Spartan King Leonidas fought against the overwhelming Persian army but was defeated. Then the Persian army moved into Greek mainland and captured and destroyed Athens. One month later, at the Battle of Salamis, the Persian fleet was defeated by the Greek fleet under the skillful command of Themistocles. Fearing the destruction of the pontoon bridge and the isolation of his land forces, Xerxes I withdrew its main force to Persia. The remnant of the Persian land forces in Greece was decisively defeated in the Battle of Plataea in 479 BC. Xerxes I was assassinated by Artabanus, the commander of the royal bodyguard, in 465 BC.

2. The Old Testament does not forbid to bow down for another man, except when the gesture is unmistakably the recognition of the supposedly divine nature of the other man. An example of bowing in the Book of Esther is when Esther spoke to the king, falling at his feet and weeping (Esther 8:3). In contrast, the Greeks refused 'proskynesis' (προσκύνησις) which was the traditional Persian act of bowing or prostrating oneself before a person of higher social rank. For the Greeks proskynesis was a sacral act of addressing a deity.

Jewish people in Persia, including herself. Although God is never explicitly mentioned in the Book of Esther, Esther is convinced that the LORD has the power to prevent things to happen or to change the course of history. Moreover, 'teshuvah' is the only possible approach for meeting God face to face, which was well understood by Esther.[3] By fasting, she and her fellow Jews in Shushan made it publicly clear that they were Jews and there was nothing to hide.[4] Not even the dark threat of anti-Semitic genocide could stop them acknowledging God and claiming their religious identity. Esther added that she might perish, and if she was going to die, it was better to put up resistance with a self-assured conscience. She knew that she was fighting for a most noble cause. In honor of her steadfast belief, Judaism has always recognized Esther as one of the seven female prophetesses.

Esther's action made the king change his mind, and Haman was put to death while the Jews won for the first time their public place as Jews in Persian society. The hidden power of 'teshuvah' transformed a moment of grief and sorrow into a festive joy and the event remained an eternal part of the Jewish calendar in the form of the Purim festival. Finally, the phrase '. . . accordingly the Jews assumed as an obligation that which they had begun to practice' (Esther 9:23) means that the Jews in Persia were again committed to God and willing to serve His plans. The impact of this event renewed their faith in God and the practice of the Jewish religion in Persia.

The book of Esther is an important one because it raises the question if we can show our true self. Someone who is honest and truly himself does not fear to show that and people who do not pretend to be someone else are more trustworthy and enjoyable. It requires that we know who we are, that we have examined ourselves and have come to an identity without fear. This quality of self-awareness is our unique personality that sets us apart from the herd and herd behavior. Yet, we also have a private life that protects us from unwanted intrusion or, in extreme circumstances like the persecution of the Israelites in Persia, putting our life in danger.

---

3. As is written in Exodus 33:11 'The LORD would speak to Moses face to face, as one man speaks to another.' However, this is not in a visible form.

4. Shushan or Susa was the place where not only Esther lived during the Babylonian captivity, but also Daniel and Nehemiah.

Daniel

Reading 52 — *Daniel's prayer on behalf of the people, confessing transgressions and seeking forgiveness.*

Daniel 9:1-19

1. In the first year of Darius son of Ahasuerus, a Median, who was made king over the kingdom of the Chaldeans

2. in the first year of his reign, I, Daniel, examined the books regarding the number of years that, pursuant to the word of the LORD had come to Jeremiah the prophet, were to be the time of Jerusalem's desolation: seventy years.

3. I turned my face to the Lord God, in prayer and supplication, with fasting, in sackcloth and ashes.

4. I prayed to the LORD my God and confessed, and said: "O LORD, great and awesome God! You are always faithful to Your covenant with those who love You and keep Your commandments!

5. We have transgressed; we have acted with iniquity; we have acted wickedly; we have rebelled and have turned away from Your commandments and Your orders,

6. and have not listened to Your servants the prophets who spoke in Your name to our kings, our princes, our fathers, and all the people of the land.

7. With You, O LORD, righteousness, and we are ashamed on this very day, on the men of Judah and the inhabitants of Jerusalem, all Israel, near and

far, in all the lands where You have driven them, for the treachery they committed against You.

8. O LORD, we are ashamed, on our kings, our princes, and our fathers, because we have transgressed against You.

9. To the LORD our God belong compassion and forgiveness, for we rebelled against Him,

10. and did not listen to the LORD our God by following His rules that He revealed to us through His servants the prophets.

11. All Israel has transgressed Your rules and turned away, ignoring You; so the curse and the oath written in the commandments of Moses, the servant of God, have been brought down upon us, for we have transgressed against Him.

12. He carried out the warning that He made against us, and against our leaders who ruled us, to bring upon us great hardships; under the whole heaven there has never been done the like of what was done to Jerusalem.

13. Just as is written in the commandments of Moses, all that hardship, came upon us, yet we did not address the LORD our God, did not repent of our iniquities or become knowledgeable through Your truth.

14. Hence the LORD saw our evildoings and was intent on bringing calamity upon us, for the LORD our God is righteous in all that He has done, but we have not listened to Him.

15. Now, O LORD our God who brought Your people out of the land of Egypt with a mighty hand, winning glory for Yourself as at this very day, we have sinned, we have acted wickedly.

16. O LORD, as befits Your abundant kindness, let Your awesome fury turn back away from Your city Jerusalem, Your holy mountain; for because of our sins and the iniquities of our fathers, Jerusalem and Your people have become a reproach to all people around us.

17. O our God, hear now the prayer of Your servant and his supplication, and let show Your shine on Your desolate sanctuary, for the LORD's sake.

18. O my God, incline Your ear, and hear; open Your eyes and see our desolations and the city to which Your name is connected. Not because we deserve to lay our plea before You but because of Your abundant compassion.

19. O LORD HEAR! O LORD, forgive! O LORD, listen, and act without delay for Your own sake, O my God; for Your name is connected to Your city and Your people!"

ALONGSIDE PSALM 51, DANIEL 9 is considered as one of the greatest prayers of the Old Testament confessing transgression and seeking God's mercy and forgiveness. The first part of the Book of Daniel tells the story of a tumultuous Jewish life at the Babylonian court while the last chapters contain apocalyptic visions. The storyteller is Daniel whose name means 'God is my judge'. He and his friends are saved from their enemies at the royal court which confirms God's will to save His people in exile. Chapter 9 is the central part of the book with its first two verses referring to Jeremiah's prophecy that the exile would last 70 years and continued by the return to Jerusalem and the rebuilding of the Temple (Jeremiah 29:10). The LORD had promised 'I will forgive their iniquities and remember their sins no more.' (Jeremiah 31:34). A remnant of the exiles continued to look forward to their return to Jerusalem and Daniel's prayer expresses their hope. Before addressing God with the question of return, Daniel, on behalf of his people, prepared himself by setting his face toward the LORD and perhaps in the direction of Jerusalem. He started to fast and put on sackcloth and ashes as a sign of humility and sorrow, an ancient custom of repentance.[1] A prayer on behalf of the people was also made by Moses and Solomon as the religious leaders of their generation (Readings 11 and 22). Daniel proceeded with admitting responsibility for committing iniquities, doing wicked things, rebelling against God, departing from His commandments and words, and failing to heed the words of the prophets when they spoke to the people.

Now the people felt ashamed and realized the righteousness of God. Shame accompanies a contrite spirit during the process of 'teshuvah'. It refers to the downfall of Adam and Eve when they rebelled against God and disobeyed His order not to eat from the Tree of Knowledge of good and evil (Reading 1). After the expulsion from the Garden of Eden they were ashamed and covered their nakedness. However, God's righteousness is also the source of His willingness to show mercy and forgiveness. Before begging for forgiveness Daniel recalled God's curse written in the Teaching of Moses if the people would not remain faithful, which had become a reality because of the people's many transgressions.[2] Jerusalem and its citizens were so severely punished that '... there has never been done the like of what was done to Jerusalem.' (Verse 12). Daniel accepted the divine judgment and punishment delivered to the Jerusalemites, now in exile with the city destroyed and

---

1. See for example Genesis 37:34, Leviticus 11:32, 2 Samuel 3:31, 2 Samuel 12:16, 2 Samuel 21:10, 1 Kings 20:31; 2 Kings 3:30, 2 Kings 19:1, 2 Kings 19:2, Esther 4:1-4, Job 16:15, Isaiah 3:24, Isaiah 15:3, Jeremiah 48:37, Ezekiel 7:18, Ezekiel 27:31, Joel 1:8, Amos 8:10, and Jonah 3:5.

2. Regarding God's curse for disobedience and unfaithfulness, see Leviticus 26:14-17 and Deuteronomy 28:15-69.

largely abandoned. Daniel's passionate plea begins with verse 16. He asks God to turn away His anger from Jerusalem and His holy mountain. The pitiful condition of the Israelites made them a mockery in the surrounding countries. He prays to restore the bond between God and the faithful and to take away the shame and disgrace. He begs for God's attention with the words 'Incline Your ear, O my God, and hear; open your eyes and see our desolation' (Verse 18). Daniel rightly declares that not the good deeds of the people in the past can justify his plea but only God's abundant mercy. This alone can save the life of the people.

The Book of Daniel ends with the belief that the eternal bond between Jerusalem and God cannot be destroyed: 'Your name is attached to Your city and Your people!' (Verse 19). Like Psalm 51, Daniel 9 seeks forgiveness based on God's abundant mercy and loving kindness, not one's own righteousness. This lesson was also the major theme of the Book of Job (Reading 46). Daniel was a righteous man and a good mediator between the hardheaded people and God. While in prayer the angel Gabriel was sent to Daniel to accept his plea.

> 22. He made me understand by speaking to me and saying,
> "Daniel, I have just come forth to give you understanding.
> 23. A word went forth as you began your plea,
> and I have come to tell it, for you are precious;
> so mark the word and understand the vision.
> Daniel 9:22-23

Ezra

Reading 53 *Ezra's prayer to send away idolatry.*

Ezra 9:1-8

1. When this was over, the officials approached me, saying, "The people of Israel and the priests and Levites have not separated themselves from the peoples of the land whose abominable practices are like those of the Canaanites, the Hittites, the Perizzites, the Jebusites, the Ammonites, the Moabites, the Egyptians, and the Amorites.

2. They have taken their daughters as wives for themselves and for their sons, so that the holy seed has become mingled with the peoples of the lands; and it is the officials and rulers who have taken the lead in this faithlessness."

3. When I heard this, I rent my garment and mantle, I plucked off hair of my head and beard, and I sat down appalled.

4. Around me assembled all who feared the works of the God of Israel because of the returning exiles' faithlessness, while I sat appalled until the evening offering.

5. At the time of the evening offering I arose from my fastening; still in my torn garment and mantle, I fell on my knees and spread out my hands to the LORD my God,

6. and said, "O my God, I am too ashamed and humiliated to lift my face to You, O my God, for our iniquities are overpowering and our guilt has grown up unto heaven.

7. Since the days of our fathers we have been steeped in guilt. Because of our iniquities, we, our kings, and our priests have been handed over to foreign

kings, to the sword, to captivity, to pillage, and to humiliation, as it is this day.

8. "But now, for a short while, there has been a clemency from the LORD our God, who has granted us a surviving remnant to escape and given us a place in His holy place; our God has restored the light in our eyes and given us with a little sustenance in our bondage."

THE BOOK OF EZRA starts with the rebuilding of the Temple by the returned exiles from Babylon. Local opposition in Judah to the rebuilding came from the Samaritans who convinced the Persian governor to stop the work of rebuilding the Temple.[1] After the complaint of the Jewish elders that King Cyrus had allowed the rebuilding of the Temple, the Persian governor wrote to King Darius with the question if such an order had been given. The Babylonian archives were searched, and it was in the citadel of Ecbatana, in the province of Media, that a scroll was found in which King Cyrus had given the order to rebuild the Temple of Jerusalem. After hearing this news, King Darius sent an order to the Persian governor in Samaria to allow the rebuilding of the Temple which was completed '... in the third month of Adar in the sixth year of the reign of King Darius.' (Ezra 6:15). The precise dating allows historians to designate the year 515 BC as the year when the rebuilding of the Temple started.

The Book of Ezra proceeds with the arrival of Ezra and some other exiles in Jerusalem.[2] Soon Ezra receives a report concerning a widespread practice of intermarriages in the land because the land of the Israelites then had a mixed population in the wake of the expulsion to Babylon. Chapter 9 describes Ezra's profound shock and subsequent regret because of the intermarriages. He publicly showed his feelings of sorrow and regret by rending his garment and mantle, by tearing hair out of his head and beard, and by sitting still on the ground (verses 3 and 4). Then Ezra explains why he is worried about the intermarriages. Apparently, mixed marriages had weakened the Israelite faith. Idolatry or the abandonment of God was the iniquity of the forefathers leading to a national disaster. Ezra is afraid that

---

1. The Samaritans originated in the early years of the Second Temple and recognized only the Torah. They rejected the prophets and rabbinic literature. This immediately created religious tension with the returned exiles from Babylon who embraced the prophets and the rabbinic texts.

2. Ezra is highly regarded in Judaism although he is not considered as a prophet. He is credited with the establishment of the Great Assembly of elders and scholars which is the forerunner of the Sanhedrin. This institution provided instructions regarding the Torah reading, the Amidah prayer or 'The Standing Prayer' (the central prayer of the Jewish liturgy), and the celebration of Purim.

the 'foreign' or non-Jewish wives would worship other idols and lead their husbands astray from God. One notable example has been King Solomon who had many foreign wives and was led astray by them. He was punished with the division of the kingdom into two separate kingdoms after his death (1 Kings 11:9-13).[3]

The temptation of idolatry was an existential threat to the returned exiles because of the expected punishment by God and the reduction of the Israelites to a very small remnant after the Babylonian exile, called 'the surviving remnant' (verses 8 and 13). Only part of the population was left in the land of Judah during the Babylonian captivity, and most of them were subsistence farmers. Considering that the returned exiles from Babylon were only a small percentage of the Babylonian Jews, the survival of the very small remnant of the nation could not be endangered by a new threat, now from the inside, by intermarriages. Hence the desperate cry by Ezra 'Will You not be angry with us till we are destroyed without remnant or survivor? O LORD, God of Israel, You are compassionate, for we have survived as a remnant, as it is now.' (Ezra 9:14).

The Book of Ezra ends with the list of names of the men who had sent their 'foreign' wives and their children away. 'All these had taken foreign wives, among whom were some women who had children.' (Ezra 10:44). Looking at the list of names it is apparent that only a small number of foreign wives were expelled after the men had divorced these foreign wives. In most cases, the foreign wives committed themselves to Judaism and the God of Israel. The sending away of the non-converted foreign wives was a matter of national emergency for the spiritual survival of the small remnant nation.

---

3. The example of idolatry by King Solomon under the influence of his foreign wives is mentioned in Nehemiah 13:26. Nehemiah makes the same point as Ezra.

Nehemiah

Reading 54 Nehemiah's prayer for success.

Nehemiah 1:4-11

4. When I heard that, I sat down and wept, mourned for days, fasting and praying to the God of Heaven.

5. I said, "O LORD, God of Heaven, great and awesome God, who keeps to His covenant with those who love Him and keep His commandments!

6. Let Your ear be attentive and Your eyes open to accept the prayer of Your servant that I am praying to You now, day and night, on behalf of the Israelites, Your servants, while I am confessing the sins of the children of Israel committed against You, sins that I and my father's house have committed.

7. We have affronted You by not keeping the commandments, the laws, and the rules that You gave to Your servant Moses.

8. Be mindful of the commandment You gave to Your servant Moses: 'If you are unfaithful, I will scatter you abroad among the peoples;

9. but if you turn back to Me, keep My commandments, even if your dispersed are over all places, I will gather them from there and bring them to the place where I have chosen to establish My name.'

10. For they are Your servants and Your people whom You have redeemed by Your great power and Your strong hand.

11. O LORD! I implore You, let your ear be attentive to the prayer of Your servant, and to the prayer of Your servants who delight to hold Your name in awe. Grant Your servant mercy today, and dispose that man to be compassionate toward him!"

At that time I was the king's cupbearer.

NEHEMIAH WAS THE CUPBEARER, a high position, at the court of the Persian King Artaxerxes II (404 to 358 BC). He was at the fortress of Shushan when some Jews arrived and told him about the dire conditions of the few remaining Jews in Judah and that the walls of Jerusalem were full of breaches and its gates destroyed by fire. Overwhelmed by emotions and in tears Nehemiah sat in mourning for days, fasting and praying to God. Nehemiah knew that an improvement of Jerusalem's situation needed God's help and the effort of many people. He started by addressing God as a humble man, knowing well how great and powerful God is. Humility is the appropriate mind-set of a faithful believer and a condition for true change as is written in Leviticus 26: 41 '. . . then at last shall their hardened heart humble itself, and they shall atone for their iniquity.' Nehemiah asked God's attention for his prayer on behalf of the Israelites. At that moment Nehemiah showed himself as a leader-in-waiting before embarking on a very special mission. He acknowledged guilt for the transgressions of the Israelites, both the present and the past generations (verse 6). The prayer of Nehemiah recalled the covenantal relationship between God and His people as sealed at Mount Sinai in an encounter between God and Moses. The covenantal promise was followed by the warning of God that, if they were to become unfaithful, He would destroy the land and scatter the Israelites among the nations—see Leviticus 26:33 and Deuteronomy 4:27 (Reading 14).

However, Nehemiah knew that God had also promised the restoration of the nation if they returned to Him; He would not forget the covenant (Deuteronomy 4:29-31). In verse 9 Nehemiah considered that God had promised to let return the faithful remnant to the land of Israel. Aware of this promise there was still hope for redemption in exchange for a return to God. Verse 10 implies that the Jewish people are the instrument of God's presence on earth and that saving the Israelites would guarantee God's uninterrupted presence. Israel can remain '. . . a light unto the nations, that My salvation may reach the ends of the earth.' (Isaiah 49:6); and 'I created you, and appointed you a covenant people, a light of nations.' (Isaiah 42:6). Finally, verse 11 introduces the plea of Nehemiah to let him go to Jerusalem, to help save Jerusalem. Nehemiah asks, 'Grant Your servant success today, and dispose that man to be compassionate toward him.' The expression 'that man' means the Persian king who had the power to let Nehemiah go to his spiritual homeland, Israel, although Nehemiah was born in Persia. The final addition that Nehemiah is the king's cupbearer implies that Nehemiah is a most trusted servant of the king, someone who holds a position to ask the king a favor.

At the request of Nehemiah, the Persian king granted him permission to go to Judah and gave him letters for a free passage as well as the protection of army officers and cavalry on his journey. In Jerusalem he succeeded in convincing the people to rebuild the walls of Jerusalem notwithstanding hostile opposition from the local non-Jewish population.[1] During the working time the builders were armed for self-defense in case of an attack. Nehemiah stayed in Jerusalem as governor before returning to Shushan. The walls of Jerusalem were rebuilt, and its gates restored. Chapter 9 of the Book of Nehemiah is a communal prayer of the Israelites, spoken by the Levites, whereby they confessed their transgressions and renewed their commitment to God. The closing Chapter 13 mentions the return of Nehemiah to Jerusalem where he finds that the people had regressed into transgressive behavior, among which intermarriages. Like Ezra, he exhorts the expulsion of the 'foreign' or non-Jewish wives (Reading 53).

---

1. F. Charles Fensham, The Books of Ezra and Nehemiah, Grand Rapids (Michigan), William Eerdmans Publishing, 1982, p. 11 mentions that not all the Jews of Babylonia went back to Judah. 'A significant number stayed behind because they had become prosperous and were satisfied with conditions in that country.' One of the remaining Jewish families, the Murashu family, started the first banking firm in human history according to cuneiform tablets.

1 Chronicles

Reading 55 — Satan induces David to transgress, and David repents.

1 Chronicles 21:1-13

1. Satan arose against Israel and provoked David to count Israel.

2. David said to Joab and to the commanders of the army, "Go and number Israel from Beer-sheba to Dan and bring me the results of the count."

3. Joab answered, "May the LORD increase His people a hundredfold; but my lord king, are they not all subjects of my lord? Why should my lord require this? Why should it be a cause of guilt for Israel?"

…

1 Chronicles 21:7-13

7. God was displeased about this matter and He struck upon Israel.

8. David said to God, "I have sinned greatly in having done this thing; but now, please take away the guilt of Your servant, for I have acted foolishly."

9. The LORD ordered Gad, David's seer:

10. "Go and tell David: Thus said the LORD: I offer you three things; choose one of them and I will act accordingly."

11. Gad came to David and told him, "Thus said the LORD: Select yourself

12. three years of famine; or three months during which you be swept before your adversaries with the sword of your enemies overtaking you; or else three days of the sword of the LORD, pestilence in the land, the angel of the LORD bringing destruction throughout the territory of Israel. Now consider which choice I shall take back to Him who sent me."

13. David said to Gad, "I am in great distress. Let me fall into the hands of the LORD, for His compassion is very great; and let me not fall into the hands of men."

THE TWO BOOKS OF Chronicles are closing the Old Testament. Their time of writing coincides with the decisive military victories of Alexander the Great (356 to 323 BC) and the rise of Hellenism in the Middle East. 1 Chronicles summarizes Jewish history from Adam to the end of the reign of King David while 2 Chronicles records the history from King Solomon to the decree of the Persian King Cyrus allowing the Jews of Babylon to return to their ancestral homeland in Judah and to rebuild Jerusalem and its Temple.[1] The anonymous author is commonly called the Chronicler who appears to be a learned man with professional writing skills and a good grasp of the religious themes of the Old Testament. The underlying idea is that God is always passionately involved in both humanity and the life of every person and that He intervenes from time to time to change the course of history. Notwithstanding the many personal dramas and national catastrophes caused by human failure and wickedness, He remains a compassionate God who wants to enforce His code of righteousness on earth and thereby save humanity. His ultimate purpose is the eternal survival of the souls of the righteous people in the World-to-Come, in the House of the LORD. The appeal to the world to accept God and His justice is part of the Old Testament, for example Psalm 22:28-29 'Let all the ends of the earth pay heed and turn to the LORD, and the peoples of all nations prostrate themselves before You; for kingship is the LORD's and He rules the nations.'

The immediate admission of guilt by David implies that he had transgressed against a known prohibition. And the hesitant question of Joab 'Why should it be a cause of guilt for Israel?' points in the same direction. Moreover, Joab carried out the order but did not count the number of Levi and Benjamin '... because the king's command had become repugnant to Joab.' (2 Chronicles 21:6).[2] In ancient Israel, neither the king nor any other ruler but God was perceived as the only 'owner' of His people. According to customary law of the Israelites, only the rightful owner had the right to count the number of goods, animals, and people. Because God owns His people, Exodus 30:11-16 contains the divine commandment of paying

---

1. Martin Selman, 1 Chronicles: An Introduction and Commentary, Leicester (Illinois), Inter-Varsity Press, 2008 explains the two Chronicle books as divine words of healing and reshaping human lives before God.

2. Joab did not count the Levites and Benjaminites because the Levites were in the service of God, and the Benjaminites were almost extinct. Regarding the small number of the Benjaminites, see Judges 21:6.

expiation money if a nation-wide census is held. The ransom money should be assigned to the service of the Tent of Meeting.

> 11. The LORD spoke to Moses, saying:
> 12. When you take a census of the Israelite people according to their counting, each shall pay the LORD a ransom for himself on being counted, that no plague may come upon them when you count them.
> 13. This is what everyone who is entered in the census shall pay: half a shekel by the sanctuary weight—twenty *gerahs* is the shekel—half a shekel as an offering to the LORD.
> 14. Everyone who is entered in the census, from the age of twenty years up, shall give the LORD's this offering:
> 15. the rich shall not pay more and the poor shall not pay less than half a shekel when giving the LORD's offering as atonement for your souls.
> 16. You shall take the atonement money from the Israelites and assign it to the service of the Tent of Meeting; it shall serve the Israelites as a reminder before the LORD, as atonement for your souls.
> - Exodus 30:11-16

David had transgressed hastily so that he knew the number of able men for service in his army. The census recorded 1.1 million able men in Israel and 470,000 men in Judah (1 Chronicles 21:5). Notwithstanding David's personal transgression, the anger of the LORD was raised against Israel because the people had not paid what was due to God.

The story of Satan inducing David to transgress, and God's subsequent punishment of the Israelites is a recapitulation of 2 Samuel 24. But there is a slight difference in the phrases. 2 Samuel 24:1 mentions that 'The anger of the LORD again flared up against Israel and He incited David against them' while 1 Chronicles 21:1 says that 'Satan arose against Israel and provoked David to count Israel'. Satan is only mentioned a few times in the Old Testament, namely in the Book of Zechariah (3:1-2), the Book of Job (1:6-9) and the Book of 1 Chronicles (21:1). He stands for 'the Accuser' or the seducing power to do evil by appealing to the evil inclination of man. In the Old Testament Satan is an instrument of God and used for a specific purpose, like in the Book of Job where Satan is allowed to test Job's loyalty to God (Reading 46) or in Zechariah 3 (Reading 38) where the High Priest is accused by the Accuser. Thus, Satan cannot do anything without the permission of God. After God struck Israel—how He did so is not mentioned—David immediately acknowledged transgression and asked to remit his guilt. Notwithstanding his plea for forgiveness, his foolish action would still have consequences. The seer Gad, acting as the spokesperson of God, offered David three choices with three different durations: famine for three years, three months for enemy forces ravaging and humiliating the country, or three days of the sword of the LORD in the form of pestilence in the land. God's message, in any of the three choices offered, meant that the census would not be reliable or usable because many people would die.

Finally, David's agonizing choice is the sword of the LORD or the direct punishment by God. It shows that David trusted God more than people regarding punishment, knowing that God is more compassionate than men. Another reason for his choice is Exodus 30:11 where God sanctioned the ransom payment with the plague. The LORD sent pestilence and 70,000 men fell in Israel. When God sent the angel to Jerusalem, He felt pity and renounced further punishment (1 Chronicles 21: 14). David had to face the terrible consequences of his foolish decision: 'David looked up and saw the angel of the LORD standing between heaven and earth, with a drawn sword in his hand directed against Jerusalem. David and the elders covered in sackcloth and threw themselves on their faces.' (1 Chronicles 21:16). Now he declared that he alone was guilty and that the people should not be punished because of his wrong action. He said, 'O LORD my God, let Your hand fall upon me and my father's house, and let not Your people be plagued!" (1 Chronicles 21:17). David's personal integrity is maintained throughout his whole life.

David gave a lesson to all future leaders, whether religious or political, to accept personal responsibility for wrong decisions and to avert as much as possible harmful consequences for the people they rule. In many dictatorships or failing states, leaders rule unopposed while the people are suffering under their horrible government. Considering that David ruled in the ancient world of absolute kings, who placed themselves above the law, his example is remarkable because it is exceptional.

2 Chronicles

Reading 56   *God promises that His forgiveness shall heal the Land.*

2 Chronicles 7:11-22

11. Thus Solomon finished building the House of the LORD and the king's palace; Solomon succeeded in everything he had wanted to accomplish with regard to the House of the LORD and his palace.

12. The LORD appeared to Solomon at night and said to him, "I have heard your prayer and have chosen this place as My House of sacrifice.

13. If I shut up the heavens and there is no rain or if I command the locusts to ruin the land; or if I let loose the plague against My people,

14. when My people, who bear My name, will humble themselves, pray, and seek My face and turn from their evil ways, I will hear from heaven and forgive their sins and heal their land.

15. Now My eyes will be open and My ears attentive to the prayers from this place.

16. And now I have chosen and made holy this House that My name be there forever. My eyes and My heart shall always be there.

17. As for you, if you walk before Me as your father David walked before Me, doing all that I have commanded you, keeping My laws and rules,

18. then I will establish your royal throne over Israel forever, in accordance with the Covenant I made with your father David, saying, 'You shall always have a descendant ruling over Israel.'

19. But if you turn away from Me and forsake My laws and commandments that I set before you, and go and serve other gods and worship them,

20. then I will uproot them from My land that I gave them, and this House that I consecrated to My name I shall cast out of My sight, and make it a proverb and a byword among all peoples.

21. And this House, once so acclaimed, everyone passing by it shall be astonished and say, 'Why did the LORD do thus to this land and to this House?'

22. And the answer will be, 'It is because they forsook the LORD God of their fathers who liberated them from the land of Egypt, and adopted other gods and worshiped them and served them; therefore He brought all this disaster upon them.'

THE FIRST TIME GOD appeared to Solomon was at Gibeon, a Levitical city located ten kilometers northwest of Jerusalem, at the start of his reign when Solomon asked God for wisdom and knowledge to lead his people (2 Chronicles 1:7-10). After Solomon's dedication of the Temple and the subsequent weeks of public feasting, he dismissed the people to their homes. It was then that the LORD appeared for a second time to Solomon, again at night. The event came shortly after Solomon had prayed to the LORD in the dedication ceremony of the Temple, seeking God's future forgiveness in case that the Israelites would turn away from God (Reading 22). God told him that his prayer was heard and that He chose the Temple as His House.

The most cited verse is Verse 14 in which the LORD confirms that whenever the people would return to Him and turn away from their evil ways, He would turn to them and forgive them. This divine promise of forgiveness would heal the land whenever it was sought. One essential condition of verse 14 is that the people would humble themselves. This kind of attitude is highly problematic since our social position is often strengthened by looking strong and successful, just the opposite of humility. Self-aggrandizement looks better for promotion and acquiring wealth and power, but not so with self-chosen humiliation. Moreover, self-aggrandizement stimulates pride and stubbornness very efficiently. Finally, this self-destructive habit shuts us off from God's awesome power in our life. Yet, the true key to a rewarding life is acting with humility and accepting God's ways and plans with our life and the life of the community. It often happens that our ideas of leading a fulfilling life proves to be wrong much later, even when we achieve riches and a highly regarded social position. Verse 14 warns that a quality life depends on our humility to allow the influence of the ways and the plans of God, rather than relying only on our ambitions and hopes. In an attitude of self-imposed humility, we allow God to enter our life and give it a valuable and fulfilling direction. Thus, the mental state of humility is an intimate interrelationship between the believer and God, and not suited for the outside world. It is the foundation for a way of walking with God under His suggestions and words. We voluntarily allow the LORD to steer us in certain choices to be made, to guide our thoughts and feelings, so that the LORD can manifest Himself in our life in a way we cannot even imagine. Once a solitary individual, we become part of a much greater plan that embraces humanity. Another condition is that we pray directly to God as our Creator and Savior. The daily habit of praying to God starts a process of an ever-stronger spiritual life that is otherwise not achievable. By our daily prayers we become truly a child of God for whom He cares so much. Our Heavenly Father remains with us every day.

Verse 15 declares that God will always be attentive to the prayers from the Temple place in Jerusalem. One can easily understand that the ruins of the Temple today—the Kotel or Western Wall—are still considered as the most favorite place to pray to God. And the Temple Mount is the most holy site in Judaism.

In that nightly appearance, God proceeded by providing an answer to Solomon's second request in his prayer concerning the eternity of his throne for his descendants. The LORD told him that this promise could be given if Solomon would walk before Him as his father David had done (verse 17). However, if Solomon would worship other gods, the LORD would uproot his descendants and leave His House at the Temple Mount. The second element of God's answer relates only to the descendants of Solomon. Verse 14 is the most important message from God and addressed to His people: He shall heal the land whenever it repents in humility and returns to Him. In our secular world we look upon our political leaders and interest groups to improve and 'heal the land' from corruption, destruction, and greed. 2 Chronicles 7 reminds us not to naively rely on political and social leaders for reforming the land and 'healing it'. Our walking with the LORD is the beneficial prerequisite for healing the land. In a healthy society, people pray God to heal the land and restore the peace.

Appendix

Structure and Indicative Timeline of the Old Testament

THE FIVE BOOKS OF MOSES

1. Genesis — 1600 to 1200 BC
1. Exodus — 1600 to 1200 BC
1. Leviticus — 1600 to 1200 BC
1. Numbers — 1600 to 1200 BC
1. Deuteronomy — 1600 to 1200 BC

PROPHETS

1. Joshua — 1200 BC
1. Judges — 800 BC
1. 1 Samuel — 600 BC
1. 2 Samuel — 600 BC
1. 1 Kings — 700 BC
1. 2 Kings — 700 BC
1. Isaiah — 740 to 686 BC
1. Jeremiah — 600 BC

1. Ezekiel   600 BC
1. Hosea   770 BC
1. Joel   830 BC
1. Amos   750 BC
1. Obadiah   600 BC
1. Jonah   830 BC
1. Micah   750 BC
1. Nahum   630 BC
1. Habakkuk   620 BC
1. Zephaniah   630 BC
1. Haggai   520 BC
1. Zechariah   520 BC
1. Malachi   450 BC

WRITINGS

1. Psalms   850 to 400 BC
2. Proverbs   600 BC
3. Job   500 BC
4. Song of Songs   900 to 200 BC
5. Ruth   600 BC
6. Lamentations   600 BC
7. Ecclesiastes   400 BC
8. Esther   400 BC
9. Daniel   500 to 160 BC
10. Ezra   400 BC
11. Nehemiah   400 BC
12. 1 Chronicles   400 BC
13. 2 Chronicles   400 BC

www.ingramcontent.com/pod-product-compliance
Lightning Source LLC
Chambersburg PA
CBHW050350230426
43663CB00010B/2067